# MURDER IN THE ADIRONDACKS

## 'An American Tragedy' Revisited

GRACE BROWN - *A portrait used at the trial for identification. It may be the one that hung in the parlor of the Brown house in South Otselic.*

CHESTER GILLETTE - *A photo taken by A.P. Zintsmaster in Herkimer just before the trial. According to some reports, Chester sold this portrait to newspapermen in order to buy new clothes and restaurant food during his stay in jail.*

# MURDER
# IN THE
# ADIRONDACKS

## 'An American Tragedy' Revisited

*by*

Craig Brandon

Published by
North Country Books, Inc.
Utica, New York

# MURDER IN THE ADIRONDACKS
An American Tragedy Revisited

Eighth Paperback Printing 2001

ISBN 0-932052-58-4


Library of Congress Number 86-5328


Brandon, Craig, 1950-
   Murder in the Adirondacks.

   Bibliography: p.
   1. Gillette, Chester. 2. Crime and Criminals—New York
(State)—Biography. 3. Brown, Grace, 1885 or 6-1906.
4. Victims of Crimes—New York (State). 5. Murder—New
York (State)—Case Studies. 6. Trials (Murder)—New York
(State)—Herkimer. I. Title.
HV 6248.G42B73  1986        364.1'523'0974761  86-5528


Published by
NORTH COUNTRY BOOKS, INC.
311 Turner Street
Utica, New York 13501

*For Emily and Benjamin*

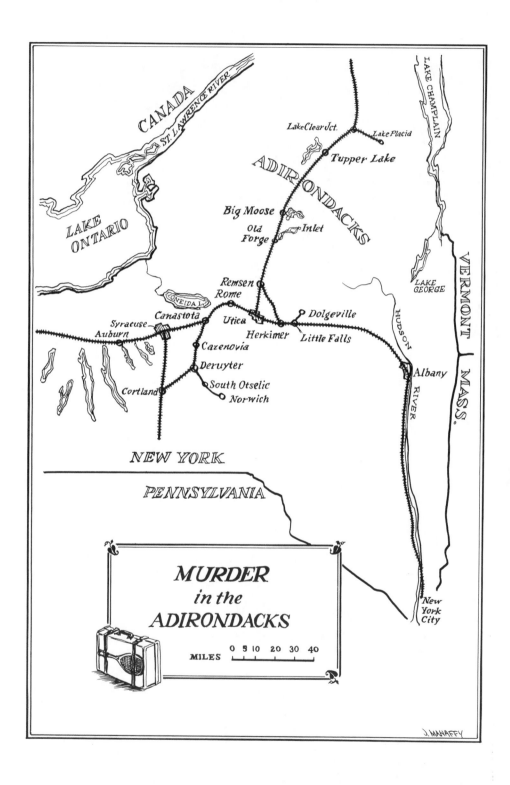

MURDER
in the
ADIRONDACKS

MILES 0 5 10 20 30 40

# Table of Contents

# *Preface*

This book was written because it was a book I would have wanted to read in 1980 when I was first introduced to the Chester Gillette - Grace Brown murder case through Theodore Dreiser's fictional account in *An American Tragedy*.

The initial research was done for a newspaper article commemorating the 75th anniversary of the famous trial and I was surprised to find that no book had been written about it. I found I had to go back to the original sources: the trial transcript from 1906 and the millions of words of newspaper copy that were written from 1906 to 1908. I had no idea at that point that the mystery of Gillette would involve thousands of miles of travel and tens of thousands of hours in libraries and historical societies across the country.

When I asked Mrs. Jane Spellman, the dedicated and personable director of the Herkimer County Historical Society about Gillette, she smiled and presented me with the dozens of files that hundreds of other amateur researchers had gone through over the years. Why, I complained, hadn't anyone ever put all of this together into a complete and readable account so that each reader would not have to go back to the original clippings? She agreed that it was a needed and worthwhile project that was long overdue. Why, she suggested, not do it myself?

Five years later, this book is the result. With Utica as a base, I found I was within a two-hour drive of most of the major scenes of the story: Cortland, where the ill-fated couple had lived; Big Moose, where the crime took place; Herkimer, where the trial was held, and Auburn, where Gillette was executed. While there was virtually no one left alive who had anything to do with the case, I soon found that scrapbooks, letters and documents had been well preserved, but were scattered throughout the area in attics, basements of historical societies and college archives. The newspapers themselves had long since crumbled, but copies were available on microfilm and I spent thousands of hours reading and taking notes from dimly lighted and out of focus microfilm machines.

But much of the information in this book was not even known in 1906. The backgrounds of Chester Gillette and Grace Brown are described herein much more completely than they were in 1906 and documents and letters that remained hidden for decades are included here in their first published version.

Not all of the story was to be found in Central New York. Gillette was born in Montana and lived in Washington State, California, Hawaii, Illinois and Ohio before coming to Cortland in 1905 and information about his early life was scattered around the country. I visited his prep school in Oberlin, Ohio and the religious community his parents helped found at Zion City, Illinois.

I would like to say that this is the definitive version of the story, but I hope it won't be. Someday, I hope, documents that I have searched for in vain but hope still exist will come to light so that the mysteries that still remain can be cleared up. Gillette's diary and the petitions submitted for the commutation of his death sentence, for example, are, I hope, squirreled away in someone's collection and will once again be brought to light. Also, I hope that one day the relatives of Grace Brown and Chester Gillette who declined to talk with me will change their minds and tell what they know.

Why spend so much time and effort on a 75-year-old murder

case? It was a question many people asked me during the past three years. Besides being an interesting story, the Gillette case is worthy of this treatment for a number of reasons. First, Dreiser scholars have sought for years to determine how much of his novel was transcribed from the original documents and how much of it was created. The lack of an accurate account of what really happened has, up to now, hampered those efforts.

But the story is interesting as history as well. It is a slice of.a vanished world, pre-World War I America, with its concerns, its justice and its way of life, all wrapped together in a nutshell. It is a compelling tale that becomes all the more interesting when the reader can count on its being accurate.

Finally, the story is an excellent example of how legends and folklore have, over a number of years, come to replace the truth. With no easily available accurate account of the trial, the fictionalized version of the story gradually came to be accepted as fact, even by those with first-hand information about the original case.

I am indebted to hundreds of researchers from across the country who looked up information in places like Hawaii, Washington State, Texas and Connecticut in answer to my written inquiries and helped make the book as complete as it is. They helped to make it the only complete version of the story that exists in non-fiction form.

I would like to thank, first of all, Mrs. Jane Spellman, who not only first suggested I write about Gillette, but who assisted and encouraged me more times than can be counted. Three other people performed the ground work without which this book would not have appeared for another decade. These are Henry Blumberg, who spent many hours researching Gillette's trial; Dr. Joseph Brownell, who researched the story in Cortland, and Mrs. Wilda Bowers, the unofficial historian of South Otselic, N.Y. who was able to answer every question I had about South Otselic at the time Grace Brown lived there.

I would also like to thank the following people who made this book possible: Maxine Alcorn of the Houston Public Library; Larry Hackman, New York State archivist; Douglas A. Olson, librarian of the Eastern Washington State Historical Society; Chenango County author Joseph Quinn; Ken Miner, South

Otselic historian; Eugene D. Levy of Carnegie-Mellon University; Anita Wright of the Cortland County Historical Society; Mrs. Sexton Beer; William E. Bigglestone, archivist of Oberlin College; Alice Marshall, director of the Zion City Historical Society; Elizabeth Bergen, a dedicated researcher; Mrs. Edwin Vosburgh, the daughter of district attorney George Ward, who gave me access to her father's collection of documents regarding the case; Jean Honour, Pharsalia Town Clerk; Jarlath Hamrock of Willet, N.Y.; Warren S. Eddy, director of the Cortland Free Library; Carolyn A. Davis of the George Arents Research Library at Syracuse University who provided access to the papers of George Ward and William O. Dapping; Donald P. Schorer, who knew Chester Gillette's sister; Raymond J. Fisher of Spokane, Wash.; Dave Walter of the Montana Historical Society Library; James C. Smith of the Salvation Army Archives and Research Center; Mrs. Captain Wes. Sundin of the Salvation Army; Barbara E. Dunn of the Hawaiian Historical Society; Paul H. Heffron of the Library of Congress; Roger E. Ritzman of the New York State Archives; the staffs of the Utica Public Library, Herkimer Public Library, Ilion Public Library, Hamilton College Library, Colgate University Library, Zion City Public Library; State University at Cortland Library; the State Library in Albany; Douglas Preston of the Oneida Historical Society in Utica; the Onondaga County Public Library; the staffs of *The Utica Daily Press* and *The Observer Dispatch*, especially Joe Kelly and Bill Farrell. I would also like to thank my writing teachers, Campbell Black, Anderson McCullough, Paul Briand and George Newman; Mrs. Genevieve Wadas and Judy Wittman who proofread the manuscript; Claire Brandon for her financial assistance; Robert Igoe and Sheila Orlin of North Country Books, and my wife Jean, who spent three years of vacations putting coins into photocopying machines in such un-vacation-like places as Oberlin and Zion City.

Craig Brandon
Grant, N.Y., August, 1983
New York Mills, N.Y., June, 1985

# *The Lady In The Lake*

Robert Morrison had been rowing and searching for over an hour when he finally spotted the boat, floating upside down, about 40 feet from shore. On the overturned keel he could see a black object that looked like a jacket and there were several objects floating in the lake nearby.

He had just rounded a point of land that jutted out into the south side of Big Moose Lake and could see into a small cove that had been hidden from his view until then. He had expected to find the boat pulled up along the shore in front of one of the rustic but ornate log houses along the lake that were known as "camps" in the Adirondacks. Sometimes the tourists who rented his boats wandered off into the woods and got lost and Morrison or some other woodsman had to go and rescue them. Until now, that was what he thought had happened to the man and woman who had rented the boat the day before.

It was a warm morning, even for July, and there were large, white, billowy clouds floating across the blue sky and reflecting in the lake, which was cold and clear and so calm the only ripple was the one left by Morrison's boat as he moved the oars. It was not at all the kind of weather, he thought to himself, that might cause a boat to tip over, even a boat rowed by a couple of people from the city.

It was July 12, 1906, the height of the Adirondack tourist season and there were more city people than woodsmen at Big Moose that time of year. The resort in Upstate New York was closer to Canada than to New York City, but tourists came from hundreds and even thousands of miles, thanks to the railroads, for the roads were nearly impassable. The camps owned by the rich from throughout the Northeast were full and the hotels were doing a thriving business. Morrison had heard the voices and seen their boats all the way over from the Glenmore Hotel at the extreme western end of the lake.

But here, after rounding the point of land, it was suddenly very quiet. There were no camps or tourists here in a part of the lake called Punkey Bay. The trees grew right up to the shore and there was no easy way to put a boat into shore. Few people came to this part of the lake except to gather the water lilies that grew in abundance in the shallow water. And it was among the lilies that the boat was now resting.

It was a boat similar to the one Morrison was rowing with his daughter-in-law, Florence, and her sister, Grace Luce. It was 15 feet long, just over three feet wide and two feet deep with three seats. The seat farthest back was removable and was more cushioned than the others as it was the favored seat of women guests. The wood was inlaid with brass trimmings and there were brass braces holding the seats in place.

During their journey across the lake, Morrison had told the two women about the strange couple who had rented the boat the day before.

The man had looked like a college student, about 22, well-dressed in a neat gray suit and white tie, with a tan complexion and an athletic build. The girl was slightly younger, but looked pale and unhappy and, Morrison thought, her plain green skirt, white shirtwaist and the black silk jacket she carried in her hand suggested she was not quite the man's social equal. But he had seen many couples of many types during his summers renting boats at the Glenmore and it was not their clothing that had made them seem unusual.

While the man had asked enthusiastic questions about the lake and the scenery, as all the tourists did, the girl just stood by, with tears in her eyes, and didn't say a word.

At first they had asked about taking a ride on the *Zilpha*, the Big Moose steamboat that carried mail and passengers around the lake several times a day. Later, they decided to rent one of his boats. The young man, who seemed to know something about rowboats, selected one of the Adirondack skiffs.

The man helped the girl, who seemed less pleased about the ride, into the boat. He sat in the front where he could comfortably reach the wooden oars in the metal oarlocks, and the girl sat in the back on the removable cloth-covered seat.

But the most unusual thing about the couple was the suitcase. Morrison had seen tourists load all kinds of odd things into his boats: rifles, musical instruments and even pets, but this was the first time someone brought a suitcase. And it even had a tennis racket attached to the side of it. When Morrison asked about it, the man said his camera was in the suitcase and that he wanted to take some photos of places around the lake. Morrison suggested the Higby Camp and the bridge over the outlet to the lake as places that might make good photographs and with that the couple rowed off. When he last saw them they were rowing to the south and east along the evergreen-covered shoreline.

That night the couple failed to return to the Glenmore, where they had registered just before renting the boat. Morrison fired his rifle into the air so they could hear the sound and know where to go in the dark, but no one showed up. He used the telephone to call other hotels and camps around the lake, but no one remembered seeing them.

This morning, after finishing his chores, he and the two women set out in search of the couple and his boat. The lake was five and a half miles long and a mile wide, but because of all the bays there were 26 miles of shoreline to search. But Morrison, knowing which way they had headed, made a good guess as to where they could have gone, and they were now rapidly approaching the boat. Morrison could see that the object on the upturned keel was the black silk jacket that the woman had carried the day before. It was spread out over the bottom of the boat in an odd manner and Morrison, for the first time, feared that the couple had overturned the boat and had to swim to shore.

The oars were floating near the boat, one on either side, about four feet away. As he drew closer he saw a man's straw hat floating in the water along with a magazine and the back of the seat that the woman had sat in the day before.

He rowed over to the side of the boat and picked up the black jacket. Pinned to the front of it was a spray of pond lilies, just like the ones in the water nearby. Inside the pocket were more of the lilies. He gave the jacket to Mrs. Morrison, grasped the gunwale and with an effort turned the boat right side up. He tied a rope from his boat to the other, which was now full of water, and pulled the boat to the nearby shore, where he turned it over to dump out the water.

Suddenly, Mrs. Morrison pointed to the metal braces on the inside of the boat. There, wound around the screws that held the seats in place was a lock of dark brown hair, each strand about eight inches long. On the other side was a similar, but smaller lock of the same hair. Morrison pulled some of it off and gave it to his sister-in-law, who twisted the strands, absent-mindedly, around the fingers of her left hand.

Meanwhile, Morrison had gone back to the lake to retrieve the hat, the magazine and the seat. The hat, which had been floating crown up near the shore, had no lining in it. Instead, there were two strings hanging from it as if the lining had been carelessly torn out.

Morrison put the seat, the hat and the oars back into the boat and rowed the two boats back across and down the lake to Covey's Point where the *Zilpha* was docked. He told the men there that he feared some tragedy had befallen the couple in South Bay the day before and that the man and woman had drowned. The *Zilpha* towed the two boats back to the Glenmore, where more boats and men were organized for a search party.

Returning to South Bay a short time later on the *Zilpha* were James Higby, the owner of the steamer and also local justice of the peace; Frank Crabb, the boat's engineer; Charles Kirwin, the bartender of the Glenmore, and about 18 other volunteers.

Also on the boat was 13-year-old Roy Higby, James' son, who was working on the boat as a purser that summer to earn enough money to buy a bicycle. His mother had told him he could go

*Big Moose Lake*

*Punky Bay, Big Moose Lake*

with the men but that he was not to go into any of the smaller boats that would drag the bottom of the lake for the bodies of the man and the woman.

The *Zilpha* was about 40 feet long with an old-fashioned steam engine and a smokestack in the center, a helmsman's cabin in the front and a covered platform in the rear with seats for about 20 passengers. Besides taking visitors to the various camps around the lake, the boat was often the only means of transportation.

When the *Zilpha* was nearly to the part of South Bay past Covey's Point where Morrison had found the boat, the motors were shut down and a large sugar bag filled with rocks and attached to a rope was thrown overboard to act as an anchor. Then the men set off in smaller rowboats in groups of two, armed with sticks on which were attached fishing lines with large hooks, weighted so they would sink to the bottom. The boats moved slowly in circles, one man rowing and the other dragging the fish hook on the muddy bottom of the lake, which was about seven to eight feet deep in this area, about 40 feet from shore.

Roy Higby and Crabb remained on the *Zilpha* and were watching the operations when Roy, staring down into the water, thought he saw a blur on the bottom. Crabb looked where Roy was pointing but said it was probably just the old sugar bag anchor. But no, Roy said, the boat was drifting away from the anchor so it would be on the other side.

Crabb went to the side of the helmsman's cabin and took down a 13-foot wooden pole with a sharp spike in the end. It was the kind of pole lumberjacks used to pole logs. On the *Zilpha* it was used to keep the boat from striking the docks when it drifted in after the motor had been shut off. Crabb gently thrust the sharp end of the pole down into the water where Roy had seen the blur.

He poked for several minutes before he was convinced that it was a body at the bottom of the lake and he called out to the men in the boats that he had found something. The men rowed back to the *Zilpha* and dropped their lines into the water where Crabb had indicated, but Crabb began to bring the pole straight up, knowing by the strain that he had hooked it onto something at the bottom.

The head and the chest came out of the water first. The skin was yellow and the eyes, which were half open, were bloodshot. The hook had caught the woman's skirt, near the top. She was dressed in a light green skirt and a white shirtwaist. One of her stockings had fallen down over her low cut shoe and a lock of her brown hair, which had been done up in the Gibson Girl fashion of the day, drooped over her face.

Crabb grabbed her around the shoulders and Kerwin took her legs so they could swing her into the boat. Right away Morrison identified her as the woman he had seen leave in his boat with the man the day before. They tried to lay her down on one of the *Zilpha's* seats, but the seat was too narrow so they laid her in the aisle on the deck.

Blood began to run out of her nose. They noticed that her lip was cut and there was some blood on her mouth. They took a piece of carpet and laid it over her and added Crabb's mackintosh before turning the *Zilpha* around and heading back to the Glenmore with their sad cargo.

Several of the men remained in the small boats to continue the search for the man, but others claimed later that after seeing the marks on the girl's face and hearing Morrison's story that they thought, even then, that the man had probably run away. He would not be found in the lake no matter how long they searched, they said.

When they arrived at the Glenmore, the men took the body, still covered with the carpet and Crabb's mackintosh, into a room off the main parlor and laid it on the bed. Mrs. Morrison took the hair she had found in the boat, wrapped it in some paper and pinned it to the black silk coat. She went back into the hallway and took down the girl's straw hat, which was still hanging on the rack near the desk where she had left it the day before.

Some of the men who had returned with the body looked at the register. The man and woman had signed it the day before, just hours after they had arrived by wagon from the Big Moose train station, and just minutes before they rented the boat. Written on the register in a man's hand was "Carl Grahm, Albany, and Grace Brown, S. Otselic."

Dwight Sperry, the owner of the Glenmore, wired the Herkimer County coroner, Isaac Coffin of Frankfort, about what had happened and then called Sheriff Richard, who said he could not arrive until the next day, the trip being about 75 miles by train and wagon.

The search for the body of Carl Grahm continued until it was dark and the men returned to the hotels and camps around the lake. That evening, the woodsmen, their wives, the tourists and the hotel employees made the incident the main topic of conversation as they sorted through the facts and tried to figure out what had happened.

While some were ready to believe the worst, that the man had thrown the girl out of the boat and run away, others said they were sure the other body would be found when the search resumed the next day. On the porches along the lakeside and in the hotel bars they went over the evidence: the mark on the girl's face, the way the coat had been found, the fact that the "accident" had occurred in one of the most remote parts of the lake and the strange way the couple had acted before renting the boat.

The wagon driver who had taken them from the station at Big Moose recalled that they had said they planned to return on the train that evening and others remembered that the girl had been crying.

But perhaps strangest of all, there was that suitcase the man had brought with him on the boat. Why had they taken that and left behind the woman's hat at the hotel?

The searching continued the next day, but by afternoon word had reached them from the Albany police that there was no one in their area with a name like Carl Grahm. More of the searchers gave up, joining others in thinking the worst. When the afternoon paper, the Utica *Observer*, arrived, they were informed that the man in the boat was probably not Carl Grahm at all, but Chester Gillette, the nephew of the owner of the factory in Cortland, N.Y. where Grace Brown had worked. The article also noted that Grace Brown had often been seen "keeping company" with Gillette. That was enough to convince everyone and the search was not resumed.

Drownings were one thing at Big Moose; there had been many of them over the years, but murder was something else. Once again, it was what everyone on the lake talked about that evening, each offering the bits of information he had seen or heard from someone else.

Some of the campers recalled seeing a boat with a man and a woman in it that day drifting back and forth in South Bay. The passengers had been reading magazines.

Irv Crego, after hearing the description of the man who had been in the boat, said he thought he had seen just such a man on the evening of the 11th, walking down the road in the dark toward Eagle Bay. The reason he remembered it, he said, was because he had never before met a man in the woods who was carrying a suitcase.

Marjorie Carey, who was in the Adirondacks from New Jersey, recalled, after hearing the stories, that just about 6 p.m. that day she had been crossing South Bay with her husband when she had heard a strange sound. At the time she thought it was a bird. Now, she told her friends, it could very well have been the last scream of that poor woman.

Few people would have thought, that evening of Friday, the 13th of July, 1906, that the same stories would be told on the lake for more than seven decades; that tourists would come to Big Moose from across the country to hear the stories and to visit the places where the things they described had happened.

If someone had told them that what happened that week would soon involve dozens of New York City reporters and millions of readers, the governor of the state and the future chief justice of the U.S. Supreme Court, no one would have believed it.

They would have called it a tall tale indeed, if someone told them that the incident on Wednesday would one day be the subject of a best-selling novel by a famous American author, that songs would be sung, that virtually unknown things like moving pictures would be made about those stories.

Yet many of them were to live to see all those things happen and all of them soon found out that, like it or not, they would spend the rest of their lives telling the story of what had happened that week at Big Moose Lake.

# PART ONE

## *The Lives*

# CHAPTER ONE

# The Factory Owner's Nephew

A century before the name Gillette became permanently associated with Cortland County's most famous murder case, it was well-known as the family name of some of the earliest pioneers; people who settled the steep hillsides and gentle valleys of the county, located in the geographic center of New York State.

The Gillettes were of French Huguenot stock and were originally from Massachusetts until John Gillette, Chester's great, great, grandfather purchased a tract of government land on Cold Brook, a tiny stream in the extreme northwest corner of the county, near the foot of Skaneateles Lake. The family, however, did not permanently move there until 1805, after which they set about clearing the land, then an almost unbroken wilderness, 10 miles over nearly nonexistent roads to the little trading village which was to become the city of Cortland.

Albertus Starr Gillette, grandson of John Gillette and Chester Gillette's grandfather, was born Dec. 12, 1822 and grew up on the family farm in East Scott. On Feb. 5, 1846, he married Harriet Osborne, the daughter of Noah Humphrey Osborne, a merchant turned farmer who had moved to a nearby farm several years before.

The newlyweds moved in with the groom's family for several years and their first son, Rembrandt W. Gillette was born there in 1848. By 1850 they had moved to their own 100-acre farm nearby. Their second son, Frank S. Gillette, Chester's father, was born there on Oct. 27, 1852. Also born there were Noah Horace Gillette in 1855 and Carrie, their only daughter, in 1858.

Just before the Civil War, Albertus and Harriet, both nearing the age of 40, made a decision many younger couples were making. They sold their farm and the buckets and kettles they had used to make maple sugar, packed up their belongings and children in a wagon and set out to seek the opportunities they had heard about in the West. For several years they lived in Iowa, probably as farmers, and two more sons, Henry C. and Ellsworth Porter were born there.

It was in Iowa, according to his later statements, that 12-year-old Frank S. Gillette had his first experience with the evangelical Christian groups that were to shape his life and that of his family. He recalled that it was a Methodist tent service and that he underwent the "born again" experience.

The Iowa farm, however, either was not successful or stories of fortunes being made on the Western frontier tempted Albertus to move his family again, for he moved to Montana after only a few years in Iowa. There was no train service to Montana and the journey by covered wagon meant traveling for weeks through the dangerous Indian territory of the Dakotas.

Montana had been organized as a territory in 1864 and in the 1870s Indian attacks were still a constant threat and concern. News from the outside world arrived weeks late and Montana residents, because of their isolation, referred to events in other parts of the nation as happening "in America" as if it were a foreign country.

Sometime before 1870, the Gillette family took up residence in a log cabin in a tree-covered mountain valley just south of Helena. Although the community had a name - "Prickly Pear" - it was really nothing more than a lumber camp. Albertus, at age 45, and Rembrandt, 22, helped to cut down the virgin timber and fashion it into the beams used to prop up the tunnels of the booming mines in the area.

Frank and Noah attended schools in Helena for a time, although no records seem to have survived, and during the summer they probably helped their father and older brother in the logging work. In 1875, Noah, dissatisfied with life on the frontier, left for New York City to accept a position with the Warner Brothers Corset Co., which had been founded by Lucien C. Warner, his mother's sister's husband. Both Noah Gillette and Lucien Warner were to figure importantly in the later life of Chester Gillette.

The remaining members of the Gillette family moved farther south to take up farming outside the village of Clancy. Although Albertus was assisted by his two remaining full-grown sons, Rembrandt and Frank, and two younger sons who could also lend a hand, he needed to hire two farm laborers to help with the work.

Sometime after 1880, Frank Gillette met his future bride, Louisa Maria Rice, a native of Millbury, Massachusetts. She had been born May 12, 1859, a daughter of Leonard Rice, a sash and blind maker, and Dulcemer S. Rice. The circumstances of the couple's meeting, courtship and marriage have not been recorded, but the ceremony probably took place sometime in the summer of 1882. Soon after their marriage they moved to Wickes, a mining town just south of Clancy, where they seem to have taken up residence in a tent.

Wickes was a boom town in 1882 because of the rich lodes of silver discovered in quartz deposits in the mountains nearby. In 1876, a syndicate of Montana and New York capitalists headed by the town's namesake, William Wickes, built an elaborate reduction-smelting works in a previously unsettled valley and Wickes quickly became the hub of mining operations throughout the state. It was noisy, dirty and a victim of all the vices that plagued Western boom towns - crime, vice, shortages of necessities and a haven for all the wrong types of people.

It was in Wickes on Aug. 9, 1883 that Frank and Louisa's first child, Chester Ellsworth Gillette was born. In later years when she talked about her son's character, Louisa said she thought "prenatal influences" may have been a factor in her son's personality flaws, but she never elaborated on what those influences were. A deeply religious woman like Louisa could have felt guilty about any number of things: an impure thought, a glass of beer, or even a simple lapse of faith. She may even have been referring to the general atmosphere of Wickes at the time she was pregnant.

But, as Louisa also pointed out later, there were some advantages as well, to spending your earliest years in a place like Wickes. Living in the wilderness brought her son much closer to nature than would have been possible in a city or even on a farm, she said. Chester showed an early fascination for small animals and insects and would often pick up worms and examine them, always being careful never to hurt them.

"As he grew up we felt that the tender side of his nature was developing," Louisa recalled later. "We never knew him to do anything cruel."

In late 1886 or early 1887, when Chester was three years old, the Gillettes moved to Spokane, Washington, where Frank's parents, brothers and sister had been living for several months. Spokane had been part of the wilderness only a little more than a decade before, but the city, then known as Spokane Falls after the waterfalls on the Spokane River which was its most distinguishing feature, quickly became a major trading center when the railroads arrived. A large section of Washington and Idaho, called the "Inland Empire," used Spokane as its chief trading area and led to its prosperity.

By the time Chester and his family arrived, Spokane was a city of 9,000 and was growing rapidly; the kind of place where fortunes could be made quickly. After decades of making ends meet through their own labor in the wilderness, Spokane presented a different kind of challenge for Albertus and his sons, one they handled much more successfully.

Most successful of all was Ellsworth Porter Gillette, the youngest son, who with his sister, Carrie, established Gillette's Restaurant at 115 W. Riverside Avenue. Advertisements for the restaurant described it as "the most popular ladies' eating house in the city - everything clean and strictly first class - single meals 25 cents, per week $4.50. You will miss a great treat by not calling on us."

Drawings accompanying the advertisements showed that men were welcome as well as ladies at the round wooden tables and

Windsor chairs. Large gas lights hung from the ceiling and were mounted on the walls on which signs were posted advertising ice cream and shortcake.

At first, the other members of the Gillette family were connected with the restaurant in one way or another. Albertus, the patriarch who was now partially retired, helped with the chores and Henry was a waiter and cook. Rembrandt and Frank operated an express company out of an office in the restaurant building.

Besides the restaurant, Ellsworth, who was known in Spokane as "Billy," opened a real estate agency just down the street, and, in 1888, he opened the Pacific Coast Tea Company at the corner of Riverside Avenue and Post Street. Frank later left the express business to Rembrandt, who Spokane residents called "Doc," and took over as clerk of his brother's tea store.

By all accounts, the Gillette family businesses, formally organized into E. P. Gillette and Co. with Ellsworth and Carrie in charge, were extremely successful and growing every day in the boom town days of Spokane in the late 1880s when fate struck them a cruel blow.

The great fire of 1889 began on August 4, just five days before Chester's sixth birthday, and it was probably one of his earliest and most dreaded memories. It began at the corner of Railroad and Post streets, just a few blocks from the Pacific Coast Tea Co. offices and Gillette's Restaurant. No one is sure how it started, but it could have been controlled quite easily and quickly except for one problem: there was no water in the fire hydrants. A later investigation would show negligence on the part of the water commissioner.

Since most of the buildings in the city were made of wood, the fire spread quickly. With no water to fight the fire, firemen confiscated a train car full of dynamite intended for nearby mining operations and tried blowing up a ring of buildings around the fire to keep it from spreading. The sound of the explosions, added to the heat, smoke and flames, created a panic. Word spread quickly that there was no water in the hydrants and soon hundreds of residents were grabbing their belongings and heading for the bridge across the Spokane River.

Frank Gillette and his brothers certainly must have helped

fight the fire, although none of them ever spoke about the experience in later life. Later, Ellsworth and Henry were members of the fire department.

Four hours after the fire was first reported, the city was in ruins. All the city's hotels and banks, the entire business district and all 32 blocks of the downtown area burned to the ground. Included in those blocks and among the first to be destroyed, were the restaurant and the tea company. Ellsworth, Carrie and Albertus, who had all lived above the restaurant, were left homeless, but other members of the family lived farther away in a residential area of the city that had been spared. Frank, Louisa and Chester, who lived on College Street, took in other members of the family while the city was being rebuilt.

Although he never specifically mentioned it in any recorded conversation, Chester must certainly have seen the fire while it was being fought. It would have been very difficult to keep a boy his age away, especially when all the adults were so busy fighting the fire. Afterwards he may have helped the other members of the family comb through the ruins to salvage what they could of the family's fortune. At midnight on the night of the fire, military laws were invoked to prevent looting. The entire burned-out area was roped off and badges were issued to those, like the Gillettes, who had property inside the restricted area.

Most of the property owners lost everything in the fire. There was $6 million in insured losses, but most of the property was not insured. The Gillettes must have had at least some insurance, especially on the property owned by Ellsworth, because he soon bounced back to prosperity.

Downtown Spokane became a tent city in the winter of 1889-90 when thousands of men were employed in reconstruction. Ellsworth reopened his restaurant in a tent at the corner of Main and Washington streets, right next to the relief committee's headquarters. Many of the hungry workers remembered years later how grateful they were for the meals provided there. The winter was one of the most severe in the young city's history, with temperatures frequently falling to 33° below zero.

Gamblers and prostitutes set up their own tents along Main Street and the area soon developed an unsavory reputation that probably led Louisa and Frank to keep Chester away from it and help out at home instead of in the restaurant.

The citizens of Spokane showed their respect for Ellsworth in 1890 by naming him fire chief, a job that was not taken lightly in a city that had so recently been made aware of how important maintenance of fire fighting equipment was.

Soon afterward, Ellwsorth gave up his tent to become proprietor of the Columbia Hotel on E. Main Street and remained there until work was finished on his new hotel on the site of the old restaurant.

Frank, left without a job after the fire, was quickly hired as an engineer on the reconstruction crews. He had no formal training in this profession, but his experience in the logging camps was beneficial and the rest he learned from other workers.

Chester, meanwhile, was enrolled in the Bryant School, an elementary school on Broadway between Fourth and Fifth Streets. Years later, after they had read about Chester's disgrace in the newspapers, the teachers at the school told a newspaper reporter that Chester had been "an unruly, deceitful pupil." In the first grade, they recalled, he had been caught several times taking things from other children. When confronted with the evidence, they said, he tried to lie his way out of it. One of the teachers sent a note home to Louisa complaining about his conduct, but Louisa didn't consider it a serious offense.

"Boys always fib in the spring," she wrote back to them.

"He was always what is called an irrepressible boy," Louisa later recalled of this period in her son's life. He was "full of activity, but one we could trust. He was always good to the other members of the family."

His second grade teacher, Mrs. E. G. McFarland, also remembered him well enough to comment for reporters years later.

"He was an average student," she recalled, "neither bright nor dull. I never had much trouble with him when he was in my grade, although I have heard that other teachers experienced considerable trouble in handling him. His parents lived somewhere near the school house and seemed to be in moderate circumstances."

Without giving up his job as an engineer, Frank became the manager of the Crescent bathhouse and was doing well financially according to his own later account. He was an elder in the new

Presbyterian Church, a more traditional type of worship than the tent service he had encountered in Iowa.

But, all of that changed dramatically one evening in 1892 when he was walking down a street and heard music coming from a room above a gun store. He went inside and found a Salvation Army "night watch" service in progress and was immediately and permanently converted.

The Salvation Army newspaper "War Cry", later described his conversion this way: "At this time he had a prosperous business which brought him considerable money, but when the call of God came to him to become a Salvation Army officer, he looked upon these things as dross, and cheerfully surrendered them for the privilege of winning souls for Jesus."

He seems to have had little trouble in converting his wife to his new religion and the two quickly entered into the three years of training it took to become an officer. Frank served as treasurer of the Spokane branch of the Salvation Army during much of that time.

At the turn of the century, the Salvation Army was a much more exotic and controversial group than today, when it is identified with street corner musicians, clothing collection boxes and Christmas kettles. The meetings, usually held on the second floor of business buildings, were always noisy and exciting affairs full of singing, clapping, shouts of "hallelujah", Bible phrases shouted out at random and, most importantly, breaks to hear the testimony of the new converts. These testimonies, delivered by former wife beaters, cheats, prostitutes, burglars, horsebeaters and outrageous characters, consisted of the most fantastic stories that could be imagined, all leading up to the climactic moment when they were "saved."

The sparsely furnished meeting houses had only a few benches and a platform, but the meetings were held 15 times a week. On the platform was often placed an open coffin, the better to get across to the listeners the idea of the nearness of eternity. Canaries were sometimes released from cages at meetings to demonstrate the freedom of the soul. Officers sometimes wore prison garb while giving their sermons. New members were attracted to the meetings by the brass bands and street corner sermons, often held in front of saloons or brothels.

But the Army also performed important community services in an era when there were virtually no public relief programs for the needy or the handicapped. The military-garbed officers and their followers set up rescue homes for unwed mothers and prostitutes, gave free meals to the poor, visited prisoners in jail and helped the indigent find jobs.

Most of the funding for these projects came through street sales of the *War Cry,* which mixed news about the Army's activities with prayers and "testimonies" from converted sinners. Other funds came from collections at meetings.

Resistance to the Army was widespread both from the non-religious and members of the established religious community and often came in the form of violence, especially in the years before 1896. Some of the more traditional ministers, disliking the Army's bizarre methods, preached against them in sermons. Many used this as an unofficial endorsement of the anti-Army activities, which usually took the form of thrown fruit, eggs and verbal abuse. But several Army members, including one in Spokane, were killed by angry mobs.

As Army officers, Frank and Louisa Gillette were required to wear their uniforms at all times. These consisted of a high-collared blue tunic with red and yellow trim and a military cap for the men while the women wore a black straw bonnet with a red band and a huge bow with black ribbons. They were pledged to accept a life of poverty, heartbreak and lonely toil.

During this time Chester helped his parents in their religious and missionary work. Rose H. Winstead, a neighbor who knew the family well, recalled that Chester often went with his parents when they visited prison cells.

"Both Chester and his mother were ever active in giving aid to the unfortunate," she said later. "Chester carried reading matter to the first man ever hanged in this city while the doomed man was awaiting the execution of his sentence." All of this would seem very ironic to Mrs. Winstead when Chester himself was in prison, some 15 years later.

In January 1895, the Gillettes, now a family of six with the addition of Chester's two sisters, Lucille and Hazel, and his two-year-old brother, Paul, set out in the Army's service on a whirlwind series of posts throughout the Northwest. For Chester, at the age of 11, it meant leaving the city he had lived in most of his life. For the rest of his life he would never live in any one place for more than two years at a time.

The Army's policy was to move its officers frequently from post to post and the Gillettes were no exception. They were involved in helping new centers to develop and increase throughout the district. Their first post after leaving Spokane was in Great Falls, Montana, where they served for seven months, then quickly moved on to Moscow, Idaho for six months. There, according to Army records, they converted 86 people. Then they moved to Kallispel, Montana, where they helped to clear off a debt incurred by the previous officers in charge.

In Whatcom, Washington, where they spent the next eight months, Louisa helped a saloon keeper, who was not a religious man, bury his wife, in an incident that shows the depth of her faith. Years later, in describing it, she wrote:

> On that day long ago the trees were bare of foliage. The
> sky was dark and lowering and everything in nature
> added to the desolation of the hour when a lone man, a
> saloon keeper, stood beside a freshly dug grave and laid
> away forever the form of his beloved wife, without a
> prayer or a passage from God's word, merely saying as he
> turned away, "That is the end of it all."

Louisa asked him if he would mind if she prayed for his wife. He consented to that and she prayed "despite the terrible wall of disbelief." Her heart, she said, cried out "give me no God at such a time as this and life would not be worth living."

After Whatcom, the Gillettes moved to Pendleton, Oregon, for six months and it was at this point, in the summer of 1897, that Chester, now 14, left his family to enroll in a boarding school. This was apparently a mutual decision between Chester and his parents after it was discovered that all the moving made it hard for Chester to keep up with his school work. More significantly, however, it may have marked the beginning of an ideological gap between Chester and the rest of the family. Even at this early stage in his life, Chester may have begun to rebel against the enforced poverty, long hours and hard work of the life chosen by his parents.

*The Crescent Building in Spokane, Washington, where Chester's father worked.*

*Spokane after the great fire.*

**LUCIEN CALVIN WARNER** -
*A self-made millionaire who loaned Chester the money to go to school in Oberlin, Ohio, in 1901-03, but did not help him later at his trial.*

**KAREN OSBORNE WARNER**
*Lucien's wife and Chester's grandmother's sister. She apparently thought highly of Chester and probably influenced Lucien's decision to send Chester to Oberlin.*

*John Alexander Dowie, general overseer of Zion City, where Chester's parents lived.*

*THE GILLETTE FAMILY - A portrait taken in 1900 for the Salvation Army newspaper. Top row, Frank, Chester, Hazel; bottom row, Lucille, Louisa and Paul. Frank and Louisa are in uniforms.*

*CHESTER'S BASKETBALL TEAM - A team portrait of the 1903 Oberlin team. Chester is holding the ball with his class year on it. 1908 is also the year he died.*

*CHESTER'S ROOMING HOUSE - This is one of three places Chester lived while at Oberlin.*

After Chester's failings in later life, Louisa was frequently criticized by other mothers for "abandoning her son" or "depriving him of the help of a Christian family." Louisa later justified the family's separation by saying, "It is said that Chester's influence could not have been of the best because of his travelling around with us in the Salvation Army work, but he only travelled with us two years and it was found that it was better for him to be located somewhere and we left him in a school among the best Christian influences."

Exactly where this school was located or who ran it is unknown. Chester later said he worked on a farm in Oregon during this time and didn't mention a school at all, but Louisa later described it as "an academy in the State of Washington." Chester, she said, was considered by the staff to be "a model young man - the professor called him his brightest pupil."

While Chester was living at the school, his family continued its odyssey throughout the Northwest, spending six months at Pendleton, Oregon, six months at Dayton, Washington, five months at North Yakima, Washington, six months at East Portland, Oregon, and four months in Oregon City, Washington, before finally arriving at Vancouver, Washington, on the Oregon border near Portland. Chester rejoined his family there briefly in 1899 when he was 16. He took a job as a printer's apprentice and lived with the family for four months before moving with them to their next post, Chico, California.

The move to Chico was more than just a change of post for the Gillettes; it was also a different division of the Army for the two officers, who now held the rank of captain. The Army was much more firmly established in California than in the Northwest and the family received immediate attention from the California officers who saw the Gillettes as struggling pioneer missionaries who had just come out of the wilderness. An article about them in *War Cry* shortly after they took up the post in Chico described Frank as "a dark-bearded, pleasant-looking man with a Salvation Army captain's braid about his coat collar."

The photograph of the family taken to accompany the article shows Frank and Louisa in their uniforms, the two daughters in uniforms similar to their mother's and young Paul in a sailor suit, all the picture of a model Army family. But standing behind them is the 16-year-old Chester Gillette, with hair neatly combed, dressed like a young dandy in a vested suit with pointed collar and a white matching tie. Clearly, this was a young man who had not adopted the Army's fondness for mundane attire and who aspired to something more in life, even if only, for now, what could be purchased with the salary of a printer's apprentice.

Louisa had begun to make a name for herself as a dedicated crusader and was very active in working with children and forming what the Army called "Bands of Love," organizations for young Army members. She recalled in later life that during this time she "brought three murderers to Christ." One was an Indian who had murdered another Indian and whom she visited at San Quentin prison. She visited another prisoner just minutes before his life ended at the end of a hangman's noose. In recalling it later, she said:

> Almost his last request was that I should go with him to
> the scaffold. I hesitated at first, not that I did not think I
> could do it, but the notoriety of it seemed more than I
> could stand. I was persuaded at last by the sheriff . . .
> He said it was a hard place for the prisoner and if God
> should give me strength he wished I would do it, so I
> consented. His execution was set for afternoon, and we
> found that our boat left at 12 o'clock, so we asked him if
> he would just as soon have his execution at 11 o'clock.
> He said he was willing to have his killing - he always
> called it killing as he did not believe in capital punish-
> ment, as I do not - at that time. We read, talked and
> prayed until the time came. He was a coward and never
> would have acted as coolly as he did through his own
> strength. The people were much infuriated with the man
> and as he sat there before his execution, I noticed that
> the expressions on the faces of the spectators showed only
> curiosity and I wondered what influences the sight would
> have on their lives.

It was at this time also that Louisa first began to write articles of her own for *War Cry*, beginning at first by retelling some of the stories of the sinners she had converted.

Her description of a murderer's conversion is typical of her writing: "Wednesday at our jail meeting, John Richards, on trial for murder, prayed and claimed victory in his soul. Praise God! He has promised to tell the truth, no matter what it costs him. Our prayers go with him to his trial."

After nine months in Chico, the Gillettes were transferred to what was to become their last and most exotic post, Hilo, on the large island of Hawaii. They left San Francisco on the ship *China* in late August of 1900 and toured the islands before taking up their offices in the barracks on Front Street. Chester, however, had obtained a job as a printer in San Francisco and did not sail with the rest of the family.

It took a week to travel from San Francisco to Hawaii and the Gillettes spent much of their time holding prayer meetings with the crew and the other passengers. "The grandeur of God's mighty creation comes over one as he realizes how many miles of this vast globe are covered with water," Louisa wrote in the next issue of *War Cry*. "And then to think how the mind of man, also God's creation, should conceive and construct the beautiful steamers by which the islands of the sea are made as near as New York and San Francisco."

Frank, Louisa, Hazel, Lucille and Paul arrived at Honolulu on September 6, 1900, just in time for the Hawaii Salvation Army's sixth anniversary celebration. They were treated to a grand tour of the islands by the other officers and later wrote that they marveled at the "singing sands" and the volcanos. All the officers on the islands gathered for a photograph which was published in *War Cry*. Frank wore a shirt with "Salvation Army" printed in big block letters on the front, like a modern-day T-shirt, while Louisa and Hazel wore their uniforms.

After the celebration, when they took up their post in Hilo, Louisa wrote, "Hilo is all right, if it does rain seven days in a week. The people keep good natured notwithstanding this fact and most of them are hopeful for the future. They are the happiest lot of people you ever saw."

Many of their group were native Hawaiians and orientals who worked on the nearby sugar and pineapple plantations. Louisa described some of her efforts in converting some of the local "bad boys" who smoked or were heavy drinkers. A local benefactor promised to donate a piano so they could have music at their meetings and the local sugar company donated a wood stove to keep the headquarters warm. Just before Christmas they put an advertisement in the Honolulu papers seeking donations of gifts for the poor children.

All seemed to be progressing well at the Hilo barracks until the spring of 1901. The Hilo weather they had complained about when they first arrived took its toll on Frank Gillette's health. The once robust and vigorous crusader never fully recovered from a respiratory ailment that left him a semi-invalid for the rest of his life. It was a terrible setback for both Frank and Louisa finding they could not keep up with the work. It even seems to have shaken their profound faith in the Army.

The 1901 annual report of the Hawaiian Salvation Army summarized the changes this way: "Our corps in Hilo has been most unfortunate in having to undergo several changes of officers. Capt. and Mrs. Gillette, who took charge after our last anniversary, were compelled by sickness to give up after a short six-months stay."

Frank's illness also brought Chester to Hilo from San Francisco, where he apparently quit his job to be with his family. He arrived late in 1900 or early in 1901 and lived with his parents, who had moved to Mountain View, just outside of Hilo. When he was well enough to work, Frank took a job with the Puna Sugar Company in Pahoa. Chester may have worked there as well, although his activities in Hawaii are largely unknown.

These were hard times both spiritually and financially for the Gillettes, who had given up all their worldly assets to the Army only to find themselves impoverished when they had to leave. The Army had been their entire life and the loss of it left them searching for a new purpose. Chester was apparently dissatisfied with the printing trade since he never returned to it, and he had no other marketable skills.

News of the family's plight was carried by letter to New York City, where it was brought to the attention of someone who could help: Lucien C. Warner, who had married Chester's grandmother's sister, Karen Osborne.

Warner was living proof of the rags to riches possibilities of American business at the turn of the century. He was born in Cuyler, New York, just outside of Cortland, on October 26, 1841, into a family that traced its ancestry back to the Mayflower, but that had since fallen on hard times. His father died when Lucien was three, leaving the two sons and the widow just $500 in goods.

Warner worked his way through Oberlin College and medical school. Later he spent most of his time touring the state, lecturing with his brother on medical problems. Among their most popular topics was "the comfort of women," which dealt with the problems caused by the tight corsets that the styles demanded that women wear.

In 1874, the brothers experimented with designs for their own corsets, which were comfortable as well as stylish. Called "Health Corsets," they sold out immediately on the tours and the brothers soon were designing factories for the mass production of their designs. They became overnight millionaires and were shipping corsets coast to coast and even overseas from their main factory in Bridgeport, Connecticut. By the 1880s, the Warners were dining with presidents, joining exclusive social groups and contributing to philanthropic causes.

In 1875, Lucien Warner hired Noah H. Gillette, Frank's brother and Chester's uncle, who had left the family while they were living in the logging camp in Montana. Noah soon adopted the initials "N.H." and worked in the credit department of the Warner Brothers offices in New York for the next 14 years. He lived with the Warners for a time at "The Stuyvesant" on E. 18th Street.

During this time, the Warners made several trips across the country and around the world and had probably visited Chester's family in 1887, 1893 and 1897.

Warner was a trustee and benefactor of his alma mater, Oberlin College, and had contributed the funds for the conservatory of music and the gymnasium. Hearing of the Gillettes' plight in Hawaii in 1901, it was no problem at all for Lucien to arrange for a place for Chester at the Oberlin Academy, the preparatory school on the Oberlin campus. Warner was always very proud of Oberlin and sent all of his children there. He was confident that the school would offset the problems Chester had encountered and set him up in a proper career.

An agreement was reached among Chester, Mr. and Mrs. Warner and N.H. Gillette. Mrs. Warner agreed to loan Chester the money for his tuition to Oberlin and N.H. Gillette loaned him the money for his clothing. Both Warner and N. H. Gillette had made their fortunes through hard work and they both seemed eager to help another unfortunate young man make his mark in the world.

So, late in August 1901, 18-year-old Chester Gillette  started the long journey from Hawaii to Ohio. He took the week-long boat trip back to San Francisco, during which he encountered a severe storm. Then he took the train for the 2,000-mile journey to Oberlin, Ohio.

Oberlin was known world wide for its pioneering efforts in the admission of blacks and women. It was one of the few coeducational schools in the country. The academy had a principal and a 15-member staff who held classes in two buildings. The tuition was $18 for the fall term, $17 for the winter term and $15 for the spring term. All entering students had to take an entrance exam in English and needed a letter of good character from previous teachers. Chester, who had not gone to school since he left the boarding school in Washington, was a few years older than his fellow students, but seems to have passed the entrance examination. The letter on his character, although it has not survived, was probably written by Warner himself, or may not have been needed since Warner vouched for him.

The aim of the academy, as outlined in the student handbook, was "the development of the individual pupil in body, mind and heart and under favorable and inspiring influences. Every young person needs to get hold of himself, of the powers that he has, that he may direct and develop them. The Academy desires to render individual assistance to this end."

Alcohol and tobacco were forbidden and "young people of bad morals" were allowed to remain only until "their character is ascertained." Parents were asked to refrain from giving students excess pocket money. Those with too much money, the handbook warned, "are almost sure to fail in study and in conduct."

Chester was permitted to enter as a sophomore, indicating that he had kept up with his studies somewhat during his travels and was not very far behind the other students at this level. Latin, which was a required subject, was new to him, so he took double classes his first year to catch up.

During his first year at Oberlin he also seems to have had an outside job to help pay his expenses, probably as a book sales-man. He studied Greek, Roman and English history, and English literature and composition, including the study of George Elliott, Walter Scott, the *Spectator*, Coleridge and Shakespeare. Algebra was required as was a one-day-a-week Bible lesson, which was graded as a regular subject.

He did very well his first year, especially for someone from such a confused social, economic and educational background. The Academy's grading system had a top score of 5 and Chester's lowest score was 4.1 in algebra, the equivalent of a B. Most of his grades were well over 4.5 and he regularly scored 4.8 in Bible, making good use of all the lessons he had been taught by his mother.

Friends and faculty members, asked to recall him in later years, said they remembered Chester as "a boy of no unusual bad character, but on the contrary was somewhat popular and quite widely known . . . He was a student of at least average ability."

Chester also made good use of the new gymnasium, named after his benefactor, which opened in the fall of 1901. The "cads" as the academy students were known, formed their own basket-ball team and Chester was one of the organizers. The academy students also had an active social life, more active than most prep schools because it was coeducational. A Thanksgiving party in 1901 that Chester probably attended featured poetry readings, pantomimes and impersonations organized by the students. Lucien Warner came to the college regularly to attend trustee meetings and was pleased with Chester's progress.

When school was let out for the summer, Chester accepted an invitation from N. H. Gillette to work in his factory in Cortland, New York, the Gillette Skirt Company. This was Chester's first visit to his old family home town and he was favorably impressed with the town and the many people who knew and respected his family there and the dozens of relatives who still lived there.

N. H. had moved to Cortland in 1890 and set up his own busi-ness after many years of working for Warner. He was so success-ful that he quickly outgrew two successive buildings and at the time Chester arrived, his factory was located in a large wooden building, a former corset factory on Miller Street. Many of the employees of the factory were relatives, since N. H. seems to have believed that relatives made more loyal employees.

It is not recorded exactly what work Chester did that summer or where he lived. The best guess is that he lived with his uncle in the house on West Court Street and did mostly manual labor in the factory. Many of the factory workers and relatives remember being favorably impressed with the well-dressed and well-groomed young man.

In September, he returned to Oberlin and took Introductory German, English literature and grammar. But he was not the same student who left Oberlin the previous spring. His grades fell off slightly and his absentee rate increased. By the spring term, his grades had dropped off drastically and he was falling way behind. His grade in English dropped to 2.1 and his German grade was 3.2.

It is unknown exactly what happened. At least part of the problem was that he had been named captain of the new Middle Academy Basketball team, the first such team in the history of the academy, and his notebook shows that he spent considerable time working on the plays and lineup of his team when he should have been studying.

It is also likely, but difficult to prove, that he was involved with a girl, either an Oberlin student or someone from the town, and was spending much of his time with her.

Oberlin students said years later that Chester's academic decline was the result of his "going with a number of fellows of doubtful reputation," and added that his character at that time was very unstable. His landlady, interviewed years later, said Chester was "a very rough, boisterous fellow."

John F. Peck, principal of the academy, in evaluating Chester's career after his former pupil was arrested in 1906, said he thought Chester had a lot of ability, but that it was wasted because he stopped working at his studies:

> The people for whom he did outside work seemed to like him. He was partially supported by wealthy friends and I considered the money well earned. (But in Chester's second year, he) went to pieces. He seemed to lose his self control. His grades were greatly lowered and I saw at that rate the money was being wasted. Accordingly, I informed his benefactors. I took an interest in the boy on their

account, but at the close of his second year I could not
recommend that they help him any further. I told him
that if he was willing to come back and do better, I
would be willing to help.

All of this must have been a terrible disappointment to both
the Warners and N. H. Gillette. They both seem to have accepted
Peck's advice and, perhaps, Chester had had enough of Oberlin
as well, for he left in 1903, never to return.

His family seems to have been unaware of his failure. After
leaving the Salvation Army in 1901, they had become followers of
a new religious calling: the Christian Catholic Church in Zion,
commonly called the Dowieites after the church's founder, John
Alexander Dowie, a character who made the activities of the
Salvation Army seem dull in comparison.

Dowie was born in Edinburgh, Scotland in 1847 and moved to
Australia, where he quickly became known as a crusader against
tobacco and alcohol and for his street corner sermons. He also
began to claim that he had the power to heal the sick through a
special gift from God. He moved to San Francisco in 1888 and to
Chicago in 1890, where he organized his church in 1896.

His claim of healing powers put him in conflict with the doctors and clergymen, who branded him a quack, but the publicity
only spread his fame and his followers soon numbered in the
thousands. Many people saw him for the first time at the 1893
Chicago World's Fair as they passed his "Zion Tabernacle" at
251 E. Sixty-Second Street. But most important in the spreading
of his fame was his newspaper, *Leaves of Healing*, where he wrote
about his plans for the establishment of a theocracy to be known
as Zion City.

Besides giving up pork, alcohol and tobacco, his followers were
required to give the church 10 percent of their incomes for life, a
doctrine that quickly filled Dowie's treasury to overflowing as
money poured out of letters from all over the world. The newspaper contained a coupon that urged the reader to fill out the
application to join the church and send in the money. The paper
also contained reports of miraculous cures and Dowie was soon
besieged by all types of sick and maimed converts seeking a cure.

Dowie, or "the general overseer" as he had taken to calling

himself, surprised his followers on the eve of January 1, 1900, by unveiling a huge map of the promised city of Zion, which was to be built on the shore of Lake Michigan, halfway between Milwaukee and Chicago or, as he described it, "halfway between beer and bacon." He had secretly bought up 6,000 acres for the city and hired professional architects to design what he called the first planned theocracy the world had ever seen. The huge Shiloh temple was to be at the center of the city with the streets, all named for characters from the Bible, radiating out from it like the spokes of a wheel.

The city opened on July 15, 1901, after a crew of engineers and volunteer workers did the preliminary site work. No land was to be for sale, however. Instead, Dowie's followers were offered leases with periods of 1,100 years. Contained in the leases were provisions that the lot would never be used for the possession of alcohol, tobacco or pork. No doctor or druggist was permitted to set up a shop anywhere within the city limits. It was to be a city completely without sin.

To Frank and Louisa, who had abandoned the Salvation Army but who were still looking for a righteous cause to which their lives could be dedicated, the stories of Zion City sounded like a dream come true. They first heard about the city by reading *Leaves of Healing* and Frank, still suffering from his respiratory ailment, was hopeful that it was a sign from God that he could be cured in Zion City.

The December 6, 1902, edition of *Leaves of Healing* contained a letter of testimony signed by Louisa M. Gillette, Zion City, November, 16:

> Dear General Overseer,
> We came here from the Hawaiian Islands where we had charge of the Hilo Salvation Army Corps for six months. We had been Salvation Army officers for eight years and a half, but from reading "Leaves of Healing," we became convinced that there was a higher platform than the one on which the Salvation Army stood, and we decided to cast in our lot with Zion and trust in God as our healer.
> It cost nearly all we had to get here and get settled, but God has blessed us richly since we came here, over

two months ago. Our daughter of eleven years has been
healed of a severe attack of the grip in answer to your
prayer. I have been healed of a tumor and my husband,
who has had consumption and has had a very bad cough
for two weeks before coming here, has been healed. To
God be all the glory.

Louisa, Lucille and Paul were baptized by total immersion in
the special tank at the Shiloh Tabernacle on October 12, 1902, as
part of a group of 53 people. Frank and Hazel were baptized on
November 12 as part of a group of 15 people.

Frank, who had been trained as an engineer at Spokane, had
no trouble finding work in Zion's boom days of 1902 and 1903.
Houses and offices were being built all over the city and a Dowie-
run lace factory produced lace which was famous all over the
world.

When Chester left Oberlin for the last time in June 1903, he
had no place to go other than to join his parents in Zion, but instead he chose to live in Chicago, just 40 miles away. At Oberlin
he had been exposed to a more traditional religious doctrine that
he seems to have been much more comfortable with. He had also
been exposed to the refined manners and habits of the young
gentlemen he met at school. He felt more aloof from his family
than ever and the last thing in the world he would have wanted
was to join such a group. Still, he stayed in touch with the family
and took a job selling books. His mother was apparently unaware
of his problems at Oberlin, for on August 27, she wrote to Professor Peck:

Chester has been home for a short time this summer
and is rather doubtful about going back next fall, as he
undertook canvassing this summer and had an unsaleable
book and poor territory. In consequence the whole summer has gone with little to show for it.

He is quite anxious to graduate from the Academy and
we would like to have him. Did Mrs. Warner say
anything to you about helping him next year? My
brother-in-law, Mr. N. H. Gillette of Cortland, writes that
she told him she expected to help him. He bought a suit
of clothes and books, the cash terms for which he still
owes in Oberlin. I suppose if you had not been away the

latter part of the term he could have found out about the
matter.

We received no report of Chester's work for the last
term. Has he been doing his best in school work? He has
been working in the harvest fields in S. Dakota for three
weeks past. May God bless you in your good work for
Him."

Peck said later that he wrote to Chester in Chicago and kept
for some time a letter in which Chester had expressed a desire to
return to Oberlin as soon as he got out of debt. But Peck never
heard from Chester again.

From September 1903 to December 1904, Chester's life is
somewhat obscure. At least part of the time he was a brakeman
on the Chicago and Northwestern railroad, a very dangerous job
in the days of steam locomotives. He worked on the route between Chicago and Savannah, Illinois, a distance of about 100
miles. He later said he was afraid when he had to stand on top of
the moving railroad cars, especially in the winter, and was once
involved in a train wreck.

But there are also indications in his later statements that he
worked at other jobs and even in other cities during this time. He
may have used his railroad employee pass to obtain free rides to
other cities. There is no indication that he ever paid back Warner
or Gillette for the money he had borrowed to go to Oberlin. Once
he stayed at a hotel in Savannah, Illinois, and left without paying. He was caught and his parents had to help pay back the
money to keep him from going to jail.

Meanwhile, events in Zion City were reaching a climax. Dowie
had declared himself "Elijah the Restorer," a reborn Old Testament prophet who was to save the world from damnation. With
his short stature, white hair and long white beard, Dowie had
always resembled the pictures of old testament prophets found in
illustrated bibles, but now he took to wearing long white gowns
that made him appear even more God-like. He carried a staff
and began to speak in Biblical phrases. And since a Biblical prophet required a monumental task, Dowie chose no less a project
than the conversion of New York City.

The "New York Visitation", as the project was called, involved
nearly the entire population of Zion City, beginning in the

summer of 1903. Eight trains were chartered and each was to take a different route to New York. Every member of Zion was put under intense pressure to go along and Frank and Louisa did not resist. Madison Square Garden was rented for a week to act as a headquarters for the conversion and Zion workers were soon busy preparing the provisions for the journey.

Thousands of Zion City residents left on October 15 from Chicago. Only a few of the older residents stayed behind to care for the children of the crusaders.

But the visitation was a dismal failure. The newspapers, notified earlier that the Dowieites were coming, made up all kinds of stories about Dowie, who needed no exaggeration to be made to seem bizarre, and Dowie spent much of his time describing his doctrines to reporters, who made fun of him in their stories. His sermons in Madison Square Garden, which had been set up as healing sessions where the sick would be made well, turned into tirades against Dowie's enemies. The many people who had shown up to watch and to be cured left the building in disappointment. When the week was over there was no evidence that a single New Yorker had been converted. Dowie became the butt of jokes throughout Manhattan, where it was said that the New York heathens had been more than a match for him.

But worst of all for Dowie and his followers, the church, once wealthy and prosperous, was now flat broke. Dowie was able to conceal that fact for several more years, but the truth was that the visitation had cost millions and the church was now deeply in debt.

In polite society, "Dowieites" had the same kind of reputation that "Moonies" have today, and all of the attention must have caused Chester a great deal of embarassment during his brief visits to his parents in Zion City during this time. But the very fact that Chester chose to stay in Chicago and not move somewhere else showed that he still felt attached to the family, if not to their religious beliefs.

Chester most likely would have gone on drifting from job to job, never staying in one place very long, a fugitive from the problems that he refused to face, except for a meeting which took place in November or December 1904.

N.H. Gillette and his son Harold, who was about Chester's

age, left Cortland in November to attend the St. Louis Exposition. Both N.H. and his son were motor car buffs and they wanted to see the display of the latest cars at the show. Being interested in science as well, especially factories, they also planned to make a tour of automobile factories throughout the Midwest. On their return, they stopped off at Zion City to visit Frank and Louisa and it was either here or in Chicago that they met Chester once again.

Exactly what occurred during this meeting has not been recorded, but N.H. Gillette, apparently forgiving Chester's past failures, offered Chester the chance to return to Cortland and take a job in the factory.

Four months later, Chester packed his suitcase, quit his job with the railroad and bought a train ticket for Cortland, New York.

# CHAPTER TWO

# *The Farmer's Daughter*

J ust 40 miles to the east of where the Gillette families and their relatives were tending their farms in Cortland County in the early 19th century, the ancestors of Grace Brown were living in much the same way on the steep hills and narrow valleys of Chenango County.

But it's unlikely that any of the Browns knew any of the Gillettes. Although the distance was not far, the roads were poor and many of the farming folk lived and died without ever travelling more than a few miles in any direction. It would take 100 years and a famous murder to tie the two areas and the two families together.

For nearly 100 years before she was born, Grace Brown's ancestors had lived along the Otselic River Valley, in the towns of Otselic and Pharsalia, in western Chenango County. Like Chester Gillette's, her ancestors were Central New York pioneers who came from New England seeking cheap land and a new opportunity.

On her father's side, she was the granddaughter of Charles Dennison Brown, a prosperous farmer who lived and died on the same farm in the Town of Pharsalia. When he was 24 years old, he married Mary Caroline Browning, the daughter of another pioneer family from Connecticut. She was only 14 or 15 years old when she married Charles but young marriages were not that unusual in such a thinly populated area as Pharsalia in the 1840s. They settled on Charles's father's farm and raised five children, the youngest of whom was Frank Browning Brown, Grace Brown's father.

After 17 years of growing up on his father's dairy farm and watching his older brothers and sisters grow up and move away to their own farms nearby, Frank married Minerva Babcock on the day before Independence Day, 1873. They moved in with the groom's father to help run the farm because the parents were elderly and their children had moved away.

Minerva, known to her friends as Bessie or sometimes Betsy, was the daughter of Charles H. Babcock, a carpenter and joiner who lived in South Otselic and later in Beaver Meadow. Her mother was the former Celinda Church, a close friend of the Brown family in later life and a favorite relative of Grace Brown.

In 1870, the farm on which Frank and Minerva Brown lived with Frank's parents was assessed at $5,700 and the goods on the farm were valued at $1,576, making it unusually prosperous for the time and place. They later hired a household servant named Sarah Alexander, a luxury that only the well-off could afford.

Frank and Minerva's first child, Carlton, was born in April, 1876, and he was followed by Ada, born the next year, Pauline, born in 1879 and Clayton, born in 1881.

Sometime after Clayton's birth, the family apparently moved to the farm of another relative just a few miles from the Brown farm, and it was here that Grace Brown was born on March 20, 1886. Her younger sisters, Mary and Frances, were born in 1888 and 1889.

In 1889 or 1890, when Grace was about three years old, the family moved about 10 miles away to a farm that had been owned by members of the Brown family for many years. It stood nearly at the top of Tallett Hill, about three miles from the hamlet of South Otselic, and consisted of 214 acres of meadows, orchard and forest which looked down the steep valley toward the west and the Otselic River.

The deed to the farm was registered to William Aden Brown, but by 1890 the ownership had become confused through a series of sales and outstanding mortgages that dated back to 1861. It's unknown how much of the legal entanglements were known to Frank Brown when he moved to the farm, but it's likely that he had some idea of the problems involved and had been assured that they would be resolved.

On March 31, 1892, William Brown sold the farm to Frank Brown for $3,400 with the agreement that Frank was to pay back the $2,900 still outstanding on the debt. The purchase agreement clearly stated that if he did not make the payments he would be forced to pay a penalty fee of $5,800.

For a farmer in the 1890s, owning a farm of your own was a symbol of security and prosperity. It made one a first class farmer, compared to the many farmers who paid rent to land-lords and thereby lost much of the profit from their labors.

Like most of the farms in the Otselic Valley, Frank's farm was basically a dairy farm, but it was a self-sufficient general-purpose farm as well. The barn was full of chickens and pigs, the garden full of vegetables and the orchard full of fruit. Since there was no railroad nearby, it was nearly impossible to deliver the fresh milk to markets in nearby cities, so most of the milk was made into butter and cheese, which didn't spoil as quickly.

For a young girl like Grace Brown, growing up on such a farm meant that the entire world and everything necessary to sustain it was just outside her doorstep. The family members all rose early to perform their assigned chores. While the young children milked the cows and fed the chickens, the adults carried the milk containers to the cheese factory nearby and did the thousands of things that had to be done each day.

The Brown children were lucky in that there was a school less than a mile away, at the top of Tallett Hill, where they could attend more often than most farm children. It was a one-room building with a single teacher for children aged four to 16. Since all of the pupils were farm children, the school tended to follow a flexible schedule that followed the seasons more closely than the calendar. There was no school during the busy times of the year like planting and harvesting and longer hours in the winter when there was less to do at home.

After school, the cows had to be brought back from the meadows and milked again and dinner had to be prepared. After dinner, despite the long day's work, the farm people of the Otselic Valley seem never to have been too tired for visiting friends and relatives on nearby farms or even in the next village.

The Brown farm house, which had a splendid view down the valley to the west, was built in a standard pattern and was much like many other houses in the valley. It was a two-story, wooden-framed house built on a stone foundation, shaded by four ancient maple trees in the front yard. Downstairs was a kitchen with a cast iron cooking stove, a dining room, and a sitting room. There also was the "best parlor", which contained a corner bookcase full of books of fiction, history, and other subjects, and a square piano used in family gatherings to accompany group singing. On the far side of the house, on the other side of the steep staircase, was the master bedroom where Frank and Minerva slept.

The upstairs belonged to the children. There were four adjoining rooms, most of them with window seats in the windows. All of that room came in handy for there were nine children living in the house by 1895. Hazel was born there in 1891 and Ruby was born in 1895.

But Frank Brown's tenure as a property owner proved to be a very short one. On February 15, 1896, just a month before Grace's 10th birthday, a notice was brought to Frank by mail notifying him that the Norwich National Bank had begun foreclosure proceedings on the ancient mortgages.

According to the court records, Frank had not made a single payment since he purchased the farm four years earlier. In addition, he had failed to take out a $2,500 insurance policy that also had been required. Since Frank apparently never filed any papers in his own defense, it is impossible to tell why he failed to live up to his side of the bargain. Certainly the $200 per year payment would not have been a great hardship for a farmer with over 200 acres and over two dozen cows, not to mention the hundreds of relatives who would likely have taken up a collection for him if he had fallen on hard times.

More likely, Frank's failure was the result of a misunderstanding of the terms of the agreement and the penalties for non-payment. The mortgages had a long history of not being taken very seriously. Since the mortgage holder and the property owner had been neighbors, the payments tended to be somewhat informal. Frank probably figured he could continue the non-payment tradition and probably ignored warning letters that the payments were due.

But in 1895 the mortgages had passed from neighbors to the Norwich National Bank, which tended to view them as serious business. Howard D. Newton, the attorney for the bank, took swift action after the notice was served and secured an order from Supreme Court Justice Burr Mattice that the property be sold at auction on March 4 and the bank bought the property.

Since the sale of the farm did not cover the debt Frank owed to the bank, he was ordered on June 16 to pay $1,738.42 in additional costs and interest dating back to April 25.

For Frank, these swift developments must have been bewildering and devastating at the same time. In just a few months he had gone from being an independent farmer to a second-class tenant farmer with the ownership of the land taken away from him and his deed now valueless. After the sale, the title of the property was held by Lucius Newton, probably a relative of the bank's attorney, a cattle breeder in Sherburne.

For 10-year-old Grace Brown, the changes were probably barely comprehensible. She must have understood very little of the conversations in the parlor between her father and relatives as they discussed what was happening to the farm. Outwardly, the farm didn't change at all. The buildings, land and cows were all exactly as they had been. But now her parents probably told her she would have to get by without new clothes as often and money would have to be watched more carefully.

Carlton, the older brother, now aged 20, left home at about this time to hire himself out as a hand on other farms. His extra income was a welcome relief to a family with too many mouths to feed.

But it would be a mistake to consider the Browns a poor family. They seem to have held on to what they had very well, despite their problems, and many years later when the family was portrayed as "poor white trash" on the movie screen, Minerva Brown successfully sued the motion picture company for slander.

For the most part, the Browns' life probably changed very

little. They went into South Otselic to buy the week's supplies, pick up the mail or deliver the milk or cheese to be sent to market. The tiny hamlet had only a few stores but it was most of the world for the Brown family.

The town had several three-story buildings, including the Cox Block and the Perkins Block, across the street. Both had general stores on the ground floor and living quarters on the second floor. The Cox Block had a Masonic Temple on the third floor and the Perkins Block had an opera house - a large hall which was used for public meetings, lectures and visiting entertainers more than operas.

All of the stores had plate glass windows and the houses had wide verandas, beautifully kept lawns, stone walks and maple trees lining the streets, some of which were three feet in diameter.

Dominating the town was the Gladding Fish Line Factory, founded in 1816 and the town's largest employer after dairy farming. Inside the large brick building, 300 machines manufactured the line used by fishermen throughout the nation.

The town also contained a print shop, a weekly newspaper, a box factory, a large harness shop, the three-story Gothic House hotel next to the Cox Block, two hardware stores, a clothing and dry goods store, several small shops, a tannery, a saw mill, several creameries and cheese factories, a bowling alley and billiard room.

For some reason that has faded into history, the entire hamlet was known as "The Burg" and the area around the Gladding Factory, near the Baptist Church, was called "Brooklyn."

A popular gathering spot was the Cox Block, where the post office was located. Besides the thousands of items stocked on the shelves and on the walls 10 feet up to the ceiling, it also had a drug store and ice cream parlor.

Farther down Gladding Street, in the "Brooklyn" area, was the Baptist Church that the Browns attended, but of which they were never official members. Some local residents later recalled that Grace was once a singer in the choir, but this is not shown on any of the records.

Right in the middle of town, at the intersection between the Cox and Perkins Blocks on the main road there was a bandstand

*GRACE BROWN'S SCHOOLMATES - Standing in the doorway are Grace Brown and Maude Kenyon, her teacher and friend (later Maude Crumb). Also in this photo are Grace's four younger sisters. Probably taken in 1901 or 1902 when school let out for the summer.*

*GRACE BROWN AT 16 - Grace is at the left dressed in a very fancy dress. The other girl is not identified. Site may have been the Brown family orchard.*

THE BROWN FAMILY - From a portrait taken at the trial. Top is Frances and Mary Brown, Grace's younger sisters, with Minerva and Frank.

GRACE BROWN'S HOME SO. OTSELIC N.Y.

BROWN FARM IN 1906 - This photo, later made into a South Otselic postcard, was allegedly taken the day after Grace's funeral.

*BROWN FARM TODAY - A photo of the Brown Farm taken in 1981.*

*VIEW FROM THE BROWN FARM - This is the view looking west from the Browns' front yard.*

*SOUTH OTSELIC AROUND 1906 - In front is the bandstand where the South Otselic band played on weekends and holidays. Behind it is the Cox Block with a general store, etc. and next to that is the Gothic House, where Grace made her phone call to Chester in June, 1906.*

*CORTLAND IN 1906 - A postcard view of Main Street in Cortland show-ing what it was like when Chester and Grace lived there.*

in the middle of the intersection. The South Otselic Band and visiting bands played concerts there during the summer. Travelling minstrel shows, magic shows and miniature circuses, which travelled the country by wagon, frequently stopped for a night or two for a performance in the Opera House.

According to local legend, it was after one of these concerts that Grace acquired her nickname. A travelling jazz band performed the popular song "Won't You Come Home Bill Bailey," and Grace, taking to the tune, sang it over and over again, until people began calling her "Billy." The name stuck, and for the rest of her life her friends and the members of her family called her Billy.

The local residents also recalled that Grace was very fond of dancing. According to a story told after her death, it was her fondness for dancing, inherited from her parents, that prevented her from becoming a member of the church, whose members looked down upon such activities as somewhat un-God-like. In any case, there was no lack of opportunities to dance and sing in South Otselic at the turn of the century.

The big event each year, beginning in 1900, when Grace was 14, was the Dairyman's Picnic, held just south of the village. It was a kind of miniature county fair with bands, dance contests and prizes for the best poultry, baked goods and needlework. There were wheelbarrow races, three-legged races, a shooting gallery and games of chance. Wagons were used to ferry people, many of whom came from miles away, from the downtown intersection to the picnic site. Old timers recalled that it was the social function of the year, a time to see old friends and make new ones, a traditional end of the summer celebration held each August.

In 1901, a year after the first dairyman's picnic, Maude Kenyon was appointed as teacher of the little one-room school house on Tallett Hill and she immediately became very important to the 15-year-old Grace Brown. Just seven years older than Grace, Maude was the daughter of a local justice of the peace and cheese factory owner. She was a cheerful, sympathetic young woman, just the kind of confidant an adolescent girl required. She was not as old as Grace's parents, but old enough to know something of life and still young enough to serve as a role model.

Grace was one of the oldest students in the school and Maude took a special interest in her, impressing on the young girl the importance of a good education and teaching her about the wonders of the world beyond the Otselic Valley. For two years, Grace shared her intimate thoughts, hopes and dreams with her teacher.

The other important events in Grace's life at this time were the weddings that seemed to occur nearly every month. Her oldest sister, Ada, was married on Christmas Day, 1899, in the Brown home. For the sisters, including Grace, it was an opportunity to dress in their finest outfits, decorate the house in celebration and welcome the minister and their new brother-in-law, Clarence Hawley, the son of a cheesemaker.

But Ada's wedding was only the first of many. Her older brother, Carlton, was married less than a year later at the home of his wife and cousin, Lena J. Brown, in nearby Pitcher, New York. Grace watched again as the rice was thrown and the bouquet was tossed.

Just six months later, her next oldest sister, Pauline, was married to Miles Loomis at a ceremony in the little parlor in the Brown house. This reduced the size of the family once again, opened up more room in the upstairs of the house, and began to weigh somewhat heavily on the shoulders of Grace Brown. The words did not need to be spoken, but they probably were anyway. Grace knew she was the oldest unmarried daughter and she knew that everyone expected her to be the next.

Her father, in talking about this period of Grace's life, said later:

> I got so I depended on her. She kept all my accounts.
> No matter how stormy the weather, Mrs. Brown or myself
> had only to mention an errand about the place to have
> her anxious to go and do it. And about the writing. What
> a letter she could write! Once I got a letter that showed
> misunderstanding. Grace sat down and dashed off a reply
> that would have done credit to a lawyer and that set the
> matter right.

But despite her talents and abilities, many of them no doubt encouraged by Maude, further education never entered the realm of consideration for Grace in light of her parents' modest circumstances. She had stayed in school longer than many of her friends and it was time to leave. In June 1902, at the age of 16, Grace left school and returned to the farm as a full-time helper.

Her younger sisters were now able to do much of the work that she had done before, and when the opportunity came up, Grace took a position as a helper on a farm at King Settlement, about 40 miles away on the other side of Norwich.

She spent six months away from home, but the experiment was apparently not successful since she never tried it again. After spending nearly all her life with her own family, she missed them and was lonely with strangers. She returned home in January 1903, in time for a family celebration at her sister Ada's house in Taylor Valley, where Clarence Hawley had purchased a cheese factory.

For the next year and a half she lived on her parents' farm, nursing her sisters when they were ill, doing the chores she had done nearly all her life, and all the time feeling the pressure that it was her turn to find a mate and settle down on a farm of her own.

On June 22, 1903, her best friend, Maude Kenyon, married Dr. J. Mott Crumb, a newly-graduated medical student and son of the local doctor. Crumb was South Otselic's resident genius and probably regarded by the young women of the village as the best catch in the township.

Born in South Otselic in 1878, he was a graduate of Norwich High School, the Fairfield Military Academy and the pre-medicine program at Syracuse University. A year before the marriage he had been the valedictorian of the University of Vermont Medical School. Returning to South Otselic, despite numerous offers to go elsewhere, he took over his father's practice and was the resident doctor in South Otselic for the rest of his life. He was also a star athlete who played on the South Otselic baseball and football teams.

Maude no doubt shared with Grace the details of her courtship throughout the pre-engagement and engagement rituals. After the marriage, Grace spent much of her free time at Maude's new house, one of the nicest in the village, at the corner of Potter and Gorge Streets.

Grace went to many of the social functions, but the right man never showed up for her. Since she was attractive, bright, popular and well thought of, it wasn't for lack of opportunities that she remained unmarried. It certainly wasn't for lack of trying on her part. By all accounts, she was more interested in fashions and looking attractive than most other farm girls her age. She may have been waiting for someone better than the farmboys and shopkeepers' sons she met at the parties and picnics. Through her reading of romantic novels and long talks with Maude about the ideal husband, she may have set standards higher than any farmer's son could hope to meet.

In the late fall of 1904 she was offered a chance to get away from South Otselic, to move to a larger town where the long-sought spouse might be waiting for her. Her brother-in-law, Clarence Hawley, had worked at several odd jobs after his cheese factory was destroyed by fire in 1902. He had since taken a position with the Cortland Traction Company, the firm that ran the street cars in the city, 40 miles from South Otselic. Soon after the Hawleys moved to Cortland, Grace came for a visit and decided to stay.

It's very likely that Grace had been to Cortland before. While many of the everyday necessities could be purchased in the South Otselic stores, any kind of major purchase or the need for something out of the ordinary, would be impossible to fulfill there. The alternatives were Norwich to the east and Cortland to the west. All her life, Grace had passed the bandstand at the cross roads in South Otselic where there were sign boards, pointing the directions to distant places. One said Cortland, 25 miles via Hawleys and the other said Cortland, 31 miles via DeRuyter. Any South Otselic farmer's daughter passing those could not help but wonder about what life must be like in the city, with its dress shops, restaurants, trolley cars and young people dressed in the latest fashions. It had to seem exotic to someone familiar only with the dusty farmers who walked the streets of South Otselic.

But despite what Grace may have thought of it, Cortland in 1905 was not a large city. It had only been a city for five years and had a population of 10,000. Its main streets, however, were filled with stores and imposing stone office buildings. There were long rows of distinguished houses along the main streets, especially Tompkins Street. The streets themselves were full of electric trolley cars, carriages and bicycles. There were even a few motorcars; expensive luxuries owned by the sons of rich men.

The Hawleys, of course, didn't live in one of the stone mansions, but in a much more modest wood frame house at 13 Fifth Avenue, in a residential area shaded by tall elm and maple trees. It was a few blocks from the main streets and about seven blocks from the business district.

Grace made herself useful during her visit by helping to take care of her newborn nephew, Robert. But within a few days of her arrival, some of her sister's friends told her that there were jobs available at the Gillette Skirt Factory.

The factory, just three blocks away at the corner of Homer Avenue and Miller Street, was not the same one that Chester Gillette had worked at during his summer vacation from Oberlin in 1902. That factory had burned to the ground in a spectacular fire on the night of January 9, 1904. The old wooden building went up quickly, throwing 150 people out of work and taking with it 1,500 skirts waiting to be shipped to stores.

For N.H. Gillette, the disaster may have been a blessing in disguise. The $16,000 in insurance costs did not begin to cover the cost of replacing the building, but it did allow him, for the first time, to design a new factory from the ground up for the sole purpose of making skirts. In the past, he had purchased used buildings and converted them for his use.

N.H. had always had an interest in science and firmly believed in progress, so, after one experience with a fire, he set about building a factory that wouldn't burn. He had heard about a new building material called concrete blocks and within a year the result was, as the cornerstone of the new factory noted, "The first concrete block building in Cortland." But N.H. was frugal as well, so instead of purchasing new wooden beams for the inside of the building, he used the charred ones left over from the fire. He took an active interest in the interior of the building so that work could be handled as efficiently as possible.

In the fall of 1904, when Grace Brown, a frail-looking 18-year-old, about 5 foot 2 inches and weighing about 100 pounds, walked into the office of the factory to ask for a job, the factory was just getting back to full production after a summer of operating out of temporary quarters. N.H. probably needed

many new workers to replace those who had found work elsewhere after the fire. N.H. was no doubt pleased to offer a job to
anyone, even a young woman whose only experience had been in
farming.

For Grace, the Gillette factory was the most modern facility in
the city and probably much talked about because of its unique
construction. When she entered the three-story building with its
rows of windows and a single tree at one side, she walked up the
stairs at the far end of the building. The only factory she was likely to have entered before was the fish line factory in South Otselic.

The heart of the plant was the sewing room in which rows of
skilled seamstresses at long tables ran dozens of machines,
sewing the skirts and petticoats together. In other parts of the
factory, cutters, usually men, used large wrought iron patterns to
trace the lines on the bolts of fabric and cut them out. Also
employed were people to carry the cut pieces from the cutting
room to the sewing room, people who took care of the bolts of
fabric and the trimming material and inspectors who made sure
that the finished product met all the specifications for size and
proper construction. Wrappers then bundled the skirts together
and got them ready for shipping. In the same room, clerks
checked in the shipments of fabric, thread and other supplies
that came in from other factories via the railroad station. There
were also the clerks and bookkeepers who kept track of the accounts and the payroll. In all, there were about 250 employees.

Since Grace had no skills as a seamstress or a cutter, apparently having even less experience in that area than most farm
girls, she probably started out for a while at one of the low-skilled
jobs before finally settling on her job as an inspector. Later,
however, she proved to be such a good worker that she seems to
have filled in at a number of jobs for other workers who went on
vacation. By the time she left, a year and a half later, she knew
how to perform many of the jobs at the factory.

She quickly made friends with the many other young women
her age, who showed her where to hang her hat and coat, where
to eat her lunch and how to collect her pay at the end of the week.
Much of her pay was spent in the Cortland dress shops, where
fashions were available that were only dreamed about in South
Otselic.

Towards the end of March of the next year, after Grace had been at the factory about four and a half months, the factory gossips passed on the talk about a new employee, a nephew of N. H., who had just arrived from somewhere in the west and who was full of stories about his adventures in such far away places as Hawaii, San Francisco and Ohio.

The April 3 edition of the *Cortland Standard* announced his arrival in its personal column this way: "Chester Gillette of Chicago, Illinois, has entered the employ of the Gillette Skirt Company and is at present making his home with his uncle, N. H. Gillette."

But the Chester Gillette who stepped off the train at the Cortland railroad station in late March of 1905 was quite a different person from the college student who had last been there in the summer of 1902. He was a mass of contradictions. The student who had studied Wordsworth and Shelley had been tempered with the hard life and rough habits of the railroad brakeman. The young gentleman scholar had been thrust into the worst kind of influences.

When he wanted to, he could still project the image of the prep school student. His uncle, aunt and cousins saw a well-dressed, immaculately-groomed, intelligent and well-spoken young gentleman, who could discuss literature and poetry at an evening soiree, always knew the proper courtesies and never stepped out of line. He was an intelligent gentleman who, through the unfortunate circumstance of his family's conversion to a bizarre religious cult, had not become all he was capable of being. All this person needed, his uncle thought, was a chance and his abilities and talents would make him a valuable asset to society.

Others in Cortland were soon to see another side of the new arrival. The former railroad brakeman could spend hours telling about his exciting adventures riding cars, surviving a train wreck, crossing the Pacific Ocean on a steamer and playing college pranks. He loved to spend his time with a group of friends, playing cards and smoking cigarettes and discussing women and dancing. He was a person who made friends easily and he soon had a large following of admirers of both sexes who loved to be with him and go on adventures with him to nearby towns. At five-foot-seven and 150 pounds, he was small but extremely athletic.

He loved to play tennis, row boats, and go for day-long bicycle rides with his friends.

Yet, at the same time, he attended services every Sunday without fail at the First Presbyterian Church, where his uncle was a member of the board of directors and a Sunday School teacher. On some Sundays he attended services more than once. He was an evening usher at the church and for the first six months of 1906, Chester was one of only three students with perfect attendance at the church's Sunday School. One of his friends who attended the school with him, Fred H. Crook, said Chester was "quiet, a hard worker and a favorite with workers at the skirt factory."

"A careless and thoughtless boy," was how his mother later accurately described him. She said he always had a "light, free-from-care way about him," and that many of his decisions were made "on the spur of the moment." He was emotionally immature for his age, especially for someone who had lived so long on his own. His main goal in life, as he expressed it to several people, was to "have as good a time as you can." His early separation from his family and his rejection of the family's strict moral code was at least part of the source of his personality flaws. He knew that many of the things he did were considered evil and sinful by other members of his family, but he never seems to have developed his own ethics to replace those he rejected. He had a serious inability to accept responsibility for his actions and this expressed itself in several ways.

Chester always spent more money than he earned and had been constantly in debt since his days at Oberlin. His salary of $10 a week at the factory was not nearly enough to pay for the expensive clothes that he bought, not to mention the luxuries like a bicycle and a camera that he bought in Cortland.

His other major weakness, and the one he considered his major downfall when he examined his life during his final days, was a fondness for young women. Chester required the constant attention of many women and those in Cortland quickly found him to be an interesting and somewhat exotic young man with connections to an established local family.

Although his lips were unusually full and his ears stuck out a little, he was always well-groomed and well-dressed. His hands, especially, were always neatly manicured. But most of all, women found him full of interesting stories and, therefore, a person who was fun to be with.

Chester lived with his uncle for only a few days, although it is not explained exactly why he left. Most likely, the Cortland Gillettes never intended for Chester to live with them and only let him stay there until he could find a place of his own. Soon after his arrival he moved in with his cousin, Fred Gillette, who had recently returned to Cortland from Iowa. He was a jeweler and the son of Chester's grandfather's brother. Right away the cousins developed a close friendship that remained long after N. H. Gillette's family had abandoned Chester.

Fred Gillette's friends were a step below his uncle's son's friends in the social pecking order of Cortland. They were working men: clerks, bankers and salesmen instead of the sons of doctors, lawyers and professional people. Chester seems to have felt much more comfortable with Fred's friends than he did with the people in the Court Street house.

Within days of his arrival in Cortland, he went to work in the factory. Although the factory was somewhat noisy, it was easy for the seamstresses, the cutters and the inspectors to talk with each other as they did their work and gossiping was a major activity during breaks and lunch hours.

Everyone knew his name the day he arrived and they knew his relationship to the owner. So, right from the start, he was treated quite differently from any other new arrival. He was related to at least half a dozen other workers in the factory and many of them had quickly risen to positions of responsibility.

So, even though he had no real supervisory position at first and was paid a very modest salary, he wasn't treated like a regular employee by his fellow workers. Like Grace, Chester seems to have worked at several different jobs when he first arrived and some of the work was familiar from his experience in 1902. Within a few weeks he found his permanent spot in the stock room.

His job there was to make sure the work was given out to the cutters and to make sure it was collected when they were finished. The stock room was on the second floor and was walled off by a partition from the rest of the room.

As an inspector, Grace's job was to examine the finished skirts to make sure there were no defects. In the normal course of the factory routine, Grace and Chester probably would not have crossed paths very often. But Chester enjoyed roaming around the plant and quickly met most of the employees in the building, especially the women.

According to an account told to a reporter after Grace's death, Chester met Grace when a ring slipped off of Grace's finger. The ring had an inexpensive gold band with an opal stone and Grace had such small fingers that the ring often fell off. One day it rolled to the feet of a worker who happened to be passing by. Chester Gillette picked it up and returned it with a bow and Grace thanked him with a blush.

By early summer, Chester and Grace were frequently seen in each other's company at the factory. Chester often found an excuse to visit her, as he did with many of the women in the factory, but eventually he began to pay particular attention to her. They often ate their lunches together at the tables in the factory and Grace often gave him most of what she had packed for herself.

Theresa Dillon, one of the factory employees in 1905, later recalled that Chester was "with her constantly. He never lost an opportunity to see her either in the factory or outside of it." At first, she said, Grace didn't care for Chester at all, but he "wouldn't leave her alone."

One of the things Chester and Grace had in common was a fondness for the popular magazines and newspapers of the day. Both of them spent much of their free time reading. Grace also showed an interest in more literary subjects, a love for which was probably instilled by her friend and teacher, Maude Crumb. Chester didn't show much interest in literature these days, but had studied it in Oberlin, and this was something Grace seemed to like in him. Some of the factory employees recalled that Grace often asked other employees about the things that she had read, and Chester, no doubt, found this an opportunity to talk about his days as a "college" student at Oberlin.

"She was trying to educate herself to be his equal," Dillon said. She said Grace was always proud that Chester had been to "college," and no one seems to have known that Chester's days at Oberlin were spent in the prep school, not at the college itself. In

*HOW IT LOOKED IN 1908 - In a photo of the skirt factory, the words GILLETTE SKIRT CO. are painted on the side toward the left, behind the tree.*

**THE SKIRT FACTORY TODAY** - *This is how the skirt factory building, now an appliance warehouse, looks today.*

*The original Gillette Skirt factory building where Chester worked in 1902.*

*Interior of the original Gillette Skirt factory.*

*NOAH H. GILLETTE -*
*Chester's uncle.*

*Logo of Gillette Skirt Factory.*

"DON'T I LOOK FINE IN MAMMA'S SKIRT?"

*GRACE BROWN'S BOARDING HOUSE - Grace Brown lived in this house from November 1905 to June 1906. It was run by Carrie Wheeler.*

*CHESTER'S RESIDENCE - This is where Chester lived from May to July 1906. His room was the upper left window. It was in this room that Grace's letters were found by the police.*

*Postcard view of Little York Lake around 1906. It was here that Chester went swimming and canoeing in 1906. He took Harriet Benedict here in 1906 and may have taken Grace also.*

*CORTLAND PRESBYTERIAN CHURCH - Chester's aunt and uncle were both involved in many church activities and Chester attended here regularly and was a regular at Sunday School.*

reality, Chester had not even graduated from high school, but he never told anyone that fact.

Ellen Melvin, another factory employee, said Chester and Grace were together nearly every day. "His business didn't keep him in the stock room," she said. "He went around the factory to the different machines where the girls work, both with and for work."

Neva Wilcox, who worked in the cutting room, remembered seeing the two of them together one day. "He had some candy and laughingly gave me a piece and said 'give it to Grace.' "

Theresa Harnishfager, who was in charge of the floor where they both worked, said Chester "spent the greater part of his time at her (Grace's) table. His place was in the stock room and she was in the other part of the room in the inspecting department." Chester's visits, she said, were causing some problems in the operation of her floor.

"I would tell him not to neglect his work and she was neglecting hers at the same time that he was up there," she said. "I used to tell him his place was in the stock room. Sometimes he would listen to what I said and sometimes he didn't."

Technically, Harnishfager was Chester's supervisor, but she knew very well that he was the owner's nephew, so she couldn't take her complaints about Chester's work to N. H. It was a problem that she had to solve on her own.

Harnishfager said Chester talked to many of the girls in the factory and it was only gradually that he seemed to single out Grace as the object of his interests. All of this seems to have been taken, at first, as a harmless flirtation, the kind of factory romance found in most plants that ends at the end of the working day and starts up again the next morning.

But after rumors began to circulate that Chester was seeing Grace outside the factory, many of the employees began to warn Chester that it was wrong and would get him into trouble. They told him not to get involved with her. Beginning in July, however, Chester began calling on Grace in the evenings at her sister's house on Fifth Avenue.

By this time, he had moved to a rented room at 21 East Main Street, just down the street from his father's cousin Ella Hoag, the paymistress at the factory. Mrs. Hoag, a widow and close friend of Chester's since his first visit to Cortland, seems to have nearly adopted him during this time. Chester's mother later said Mrs. Hoag was "like a mother to him," and she was one of the few Cortland people who did not abandon him later.

Chester had used some of his first earnings from the factory to buy a bicycle, or a "wheel" as he called it, and used it to ride all over the countryside and to nearby cities. He seems to have thought nothing of riding the 25 to 30 miles a day to visit Ithaca or other nearby cities.

A neighbor on East Main Street recalled seeing him go by on his bicycle frequently. The street was paved only with boards and he rode over them so fast that he made a loud noise that raised objections from his neighbors. Sometimes, they recalled later, he had a tennis racket slung over his shoulder on his way to play with friends at the YMCA or at the Normal School, where he knew several of the students and faculty members.

It was just 10 blocks from his rented room in the home of John and Catherine Lonergain at the corner of East Main and Harmon Avenue to Clarence Hawley's house on Fifth Avenue and Chester made the trip often. Ada Hawley later said that Chester "usually came to our house around eight or nine (at night). I think he came once a week at first, then he began to come oftener. I think some weeks he would come twice a week."

During the visits, she said, Chester would sit and talk with Grace in the parlor where they were often left alone. Ada seems to have been too kind a sister to Grace to insist that she have a chaperone. The odd thing about their relationship, Mrs. Hawley said, was that they never went out. The only times she could ever recall their leaving together was to go out for a ride. Chester never took her to dances or parties, even though Grace had been invited to many of them by her friends at the factory and was an excellent dancer.

During his visits, Ada said, Chester amused them all by telling funny stories and detailed accounts of his adventures in the West and in college.

Left alone after the Hawleys had gone to sleep, Chester and Grace kissed and held each other on the couch in the parlor. Chester had certainly had some experience with sex during the last few years and he attempted on many evenings to seduce her.

According to his own account later, Grace said "no" many nights and successfully fought him off before finally giving in, sometime in the late summer or early fall of 1905. After that, they made love frequently in the parlor late at night.

But Chester spent most of his nights away from Grace, mostly with his cousins and their friends. He frequently played tennis on weekends and went on group outings with other friends who owned bicycles. Most of all, however, he enjoyed swimming and boating on the nearby lakes and the parties with the young people he had met through friends at the factory and through Fred Gillette.

In early September, Ada Hawley went to South Otselic to visit her parents and brought along her son, Robert, then two years old. Frank and Minerva, who had not had a baby in the house for several years, made such a fuss over their grandson that Ada agreed to leave him with them for a few days while she returned to Cortland.

But on Saturday night, just after Ada left, the baby became ill. Frank and Minerva, who had seen many sick children, didn't consider it very serious until the next night, when Dr. Crumb was called. He did all he could, but Robert died on Monday morning. Notified by telegram, Clarence and Ada, along with Grace, took the train and the stagecoach to South Otselic. The funeral was held Wednesday at the Brown home with the Rev. J. A. Whitney officiating. Among those attending the funeral were Grace's other married sister and her husband, Miles Loomis, Clarence's parents, Minerva's brother from Hamilton and Fred Brown and his family from DeRuyter.

The death seems to have had a terrible impact on the entire family. Frank and Minerva certainly felt responsible for their only grandchild's death and Ada Hawley was hysterical over the death of her only child. She insisted that Clarence quit his job with the Traction Company at Cortland and the couple moved to Otego to live with Clarence's parents.

Grace, too, seems to have been very much affected by the death of the child that she had looked after for the past year or so. With the Hawleys moving away, she had no place to live in Cortland and for a while considered not going back at all. Her father said later:

When Grace came home after her sister moved to
Otego, when Mrs. Hawley's little boy died and she
wanted to get away from the scene of her grief, it was not
intended that Grace return to Cortland . . . But I got two
letters, one from N.H. Gillette and the other from Mrs.
Harnishfager, asking that she be allowed to return, so
much did they think of her. Under these influences, and
because it was arranged that she should board with one
of the most respectable families there, that of B.H.
Wheeler, I consented that she could go back.

Frank, however, apparently did not know that Grace had
another reason for returning to Cortland: Chester Gillette.
Chester wrote a brief sympathy note to her while she was home,
which served to remind her that he cared about her and that she
could not see him if she stayed in South Otselic. Perhaps, also,
Chester influenced his uncle or Theresa Harnishfager to write the
letters to Frank Brown urging Grace to return. Chester may also
have been involved in helping to find a room for her at 7 Wheeler
Avenue, just around the corner from the factory.

After Grace's return, Chester continued to visit her in the
parlor of the Wheeler house and they continued to make love in
the evenings after the Wheelers had gone to sleep. Carrie
Wheeler, the landlady of the house, said Chester visited about
twice a week, not always on the same night and usually on week-
day nights. Only a few times did he come on the weekends, she
said.

In mid-October, Grace went back to South Otselic for a week-
long visit, during which Chester wrote her a letter:

Oct. 17, 1905

Dear Billy,
    . . . You don't know how lonesome it is now, with less
work to do and nothing to do evenings. Last Sunday was
the dullest day I have known for a long time although the
weather was fine. . .
    Saturday evening was fine, and I wished that you were
here then, as I have wished since. These nights are too
fine to last, so improve them while you can. I know we
were out awfully late, but we did the best we could under
the circumstances. I shall never let it happen again if I

can help it . . .

Dear, how I miss you, but not for the work you did. You always accuse me of that although you don't believe it.

Sunday I went to church three times, something I haven't done in a long time. I read all afternoon, and church in the evening. I went to bed about nine, but laid awake two hours thinking of everything, principally you.

Your letter was fine, the best I have gotten in a long time. I wish I could receive another one or that I could write one half as good . . . Hurry back as you don't know how lonesome it is here.

With love, Chester

But by the fall of 1905, a slow change had begun to take place in Chester's activities in Cortland. After nine months of only haphazard contact with the upper level of society in Cortland, he began to be invited to private parties and dances and dinner engagements with people from the Normal School.

His initial introduction to this group of people seems to have come through his cousin, Georgia Hoag, the 17-year-old daughter of Ella Hoag. Chester had visited the Hoags several times a week, more often than he visited Grace, and it was there that he met Josephine Patrick, the 17-year-old daughter of the Cortland County Clerk, who lived at 13 East Main Street, next door to the Hoags.

Chester probably had known many of Georgia's friends for some time, but it wasn't until the winter of 1905 that he began to spend a great deal of time with them. He went to parties and to the theater, quickly winning them over as he turned on his charm.

At one of these parties he met Harriet Benedict, daughter of prominent lawyer Byron A. Benedict, who lived at 53 North Main Street, just around the corner from where Chester, the Hoags and the Patricks lived.

Harriet, who was 18 when Chester met her, had just graduated from the Central High School with 24 other students. She was a member of Delta Epsilon Sorority, which limited its membership to the daughters of prominent families. Among the other members were Josephine Patrick and Georgia Hoag. At her high school graduation on June 19, she had been elected "class reciter" and read the "Romance of a Rose" by Noah Terry. She was considered by many young men of Cortland to be one of the most beautiful young women in the city.

In September, she had enrolled in the Cortland Normal School, a teacher training college, and had attended most of the school dances and social functions. At one of these, there was a poster for sale that she wanted, but had no money with her. Chester purchased it for her, but then took it home with him, prompting her to write a note a few days later saying, "Where, oh where is my poster?"

Speaking of the incident later, Harriet said, "I dropped him that note in relation to a little poster he had promised me. He merely said that I might have it. It was a very pretty poster. He knew I admired it. I got it. I wrote that note, a few lines to remind him of it, presently I got it."

After that, Chester took her to several parties, including some private parties organized by Normal School students at Dillon's Dancing Academy and at least one party at N.H. Gillette's house.

The extent of the relationship between Harriet and Chester remains one of the mysteries of the story. There are many legends built around a supposedly deep romantic involvement and even a marriage proposal. Those who choose to believe this rationalize the lack of evidence of it by contending that Harriet and her father covered it all up after Chester's arrest. But it is known for certain that Chester went out with many women during this time and Harriet was only one of them. Later circumstances were to make it appear that the relationship was more serious than it was.

Chester and Grace probably both attended the skirt factory's Christmas party on December 7 at the same Dillon's Dancing Academy where Chester had attended several parties. About 200 to 250 employees danced and celebrated together. If they did attend and dance together they must have made some attempt to remain apart from each other to save their "secret."

For Christmas, Grace gave Chester a gold seal ring that she told friends had cost her $9.50, about a week and a half's pay for her.

In January, Frank Brown and Frances, Grace's 15-year-old sister, visited her in the Wheeler house. While he was there, Frank said he made several inquiries about Chester.

"I heard only good reports and was told that he was steady," Frank said. "We never thought there was anything wrong." The day they were there, Chester called about noon and was introduced to her father and sister. Chester spoke to them as briefly as possible and then took Grace into another room.

"He came to the door," Frank said. "Grace went there and let him in. I went to the door and she introduced me. She said, 'this is my father, Mr. Gillette.' She showed me to my room about that time."

"I don't like him," Frances said she told her sister later when they were alone. "He doesn't look at you straight. He has a shifty eye." Later, in describing him, she said, "When he came to see her he never took any notice of the rest of us and he seemed all the while as if he was afraid of something. And then he never gave Grace any presents. He gave her one little picture that he bought at the 10-cent store, a string of blue glass beads and a burned wood box. And once he bought her a magazine to read on the train coming home . . . The only time he ever took Grace anywhere while I was there, she loaned him $5 to pay for the rig."

By this time, Chester was leading a double life. His life was made up of two different worlds with only a very few people in one even knowing the existence of the other. At work, he would talk with Grace and would go to her house two nights a week to make love with her. But on the other nights, he attended full-dress parties with young ladies and gentlemen from the Normal School.

But the few people who did know what he was doing cautioned him that it would all turn out badly.

"I said if he went to see her (Grace), I would not if I was in his place," said Ella Hoag. "I didn't think it was a good plan to go with girls you don't go out with or take out in company. I asked him if he had ever went to Mrs. Wheeler's. He said once. I never saw him outside the factory in company with Grace Brown. I saw him in company with other girls."

Albert Gross, general foreman at the factory and a close friend of Chester's, said he advised Chester not to go out with Grace.

He had seen him out with other girls in the evening and saw him spending much of his time with Grace during the day. But Chester ignored all these warnings and most people at the parties he attended said later they had never heard of Grace Brown and had no idea Chester was seeing anyone from the factory. But the gossips at the factory knew all about it and felt it was their duty to tell Grace about it, advising her to forget him.

Theresa Harnishfager, who had seen Chester at some of the parties, often with Harriet Benedict and Josephine Patrick, said she once asked Chester why he never took Grace out to any of the parties. All Chester replied, she later testified, was, "I am having my fun." She warned Chester about the gossip, that everyone knew of his nocturnal visits to the Wheeler house.

"Chester," she told him, "hereafter when you are up to see Billy Brown, be careful what neighbors are watching or happen to see you." But Chester denied that he had been to the house. "You know you need not try to hide yourself, we all know it," she told him. But all Chester would say was, "That is my affair" and told her to mind her own business.

Harold Gillette, N.H.'s son, also heard rumors and called Chester into his office one day to ask about them, but Chester said he had not been to see her.

It didn't take long for the stories of the parties and the young women to reach Grace. Theresa Dillon said she asked Grace about those rumors and Grace told her, "Chester is so truthful. He never told me a lie in his life. If he goes anywhere with another girl, I always know and don't care. I want him to have a good time and enjoy himself and, of course, he goes a lot of places I can't."

Chester seems to have told Grace that since he was invited to these parties that he should be permitted to go and have a good time, with the assurance that he would save all his love for her. They were the beliefs of a young girl, in the midst of her first love affair, trying desperately to believe what she wanted to believe, that she was his only real love and the rest was all just having some fun.

Events continued in this way for four months or so, until an event occurred which changed everything. Grace discovered she was pregnant. Suddenly, Chester's trustworthiness and truthfulness became all important and would have to be put to the test. Suddenly, instead of wanting Chester to love her and to marry her, Chester *had* to marry her. But at the same time, the other factory workers noticed that Chester no longer spent as much time with Grace and that he no longer went looking for her. Now, it was Grace Brown who roamed the factory, looking for Chester.

"Her whole life was bound up in him," was how Theresa Dillon put it, "and as soon as he knew it, he began to grow tired."

# CHAPTER THREE

# *Love Letters*

The options open to a 19-year-old, pregnant, unmarried woman in 1906 were few. There was surprisingly little compassion and virtually nowhere to seek help. Instead, she was held up as a public symbol of immorality to be made an example of, to show other young women what their fate would be if they showed a similar weakness.

In other parts of the country, those attitudes were beginning to change as the public began to see such women as victims rather than objects of public ridicule. The Salvation Army, for example had begun setting up homes for unmarried mothers who were abandoned by their families. But Cortland in 1906 had no such homes.

Abortions were available, even in small cities like Cortland in 1906, but they were illegal and considered morally wrong by most doctors and most of society. A doctor who performed such an operation risked his license, his social standing and his reputation, and few doctors were willing to take such a risk to resolve a young woman's moral dilemma. For the daughters of the rich or the influential, such avenues were available, but for others they were solidly closed.

That left only marriage as the honorable resolution of the problem and, all too frequently, young women often viewed pregnancy as an alternate route to the altar. For many women pregnancy was a race against time. She had, at most, four months when she could keep her condition hidden and desperately seek a husband and save her reputation.

Grace Brown had certainly heard of, or even known personally, some farm girls who had won their wedding rings in just such a fashion. It was quite common, especially in rural areas, for a woman to bear her first child not quite nine months after her marriage, and such an event, then as now, was a prime source of community gossip. The woman explained that the child had come early, but everyone knew what had really happened.

The popular novels that Grace Brown had been exposed to did not hesitate to use the dilemma in their plots. For example, she might have read about Jude Farley, in Thomas Hardy's *Jude the Obscure* who married because he thought his future wife was pregnant, only to find out later that she had been deceiving him. Or, she may have read *Tess of the D'Urbervilles* who ruined her reputation and later her marriage by bearing an illegitimate child.

For Grace, the discovery of her pregnancy came just at the time when she had begun to feel that she was losing Chester to the series of young women he was dating in the spring of 1906. During late April and early May, as she waited for her body to confirm her suspicions, she probably saw it as "the worst thing that could happen," but also as a trump card in the game she and Chester were playing; one that could lead to his doing "the honorable thing" and marrying her.

But this card would have to be played in just the right manner, and Grace must have spent many sleepless nights deciding just how to break the news to him so that he would not feel trapped into abandoning his other life of parties and outings with his friends.

Neither Chester nor Grace ever talked to anyone about the day she told him the news, so it's unknown what his initial reaction was. But from what happened afterward, it's likely that he was indecisive and advised her not to make any quick decisions. He advised her that they think of all the alternatives before making a move. That was not what Grace wanted to hear and she demanded a more substantial commitment. The best Chester could do was to talk about vague plans of running away together.

Chester was never one to make quick decisions and he always put off problems for later in case they might work themselves out. It is possible, but unlikely, that he never actually promised to marry her at all. Throughout this time, what he was looking for was a way out that involved neither matrimony nor public exposure.

After Grace told him the news, Chester continued to visit her twice a week, but he also continued to attend the parties with other young women. Chester's refusal to resolve Grace's problem caused a drastic change in her personality that was noticed, if not understood, by her friends and co-workers. Instead of the carefree, singing and laughing country girl deeply in love for the first time, she became a sickly, brooding, desperate woman who burst into tears at the slightest provocation. Most of her co-workers thought Chester's evening adventures with other women were the reasons for her tears, and no one seems to have guessed the real reason.

On May 5, Chester moved from his rented room at 21 East Main Street down the street to 17½ East Main Street, the home of Myron P. and Elizabeth Crain. Crain was a cigar manufacturer who worked out of a shop behind the house and his wife rented out the two rooms in the upstairs front of the house. Chester rented the room in the eastern half of the house, with a window overlooking the street.

A week later, on May 12, Josephine Patrick, Harriet Benedict and Hazel Peck, all friends of Chester's, helped with refreshments at a benefit for the Cortland Hospital Benefit Fund and Chester may have attended.

On the Decoration Day holiday, Thursday, May 31, the factory was closed and Chester went to Glen Haven, a resort overlooking Skaneateles Lake. With him were Georgia Hoag and two of their friends, William Short and Iva Dunfee. The 17-mile trip from Cortland was made in a horse-drawn wagon, probably driven by Chester.

But while Chester was out having a good time, Grace stayed at home, suffering from morning sickness and the constant worry over how her fate was to be resolved.

It is possible that sometime in late May or early June Chester made an attempt to take Grace to an abortionist. The evidence for this is very slim, however, and much of it is little more than local legend. The best evidence centers around a single question asked at Chester's trial: Had he taken her to see Dr. Santee? Chester said he had not.

Dr. Ellis M. Santee was one of the most prominent physicians in Cortland. Born in Hughsville, Pennsylvania, in 1862, he was a graduate of Hahnemann Medical College in Philadelphia and the Homeopathic Medical College in St. Louis. He moved to Cortland in 1890 after marrying Bulah Barber, daughter of Cortland aristocrat John S. Barber. Besides his home, the former Barber mansion on Groton Avenue, he owned a summer cottage, "Elm Bluff," at Little York Lake. It was here that, according to the legend, Chester took Grace to him, asked that the operation be performed and was refused by Santee. At the time of the trial, Santee was in Washington on an assignment for the federal government and he did not testify. He never talked about the incident if it did occur.

Grace continued to insist to those who told her tales that she had the utmost confidence in Chester. But one day during the week of June 10, a single incident occurred that brought all her worries out into the open.

Josephine Patrick, who had just been dismissed from school for the day, hitched up her father's horse and cart and drove over to the factory. Her plan was simply to invite Chester to a party at Little York that night to celebrate the beginning of summer vacation.

"I drove to the side door of the factory," she recalled later. "I sent for Mr. Gillette. He came out. I had a talk with him in reference to a party of four that were going out to Little York that evening." She stayed in the cart and talked to Chester for about 15 minutes, then she drove away and Chester went back into the factory. To Chester, it must have seemed a harmless incident, but he didn't see Grace and the other factory workers looking out the windows at the fashionably dressed young woman in the cart.

Robert Wilcox, the skirt trimmer who was working with Grace

that day, recalled that Grace was helping him cut out patterns later that day and that she was crying. He asked her what was wrong.

"I think she said 'if you went to the window you would see,' " he recalled later. "I said she shouldn't care about such things. She said she couldn't help it. She was crying while she was working."

Since Grace's table was on the opposite side of the room from the window where she could see Chester and Miss Patrick, he said, she must have been called to the window by someone else. After Chester came back in, he said, she waited about five minutes and then went to the stock room to talk with him about it. When she came back, a few minutes later, he said, "she went to her table and buried her face in her skirt."

Although it was probably one of many confrontations between Chester and Grace during this time, it was certainly the most public one. For probably the first time, Grace actually saw Chester talking with one of the young women that up to now had only been pointed out to her on the street or heard about through stories from friends. Also, everyone in the factory who hadn't been aware of Chester's activities now knew all about them. They all thought she was a fool and many told her so. Within a day or two after the incident, Grace told her fellow workers that she was going to take a vacation.

"I well remember the day Grace came to me and said she was going on vacation," said Theresa Harnishfager. "I asked her for how long and her answer was a vague one. She was preoccupied and troubled. 'It may be two weeks, it may be that I shall never come back,' was her reply."

William Steinberg, another factory worker, said that one day just before Grace left the factory, Grace called Chester, as she often did, on the speaking tube. Steinberg asked her, "Billy, what are you jollying Mr. Gillette about?" She told him they had talked about going away to the North Woods and waiting on table somewhere. Just before she left, he said, she told him, "Stein, I may never be back."

Elda Hoag, the head of the white department, said Grace's last place of employment was in the boxing department, where the finished skirts and petticoats were packed up for shipment to stores. A few days before she left, Mrs. Hoag said, Grace "said she wished she could die and hoped she would never see the sun rise again."

Grace told a similar story to Maggie McMahon, the chief of the special department. "A few days before she left Cortland she told me she was going to the North Woods and might never come back," she later testified. "She said her health was not very good. She said N. H. Gillette told her she might have her place back if she returned." At another time, she recalled, Grace was crying and said, "I want to die. I wish I might not see the sun rise again." When another worker came in and told her Chester was going with another girl, she told Grace "not to cry about that . . . there were other men. Grace said if she didn't get this one she didn't want any. I told her she was a little fool."

Despite Grace's objections, Chester went to the party at Little York that night, although Miss Patrick did not attend. Among those who were there were Georgia and Ella Hoag, but not Harriet Benedict.

That Friday evening, Chester may have given in to Grace's demands that she, too, be taken to Little York Lake to prove that she was the equal of the other women he had met there. Although Chester testified that he had never taken Grace to Little York, and there seems to be no reason why he should lie about it, his testimony conflicts with that of Albert Raymond, the owner of Raymond's Hotel on the lake, who positively identified Chester and tentatively identified Grace from photographs shown to him later. Raymond was also somewhat uncertain about the date that he saw them, but if it was Friday, June 15, as seems probable, it was the night before Grace's last day at the factory and the night when most of Chester's friends were attending a women-only sorority party. The Delta Epsilon Sorority held its annual alumni banquet that night in Maccabees Hall and among those attending were Georgia Hoag, Josephine Patrick and Harriet Benedict. Chester, then, could be certain that none of them would happen to be at Little York that night and it also would have been an evening when he found himself with nothing else to do.

Chester hired a horse and buggy to make the 7-mile journey to Raymond's, even though it would have been far less expensive to take the 25-cent trolley, but that would have meant running the risk of running into someone embarassing. Raymond said Chester drove up with a woman and had the horse put in the barn at about 9 p.m., when it was starting to get dark. Chester then asked about renting a boat. Apparently there was nothing unusual about renting a boat at such a late hour since most of Raymond's 16 boats were already rented out. Chester asked specifically for one of the new, steel boats with the round bottoms that he knew from experience were easier to row. But those were all rented out so Chester accepted one of the flat-bottom, wooden boats, No. 12.

Chester and Grace rowed around the lake for less than an hour in the twilight before returning. Chester asked that the horse be brought back around. "The lady stood by the oak tree in back of the buggy," Raymond said. "It was quite dark. I hitched the horse and turned around so she could come up and get into the wagon. I turned the light onto her countenance so I could see. He said 'Well, we must go.' I could see she was crying."

The next night, Saturday, after Grace had finished her last day in the factory, she and Chester spent several hours on the front porch of Mrs. Wheeler's house in what was certainly a stormy argument over what they would do to resolve Grace's problem. Mrs. Wheeler recalled seeing them together several times when she looked out the window. "I can't tell whether she came into the parlor that night or not," she said. "Grace came in that night somewhere between 11 and 12 and went upstairs."

They were certainly discussing their plans for the future, but it will never be known exactly what was said or what was promised. From her letters and Chester's later testimony, it is known that they talked about running away together in a week or so to the Adirondacks. The plan most likely involved them living there for some time together, probably until the baby was born. The question of marriage, which would have been central to those discussions, may or may not have been left unsettled. Chester later testified that he never promised to marry Grace and there is nothing in Grace's letters to indicate that the promise was ever made.

Several people, including Theresa Harnishfager, said later that Grace had told them that she planned to marry Chester. No one was produced later who would testify to that fact under oath, even though that would have greatly helped the prosecution's case. The question, an important one, remains a mystery.

Grace remembered the Saturday night discussion as a particularly painful one, as she indicated later in her letters to Chester, but he seems to have insisted that she go home for a few weeks, sew some new clothes and relax before they made their final plans. At the very least, he must have implied that eventually they would run away together to the Adirondacks and live together until the baby was born.

Whether there was an actual promise of marriage or not, Grace must certainly have not given up hope that once Chester lived with her for half a year and saw their child, that he would want to marry her, even if he would not accept that fact now. But if he did not, she had the option of leaving the baby at an orphanage and returning either to her family or to her job in Cortland, as N.H. Gillette promised she could.

After spending Sunday alone at her boarding house and saying goodbye to her friends, Grace walked the few blocks to the Lehigh Valley Railroad Station and boarded an early morning train for Cincinnatus, where she could take a stage to South Otselic.

Grace's arrival back home for an extended stay would have been an event for celebration at the Brown household except for the fact that her sister, Pauline Loomis, was ill after having her first child and Minerva spent most of her time caring for her daughter in her son-in-law's home. The Browns had never really resigned themselves to the fact that Grace had moved away for good and seem to have looked upon her life in Cortland as only temporary. Frank Brown listed her as living with the family on June 1, 1905, in the state census, and as a result, Grace Brown appears on the record twice; once at Mrs. Hawley's house on Fifth Avenue and once in South Otselic. Obviously, she considered Cortland as her home, while Frank considered South Otselic her home.

When they first saw her, they noticed right away that something was wrong with her. She had lost a lot of weight, was extremely pale and cried constantly. She spent much of the next three weeks in her room, gazing out the window she had looked out of most of her life, down the hillside toward the village.

For someone who had always shared every event and every thought with her parents and sisters, it was an especially hard burden for Grace to keep the biggest problem of her life a secret. She lived in terror from day to day that someone would notice that she was pregnant. Her father, for example, threatened to call Dr. Crumb at one point because she looked so ill.

At other times, however, she seems to have forgotten her troubles, if only for an hour or two, and become the innocent country girl she had been, picking strawberries and flowers, visiting her old friends and cooking the family's supper.

But she was too physically weak to do those kinds of things for long and soon she was back in her room, in her kimono, sitting on the window seat and writing yet another letter to Chester, begging him to come for her as soon as possible and take her away from the misery of her illness and secrecy.

The letters that she wrote, nearly every day, echo her desperation. They are loving, yet firm, full of praise for him, yet constantly reminding him of his duty to do the honorable thing. There are subtle and not so subtle hints that if he should back out of the deal, she would have no choice but to expose him by coming back to Cortland and telling everything.

But she also described, in great detail, some of her activities during the three weeks, including step by step updates on the dresses she was making for her trip. They also contain the outlines of the plans, as much as they were, for their trip, indicating that the plan had not been worked out in any detail that night on Mrs. Wheeler's porch.

Chester's plan was that she go to Hamilton with her parents, who wanted to spend the summer with Minerva's brother, Charles Babcock, who ran a hotel there. Frank seems to have been on the verge of giving up the farm he had bought only in 1892. The Browns, it seems, had been faced with one sickness after another since the death of Robert Hawley the year before, and had become discouraged with the hard work and few rewards of running a rented farm. But it would take a final tragedy, only a month away, before he would finally decide to give it up for good.

For Chester, Grace's departure was a tremendous relief from

the threat to his lifestyle and career that Grace posed and he began a series of outings and parties unencumbered with worrying about Grace. The weather was fine and the trolley car to Little York provided an excellent opportunity to go for canoe rides with his friends, both men and women. Most of these activities have not been documented, but there is no doubt that Grace received a running account of them, almost daily, from her former co-workers.

In his infrequent letters back to Grace, he denied some of the stories and dismissed others as exaggerated. He was, he maintained, simply having some harmless fun and Grace, for the most part, chose to believe him and not the stories, just as she had done when she lived in Cortland.

Most of Grace's letters were written late at night by the light of an oil lamp in her old bedroom when her younger sisters were asleep nearby, but some of them were written downstairs in the kitchen after the family had gone to bed.

Interesting and informative of her feelings as the letters are, they are also frustrating for what they do not say. Grace avoided writing about several topics that weighed heavily on her mind for fear the letters might fall into the wrong hands. She never wrote about her pregnancy other than in vague terms of her feeling ill or tired, but several times she makes it clear to Chester that he is responsible for her "illness." But more disappointing is her lack of any mention of marriage or what their future plans were, information which would have done much to show exactly how definite they really were. The closest she ever comes to discussing their future together is when she writes of an incident in which she inquired about some quilts she made as a girl. Her sister said she thought Grace wouldn't need so many for just she and "somebody else."

If, as many believed later, Chester promised to marry Grace and they were secretly engaged, it seems very odd that she never mentioned it or even hinted about it more strongly in her letters.

When Grace talked about Chester's "promises" in the letters, they always can be interpreted as referring to the trip itself, not to marriage. Just getting away from her family and friends seemed to have become an end in itself for her. When she talked about the future at all, it was in vague, rather than specific terms; of living in a shack somewhere with him, or working hard with little pay to help support them. She talked only of giving up her summer, not the rest of her life, and of Chester doing "just this one thing," for her. The lack of any definite plans was shown when she wrote, "I wonder where we will be two weeks from now?"

Chester, meanwhile, spent the three weeks in Cortland discussing several alternative plans for his vacation. Bert Gross said later that Chester discussed visiting his sister in Connecticut, but abandoned the idea as too expensive. Chester later told N.H. Gillette he was considering going to either the Adirondacks or the Thousand Islands, just two days before he met Grace at the beginning of their trip at DeRuyter.

But for all their faults, the letters remain the best source of what Chester, and especially Grace, were thinking about each other at the time and they contain invaluable clues to determining what happened later. Grace's first letter was written on the night she left Cortland after visiting her sister in her sick bed near Cincinnatus:

> Monday night
>
> My Dear - I have often heard the saying "it never rains but it pours," but I never knew what it meant until today.
>
> . . . Dear, what shall I do? I am about crazy tonight. You will have to come for me before then. (A week from Saturday). I could go up there first and you could come before they do.
>
> Chester, I have done nothing but cry since I got here. If you were only here I would not feel so badly. I knew I should worry all the time. I do try to be brave dear, but how can I when everything goes wrong? I can't help thinking you will never come for me, but then I say you can't be so mean as that, and besides you told me you would come and you have never disappointed me when you said you would not. Everything worries me and I am so frightened, dear. It won't make any difference to you about your coming a few days earlier than you intended, will it dear? It means so much to me. I will try to have my dresses made if I can, and I will try to be brave dear.
>
> Perhaps you will never know what a task it was for me to come home, but we can't help things now, and we may as well act like human beings . . . I won't be trouble to

you for long anyhow . . . Chester, do you miss me and
have you thought about everything today? Have as good a
time as you can, dear. I can't go out at all. I have
changed my mind about writing. Can't you write more
often than three times a week? I get so lonesome, dear.
You won't miss me so much, on account of your work;
but, oh dear, please write and tell me you will come for
me before week from Saturday. I will come straight back
to C. (Cortland) if you don't come before then.

   . . . I don't believe I will sleep a wink tonight. Please
write often and in every one of your letters I wish you
would tell me not to worry about your coming for me.

   If you were only here, dear. I am so blue. Everyone is
in bed except the nurse and so I will stop. Please write
often, dear, and tell me you will come for me before papa
makes me tell the whole affair, or they find it out
themselves. I just can't rest one single minute until I hear
from you. This is a horrid letter, but I can't write a
better one, I am so blue.

                       Lovingly, your G.W.B

The next night, she wrote him another letter, still without
hearing from him.

My dear Chester - I am writing to tell you I am coming
back to Cortland. I simply can't stay here any longer.
Mama worries and wonders why I cry so much and I am
just about sick. Please come and take me away some
place, dear. I came up home this morning and just can't
help crying all the time, just as I did Saturday night. My
headache is dreadful tonight. I am afraid you won't
come, and I am so frightened, dear. I know you will
think it queer, but I can't help it.

   You have said you would come and sometimes I just
know you will, but then I think about other things and I
am just as certain you won't come.

   I want you to write to me dear, just as soon as you get
this and tell me the exact day you can come. I will come
back as soon as I can if you don't come in a little while. I
can't stay here, dear, and please don't ask me to any
longer.

   . . . Chester, there isn't a girl in the whole world as
miserable as I am tonight, and you have made me feel so.

Chester, I don't mean that dear. You have always been awfully good to me. You just won't be a coward, I know.

My brother and sisters are at a swell reception tonight, but they can't get over my crying. I do so wish you were here. I can't wait so long for letters, dear. You must write more often, please, and dear, when you read my letters if you think I am unreasonable please do not mind it, but do think I am about crazy with grief and that I don't know just what to do. Please write to me dear.

Lovingly, you know whom.

Grace's letters were taken into the post office in South Otselic by her father and, according to the post marks, probably reached Chester the day they were mailed, that is, the day after Grace wrote them. When they arrived at 17½ East Main Street, Mrs. Crain placed them on a shelf near the front door where Chester got them when he came home from work each evening. He probably read them right away, while he got ready to go out on his evening escapades. He would have found them easy to ignore, except for the references to coming back to Cortland. That he must have taken very seriously. But it took several days before he replied. In the meantime, Grace wrote him a third letter:

Wednesday night

My dear Chester - I am just ready for bed, and I am so ill I could not help writing to you. I never came down this morning until nearly 8 o'clock and I fainted about 10 o'clock and stayed in bed until nearly noon.

This p.m. my brother brought me a letter from one of the girls [at the factory], and after I read the letter I fainted again. Chester, I came home because I thought I could trust you. I don't think now I will be here after next Friday. This girl wrote me that you seemed to be having an awfully good time and she guessed that my coming home had done you good, as you had not seemed so cheerful in weeks. She also said that you spent most of your time with that detestable Grace Hill. Now, Chester, she does not know that I dislike Miss Hill and so did not write that letter because she knew it would make me feel badly, but just because she didn't think. I should have known, Chester, that you did not care for me. But somehow I have trusted you more than anyone else. Whenever

the other girls have said hateful things to me of you I
could not believe them. You told me - even promised me
- that you would have nothing to do with her while I was
gone. Perhaps, Chester, you don't think, or you can't
help making me grieve, but I wish things were different.
You may say you do, too, but you can't possibly wish so
more than I.

I have been very brave since I came home, but tonight
I am very discouraged. Papa was frightened today and
insists on having a doctor up in the morning.

I presume you won't think you can come for me when I
ask you to, Chester. If I could only die. I know how you
feel about this affair, and I wish for your sake you need
not be troubled. If I die I hope you can then be happy. I
hope I can die. The doctor says I will, and then you can
do just as you like. I am not the least bit offended with
you, only I am a little blue tonight and I feel this way.
My brother has a gentleman friend here from Sherburne,
and the whole party of them went after strawberries
tonight. When I saw the party start and I knew I couldn't
go, I cried and cried ever so long a time.

Chester, please don't think I am unreasonable. I wish I
could hear from you, and I wish - Oh dear, come please
and take me away. You won't ever know how much I
wish you would come, Chester. I do want you to have a
good time, though, and I won't be cross. I think when I
see you dear, I shall be so glad I can't live. I hope you
will be glad to see me. I want you tonight and I am so
blue.

Lovingly,

The Kid.
P.S. Write often please.

It's unknown who wrote Grace the letter informing her of
Chester's activities in Cortland, but it was most likely one of the
factory workers who was close to Grace. The letter was not
preserved with the others. Chester's relationship with Grace Hill
is also somewhat obscure. She was a seamstress, the 19-year-old
daughter of Fanny Hill, a widow, who lived at 199 Clinton Street.
Since she is not mentioned in any of the social listings, she was
probably not much higher in the social circles of Cortland than
Grace was. Grace Hill was subpoenaed to testify at the trial but

*A photo of Chester on Little York Lake taken with his camera by Harriet Benedict on July 4, 1906. The photo was in his camera when he was arrested.*

*CHESTER - Another photo taken from Chester's camera. The location is not listed, but it is probably also Little York.*

CHESTER - A photo of Chester probably taken around 1905. It was the first photo released to the press and probably came from his own wallet.

HARRIET BENEDICT - A portrait of the woman rumored to be "the other woman."

was never called and the newspaper reporters seemed to ignore her. As a result her part in the story was never told.

Finally, on Friday morning, after not hearing from Chester for nearly a week, Grace took the family wagon down the dirt road into South Otselic and stopped outside the Gothic House, the semi-fancy hotel near the main intersection of town, and asked to use the telephone.

In 1906, the telephone was just beginning to come into use and only about five percent of the homes in the United States had them. They were considered rather novel devices, especially when used to call for long distances. The telephone in the Gothic House was in an open booth, near the front desk, where the customers could use it.

Grace knew most of the people in the Gothic House, the clerks and many of the tenants and they considered it somewhat unusual that Grace would want to place a telephone call. They knew she was calling Cortland, but they knew she had many friends there, so few seemed to think there was any cause for alarm. Grace, however, appeared very disturbed about something and, of course, she looked very sickly.

But if the use of the telephone was considered slightly unusual on the South Otselic end, it created a tremendous amount of excitement on the other end, at the Gillette Skirt Factory. Rena Dailey, a student at the Normal School who was working at the factory over the summer as a billing clerk, knew both Chester and Grace and, of course, knew right away who was calling when it was announced in the office that there was a call for Chester Gillette from South Otselic. Within minutes, everyone in the factory knew that Grace Brown was calling from South Otselic and wanted to talk to Chester.

"I went upstairs for him," Miss Dailey said, "told him long distance wished to talk with him. He came downstairs and answered the phone. I went back to my work. . ."

However, she remembered that Chester said, "No, no, yes, yes, that was not the night." "I think he said something about Friday but I couldn't swear to it . . . He wasn't at the phone more than three or four minutes."

Several people in the Gothic House recalled hearing the other side of the conversation and that Grace was crying, saying that someone had deceived her.

Chester could not say much in the Gillette office with so many people listening. He certainly must have received quite a few looks and winks on his return to his work that day.

Although Grace didn't receive it until late Saturday night, he had written a letter to her, dated Thursday, and he probably told her about it in the phone conversation. He may have led her to believe he had also written to her on Tuesday and mailed it Friday as her next letter implies:

> June 23, 1906
>
> My dear Chester - I am just wild because I don't get a letter from you. If you wrote me Tuesday night and posted it Wednesday there isn't any reason why I shouldn't get it. Are you sure you addressed the letter right? I have been home nearly a week and have not had one line from you. Don't you think it funny dear? I wrote Monday, Tuesday and Wednesday. You must have three from me. I have been busy all yesterday and today. When I didn't hear from you Thursday morning I cried, and as a result I had a nervous headache and stayed in bed all day. You can't blame me dear for, of course, I thought of everything under the sun . . . . I was so tired I went to bed for an hour after getting home. Then I went downstairs and got dinner all alone. Now, dear, I know you are laughing, in fact I can hear you almost; but, honestly, I had splendid luck. My brother, who seldom says a word of praise for anything, said 'It's not half bad, Billy'. This is a whole lot for him to say . . .
>
> I miss you. Oh dear, you don't know how much I miss you. Honestly, dear, I am coming back next week unless you come for me right away. I am so lonesome I can't stand it. A week ago tonight we were together. Don't you remember how I cried, dear? I have cried like that nearly all the time since I left Cortland. I am awfully blue.
>
> Now, dear, let me tell you. You will get this one some-time Monday. Now, you please write me Monday night and post it Tuesday morning, and then I will get it or ought to Wednesday morning. I just want to see what the trouble is why I don't hear from you. I was telling Mama yesterday how you wrote and I never got it, and she said, 'Why, Billy, if he wrote you would have received it.' She

did not mean anything, but I was mad and said, 'Mama,
Chester never lied to me, and I know he wrote.' . . .

Well, dear, they are calling me to dinner, and I will
stop. Please write or I will be crazy. Be a good kid and
God bless you.

Lovingly, The Kid

Finally, the next evening, Saturday, Chester's first letter arrived, but Grace was very disappointed about both its length and tone after pouring her heart out to him all week. Out of all the things he mentioned in her letters, the only thing he responded to was her threat to return to Cortland:

June 21, 1906

Dear Grace - Please excuse paper and pencil, as I am not
writing this at home and have nothing else here. I received your letter last night and was just a little
surprised, although I thought you would be discouraged.
Don't worry so much and think less about how you feel
and have a good time.

Your trip with your father and mother ought not to
make any difference as you can go from wherever they
are at any time. It will also do you good like that, as you
will be moving and have enough to interest you. I am
sorry you are worrying so, as there is no cause for so
doing.

The only disadvantage of your trip is the financial
matter, but you may be able to get around that . . .

I cannot get away before the 7th or 8th, and I do not
think there is any need to worry before then. I also think
you should go with your parents and write while with
them and we can make arrangements then.

Yours lovingly, C.

Grace expressed her disappointment in the letter she wrote the next night:

Sunday night

I was glad to hear from you and surprised as well. I
thought you would rather have my letters affectionate,
but yours was so businesslike that I have come to the
conclusion that you wish mine to be that way. I must tell

you, tho, that I am not a businesswoman and so presume these letters will not satisfy you any more than the others did. I would not like to have you think I was not glad to hear from you, for I was very glad, but it was not the kind of letter I had hoped to get from you.

I think - pardon me - that I understand my position and that it is rather unnecessary for you to be so frightfully frank in making me see it. I can see my position as keenly as anyone, I think.

You say you were surprised but you thought I would be discouraged. I do not see why I shouldn't be discouraged. What words have I received from you since I came home to encourage me? You tell me not to worry and think less about how I feel, and have a good time. Don't you think if you were me you would worry? And as for thinking less how I feel, when one is ill all the while, some days not able to get downstairs, one naturally thinks about one's self and the good time. If one can have a good time when one is ill and stays in one's room dressed in a kimono all the time, I fail to see where the good time comes in . . .

As to the financial difficulty, I am the one who will be most affected by that. You say your trip. Won't it be your trip as well as mine? I understand how you feel about this affair. You consider me as something troublesome, that you are bothered with. You think if it wasn't for me you could do as you liked all summer and not be obliged to give up your position there. I know how you feel, but once in a while you make me see all these things a great deal more plainly than ever. I don't suppose you have ever considered how it puts me out of all the good times for the summer and how I had to give up my position there? I think all this is about as bad for me as for you, don't you?

The girls write me that you are planning on another trip for the Fourth of July. They never wrote me how they knew of it. Perhaps you told them. Is that the reason you cannot come before the 7th or 8th? Chester, I didn't mind being snubbed and put aside Decoration Day for the other girls, but I do mind it the Fourth. I have always had to be put aside for other girls on such occasions and presume it will always be that way. This is the truth, isn't it? You ought not to be angry with me for that. I hope,

honestly, I hope you will have the most pleasant day of
your life. I presume that you think that you are so soon
coming to the unpleasant days that I ought not to care
for that once. I don't care the least, but only I think the
girl would feel highly edified if she knew you were going
away so soon, don't you? Perhaps you are not going any
place the Fourth, but I don't see why the girls wrote me
about it then.

I think I shall be back the last of the week. I can't tell
you just when. That depends on when my dresses are
done. I won't interfere with your plans.

I was ill nearly all day yesterday and at night the veins
in my temples were frightfully swollen. Mama bathed
them in cologne and they are not as bad today. They
were swollen because I cry so much.

If you care to talk over any plans, I shall be glad to see
you any evening. Chester, I don't suppose you will ever
know how I regret being all this trouble to you. I know
you hate me, and I can't blame you one bit. My whole
life is ruined, and in a measure, yours is too. Of course it
is worse for me than for you, but the world and you too
may think I am the only one to blame, but somehow I
can't, just simply can't, think I am, Chester. I said no so
many times dear. Of course the world will not know that,
but it's true all the same.

My little sister came up just a minute ago with her
hands full of daisies and asked me if I didn't want my
fortune told. I told her that I guessed it was pretty well
told.

Now I don't want you to mind this letter, for I am blue
tonight, and get so mad when the girls write things about
you. Your letter was nice and I was glad to get it. I simply
feel "out of sorts" tonight. You know if I was there tonight and was with you, I would have to quarrel with you
anyhow, then you would make me good natured again.

Please write me often and I will be back soon. I wish
for your sake things were different, but I have done all I
can do to prevent your being bothered. I know you will
be cross when you read this, but you won't be angry and
blame me will you? When you are cross just think I'm
sick and can't help all this. If you were me you couldn't
help finding fault, I know. I don't dare think how glad I

will be to see you. If you wrote a letter like this I
wouldn't write you in a long time, but I know you will
just forget it and be your own dear self. You know I
always get cross in the beginning. It was that way
Saturday night, so don't be angry dear, please.

Lovingly, Kid

Although her friends in Cortland were correct about Chester's
plans for the Fourth and Grace was justified in her assumptions,
the next day she thought better of being so harsh with Chester,
her only hope of avoiding the full consequences of her pregnancy.
But when she woke up, she found her parents had already mailed
the letter, so that night she wrote a letter in apology for the
previous one.

Dear Chester - I am much too tired to write a decent
letter or even follow the lines, but I have been uneasy all
day and I can't go to sleep because I am sorry I sent you
such a hateful letter this morning, so I am going to write
and ask your forgiveness, dear. I was cross and wrote
things I ought not to have written. I am very sorry dear
and I shall never feel quite right about all this until you
write and say you quite forgive me. I was ill and did not
realize what I was writing and then this morning Mama
gave my letter to Papa before I was down, I should not
have had it posted but it went long before I was awake. . .

Where do you suppose we will be two weeks from
tonight? I wish you would write and tell me, dear, all
about your coming. . . .

I was pleased yesterday morning. You know I have a
lot of bed quilts - six, I guess - and I was asking Mama
where they were and saying I wished I had a dozen, when
my little sister said: "Just you and someone else will not
need so many." Of course my face got crimson and the
rest of the family roared.

Mama is so nice about fixing my dresses. She has them
all up now in nice shape. You remember the white dress I
wore and you once asked me why I didn't have a new
yoke? Well, she has almost made a new dress out of
that . . .

Chester, I need you more than you think I do. I really
think it will be impossible for me to stay here any longer

than this week, I want to please you, but I think,
Chester, it would be very unwise. If I should stay here
and anything should happen I would always regret it for
your sake. You do not know Papa as well as I and I
would not like you to be disgraced here. We have both
suffered enough and I would rather go away quietly. In a
measure, I will suffer the more, but I will not complain if
you will not get cross and will come for me.

I must close. Write me Wednesday night, dear, and
tell me what you think about everything. Let's not leave
our plans until the last moment, and, above all, please
write and say you quite forgive me for that letter I sent
you this morning, I am sorry and if I were there I know
you would say it would be O.K.

Lovingly, The Kid

On the same day Grace wrote that letter, Chester was writing
to her from the factory, his second letter in nearly two weeks:

June 25, '06

Dear Grace - I am writing this from here [the factory] as
I was not at home yesterday. Three of us fellows went up
to the lake and camped in a small house that one of the
boys owns. We had a dandy time even though there were
no girls. We went in swimming in the afternoon and the
water was great. I went out in the canoe in the evening
and wished you had been there.

Perhaps I wrote too harshly Friday about your
telephoning and, you worry, but it was entirely
unnecessary and not at all satisfactory because I couldn't
say what I wanted to. Don't do such a foolish thing
again.

Above all things, don't worry and cry so or you will be
down sick in a very short time.

I can't get away the seventh or at least I will. Don't
fret until then. If you do not see me after the eighth or
ninth then get worried, but not until then.

In the meantime, have as good a time as you can so as
to have something to think about.

As I wrote before, I think the best thing is to go with
your mother on their trip and then matters can be
arranged according to where you are. That may make

things better for us and will keep you interested. Write
often dear and enjoy yourself.

Love and kisses from

P.S. The girl that wrote all that to you later told me
about it and said she stretched things in order to get you
to believe them. She kindly told me the things she had
told you and said you were foolish to believe me rather
than her, but that you always did. Of course, if you are
going to believe her I might as well not say anything and
see what you would think then.

The things you wrote were not so, at least some of
them were not, and especially those G.H. said. She isn't
here half the time so that would stop a great deal even
tho I did do what E. says. Please forgive anything harsh I
have said and don't worry for two weeks.

Lovingly, C.

Exactly who went with Chester on that excursion to Little York
is unclear, but it's unlikely that there were no girls there, as
Chester told Grace. Certainly, Grace's friends later told her that
there were girls there. The "G.H." Chester refers to in his letter
is Grace Hill and "E." is probably Ellen Melvin.

Grace didn't write for three days, the longest hiatus since she
had left Cortland. Apparently, she was waiting for Chester to
answer her previous letter, since she wrote again after hearing
from him:

My dear Chester - I wish you could have known how
pleased I was to hear from you today. I should have had
your letter yesterday morning, but somehow it was late;
and, dear, I have never received any letter from you
Friday. All the letters I have had from you in the nearly
two weeks I have been home is one - just one - and it was
written June 21. I can't imagine where the others are,
and I have written you every day except three. I wonder if
you have all mine? Where do you suppose your letter is?
I remember you told me over the phone Friday morning
you would write that night and I thought it strange I had
not received it . . .

I think I shall die of joy when I see you, dear. I will

tell you, I am going to do a whole lot better dear. I will
try and not worry so much, and I won't believe the horrid
things the girls write. I presume they do stretch things,
dear. I am about crazy, or I could reason better than I
do. I am awfully pleased you had such a jolly time at the
lake, dear, and wish I had been there too. I am fond of
the water although I can't swim.

I am crying and I can't half write. Guess it's because
my sister is playing her mandolin and singing "Love's
Young Dream." I am a little blue.

Chester, my silk dress is the prettiest dress I ever had,
or at least that's what everyone says. Mama don't think I
have much interest in it. I am frightened everytime it's
fitted. Mama says she don't see why I should cry every
time they look at me . . .

Chester, dear, I hope you will have an awfully nice
time the Fourth. Really dear, I don't care where you go
or who you are with, if you only come for me the 7th.
You are so fond of boating and the water, why don't you
go on a trip that will take you to some lake? I was cross
and ill when I wrote about it before, but really, I don't
mind the least bit, and I hope you will do it.

Are you working awfully hard? I presume you are as
thin as I am. My brother says he has never saw me so
thin in his life. He says my eyes are larger than ever, but
he had to dodge one of my shoes when he said it. They
are not so small but that he would have felt one had it hit
him. The girls [her sisters] have all come up and I don't
suppose they will be still for one minute . . .

Do you miss my poor little self in the factory? Don't it
seem funny not to chase for boxes for me and have me
ask you for your shears? I miss you dreadfully, dear, and
I find myself wondering what you are doing, and if you
are tired, and if you miss me. Now, I wish you were here
this very minute. I would - oh, I would give you such a
great kiss, you would be surprised . . .

I know you will be awfully good to me dear, for I will
die in a short time. I know I will and then - Oh, I think
you will always be glad you were good to me. I must close
and get in bed. I am cold and awfully tired.

Of course, dear, I would forgive all the harsh things
you have said, but I don't remember as you have said

any, and you have so much more to forgive than I. Oh,
how I do wish you were here. With lots of love and kisses
from,

The Kid

P.S. I can't wait until I see you, dear, and of course I
will worry a little, but I will try to be brave.

Grace wrote him Sunday night, July 1, and again the next
night without hearing from him:

My dear Chester - This has been such a crowded day that
I am almost too tired to write, but I will try for I am a
little anxious about our trip and your not writing.

I cannot see why I do not get your letters. It worried
me dreadfully. Where do they go? I thought surely if you
wrote Thursday I would get it sometime Saturday, but I
did not get a line. Mama was in the village after the mail
came, and I did feel so disappointed, dear. I can't help
thinking you wrote, and I am frightened, for I think
maybe if you did write about our trip I won't get the
letter.

You would not know me dear. I was down at the
village Friday morning and I would speak to people, and,
instead of speaking, they would stare and then tell me I
was too pale to be out of bed . . .

Now, my dear, let me explain. If anything should
happen that I can't go to Hamilton, I will go to
DeRuyter. This is the only place I can think of where I
could go. I do not know but I will go up there, but will
phone you if I go to DeRuyter, dear. You must come
Saturday, dear, for I can never stay any longer. I have
done my best and been as brave as possible these last
weeks, but if you should not come I will do something
desperate. Oh dear, dear, dear! I can't see anything but
just trouble. What if I should not be able to travel?
There are so many things to think about. If I had
strength dear, I do believe I should walk to the river and
throw myself in. It would be rather cowardly, and I
despise a coward, but I would not be a bother to you any
longer. Oh Chester, the thought that I am in your way
just drives me crazy. How I want to die no one but myself
knows.

When you told me you wanted me to come home for
one week it made some difference. I did not think it
would, and now I do not imagine what three weeks will
do. If you care at all dear, you will not make me suffer
any longer than Saturday - I mean about coming. I don't
believe I can bear any more suffering in silence. Oh dear,
if you were only here so I could talk to you and you
would pet me, dear, and tell me not to worry. I think
when I see you I will die of joy. I cannot tell how I really
and truly need you, and I presume you will never know
what I have suffered. Of course, dear, do not think I
never think of you worrying, for I do. But dear, you don't
feel ill as I do. But it's only for one week longer. You
would smile if you know how I am trying to get strong,
for I don't care how rough my life after next Saturday. I
think I would carry packs like women peddlers, but I
shall certainly die if you don't come. Dear, don't make
me suffer any after Saturday, please. I just can't bear it,
and I don't think I deserve it, do you? I don't suppose I
will be home for some time, will I? Maybe not until I am
sent home dead. You know, dear, you promised me that.
Now I wish I were with you, dear. Now I need you. I wish
I could hear from you, and it worried me for fear you
don't get my letters.

Now, dear, I will close, but if I go to Hamilton, I will
either write or phone you, and the same about DeRuyter.
And you must not fail to come. I will be so glad to see
you, I will promise not to quarrel for a long time. Write
as often as you can dear, and please come. This is rather
a blue letter, but please forgive that, dear, it has been
such a trying time.

Monday night

My dear Chester - I hope you will excuse me if I don't
follow the lines for I am half lying down. Have worked
awfully hard today because I won't be here today. This
morning I helped Mama with the washing and then
helped with the dinner. This p.m. I have been after
strawberries. It was fun, only I got so awfully tired. The
fields here are red with berries.

Tonight Mama is canning them and making bread and
cookies. We have had berries nearly every day since I

came. Mama says I am getting to be a splendid cook.
What do you think of that? I got supper alone tonight
and had potato dice and French toast and a whole lot of
good things.

I cannot help worrying about your letters. Of course,
when I don't hear from you I imagine you have gone
away. I think another week would kill me dear. Thank
heaven I don't always have to live like this. You have no
idea how badly I feel. I don't know what I should do if
you did not come Saturday . . .

Nothing would suit me as well as life in a little shanty
in the woods for a time, anyhow. Maude will tease me to
stay, and I don't want to, and I always get confused when
people ask me why I can't stay or go.

Chester, I shall phone you again if you don't write
pretty soon . . .

I don't feel nearly so well tonight, dear, and I am so
frightened, dear. How I do wish you were here. I have so
much to tell you that I can't put on paper. I wish I could
go somewhere the 4th, but that is only one of the little
crosses, isn't it dear? There will be lots of things harder
to get along with than that.

I wish, dear, I do wish you could read some of the
letters from the girls. It is no wonder I write blue letters.
I don't believe what they say now dear. I wish you could
have read one letter giving an account of your trip to the
lake. Of course, I had received your letter telling me
about it, so I did not believe the other one, but it was so
different. I was awfully glad I had your letter first,
though.

I hope you will have a nice time the 4th, dear, for you
ought to have. I don't mind staying here alone all day;
that is not so very much. I shall be all alone all day.
Don't you wish you were going to be here? I will have a
long daydream of you, dear, and all about how good you
are to me, and, dear, I hope the first minute you see me
you will give me a good pounding. It's just what I
deserve. I never felt so ashamed of anything in all my life
as that letter I sent you. Oh dear, why did I do it, dear?
Won't you forgive me? I do so wish I could die. Is it
wicked to want to die? My head aches and I am so blue.
Oh dear, if you were only here and would kiss me and

tell me not to worry any more I would not mind this, but
with no one to talk to, and ill all the time, I really believe
I will be crazy. I will never be cross again, dear, and I
will never scold, and I will try so hard to please you.
Darling, if you will only write and tell me that you will
surely come Saturday and not to worry.

I am crying so I can't see the lines and will stop. You
will never know, dear, how badly I feel or how much I
want you this very minute.

With love and kisses. The Kid

Chester wrote Grace one last letter, a week after his previous
one, dated the same day as the preceding letter from Grace:

Dear Kid - I certainly felt good when I got your letter
although I also felt mean as I hadn't written all week.

Wednesday and Thursday I had to work on the payroll
and Friday a friend came and stayed all night. Saturday I
went up to the lake and am so burned tonight I cannot
wear a collar or coat. We went out in the canoe and to
two other lakes, and, although the canoe was heavy to
carry, we had a good time, but my arm's awfully burned.

I think it is best that you should go to Hamilton next
Monday and meet me there. It would be better to go
where we are not known and so we can leave there that
day, although I don't know where we can or will go. I
have really no plans beyond that, as I do not know how
much money I can get or anything about the country. If
you have any suggestions to make I wish you would and
also just when and where you can meet me.

I have said nothing more about going away but shall
simply leave Sunday. As for my plans for the Fourth, I
have made none as the only two girls I could get to go
with me have made other arrangements because I didn't
ask them until Saturday and today, so that someone is
mistaken. I hope you are having a good time and hope
you will the Fourth.

I tried to find time to write this today, but I could not
possibly start it as I have more than I can do. Don't
worry about anything and tell me about what I ask about
the time and so forth.

Love and kisses from<br>C.

The day after he wrote that, however, Chester's bad luck in finding a date for the Fourth changed very much for the better. According to her later testimony, Harriet Benedict was walking down a street in Cortland when Chester came up to her.

"He asked me if I had any engagement for the Fourth of July," she said. "I said I had none for part of the day. Then he asked me if I would like to go up to Little York Lake for a while and I said yes."

At exactly the same time Chester was making a date with Harriet, Grace was at Maude Crumb's party for her brother, Cleveland Kenyon, a medical student who was home on vacation. Maude also took time to help with the finishing touches on Grace's silk jacket, part of the dark suit she was so proud of. Also, Grace apparently asked her father for some money, hoping to help Chester finance their trip, but her father, because of his "stubborness," refused to give it to her.

That evening, the eve of the Fourth of July, Grace wrote to Chester:

> Dear Chester - your letter was received tonight and I will
> try to write a few lines before I get in bed.
> I have been at Maude's all day and have had such a
> good time. Her brother was there as a matter of course,
> and we had the swellest dinner party. Her brother is fine.
> He was class orator at Syracuse last year, and is in Utica
> three days in the week. We had beer twice and it was
> fine.
> Maude has been helping me on my silk coat. It is a
> beauty. It looks like a real tailored affair because it is so
> plain. But it is awfully pretty.
> We were after roses this afternoon and I got a great
> heap of white and red ones. I am so awfully tired tonight.
> You have been at Little York Lake for two days now,
> haven't you? I am very glad you have had a nice time.
> You did not say if there were any girls on this last trip. I
> am very sorry you have no girl for the Fourth.
> In your last letter you said you could get away the 7th,
> or at least you would. In tonight's letter you meet me
> Monday. I expect any time to hear you can't come for a
> week or two yet. I am awfully sorry, but I have planned
> on Saturday and shall be in Cortland that night unless

you meet me. I am awfully sorry, but I can't help matters now . . .

I don't think I have any suggestions, Chester, only those I have already given you about DeRuyter. I don't think there will be any danger of our going there for we can get a train out of there that night. I have made so many suggestions and somehow none of them have pleased you that I am discouraged to say the least.

At present, dear, I am, vulgarly speaking, hopelessly dead broke. Papa and I - well, we don't agree on some things and this is one of them. There is no earthly reason for what I call his stubborness, but never mind that, dear, if I don't mind so much. I will try again and see what I can do. Don't think you have to keep me so awfully well, for I can give up lots of things if I have to. I expect to live differently and I will try awfully hard to get along, dear. Just take me away and then plan on other things.

If it would do any good I would wait and go to DeRuyter Monday morning. Then you take the 9:43 from Cortland and meet me there. I won't go down to Aunties [Mrs. Fred Brown, who lived in DeRuyter] and I think it will be all right.

But one question is this: I probably won't hear from you again and how am I to know? I do not like waiting until Monday at all. I am very much displeased about it, for I think by staying here these weeks I have done enough, or rather, my share.

I don't know what you think, but I do know that I shall come back to Cortland if you don't come, and I shall never go away like this. It is rather too much to ask of me anyway. I am not angry dear, but I am very much discouraged. I guess anyone would be. I was boiling mad when I found out that you did not want to come until Monday. But now, if you want things that way you can have it. I will make my plans here into a cocked hat, but then I can get along. It's only me, you know, and I don't mind.

Just the same about those letters you did not write. I spent three or four whole sleepless nights over them, but that was nothing for me. You were busy and are forgiven.

It was nice of you to hope that I would have a nice

time the 4th, but I don't believe I shall be able to go out
of this room.

I had a letter from one of the girls today and so I do
not feel very good natured tonight.

Do not worry about money matters dear, because I do
not care if you have one cent. All I ask of you is to come.
I am sorry I cannot go to Hamilton, but I can't dear, and
the next best plan is DeRuyter. I will make things all
right there too. I am the one who will have to suffer and
so I don't care about the money. I don't think you need
to do so. Please don't worry about that for I am not
worth it. I shall write you again tomorrow night and tell
you more.

My sister has been teasing me to come and get in bed
for a long time. I wish I could hear from you again often.

With love and kisses,<br>Kid

The next day, Wednesday, July 4, began as a cloudy day in
Cortland, threatening what was then considered to be the biggest
holiday of the season. But just before 10 a.m., the hour of
Chester's date with Harriet Benedict, the weather cleared and it
turned into a perfect summer day.

The *Cortland Standard* reported record crowds that day at
Little York, with 3,000 coming from Cortland alone, about a
third of the entire population of the city. It was the first big holiday since the trolley line had been extended from the city to the
lake, turning a resort that had previously been open only to those
with carriages into one that anyone with the 25-cent fare could
afford to visit. It was a day that the Little York proprietors
like Raymond's Hotel and the Cortland Traction Company had
planned for weeks.

All the rowboats on the lake were in continuous service. The
Cortland City Band, in place at the brand new pavilion at the far
end of the lake, provided the music for dancing and listening as
vendors distributed coffee, sandwiches, fried cakes, cookies,
lemonade, ice cream and soft drinks. It was the only day of
the year on which firecrackers were legal and youngsters took
advantage of the reprieve by setting off a constant barrage that
terrorized the horses and resulted in several injuries in the crowd.

Among the hundreds of boaters out rowing across the smooth waters of the lake, listening to the music, the laughter and the fireworks were Harriet and Chester. The scene was recorded for posterity because Chester brought along his new Kodak, one of the new light and inexpensive cameras that were just becoming available. He put down the oars for a moment to snap a picture of her as she smiled in the other end of the boat. Later, she borrowed the camera and took a photo of Chester, who posed as a gallant oarsman.

They had taken the trolley with the rest of the crowds and after paddling around the lake for an hour or so, went to Raymond's for dinner, which most likely consisted of one of the famous chicken dinners that were the hotel's specialty.

While they were waiting for the dinner to be served, Harriet took Chester over to the register on the front desk where out-of-town visitors were asked to write their names and addresses, to show from how far away they had come. Harriet picked up the pen, and, with a smile, wrote "Harriet Benedict, New York City," and "Chester Gillette, San Francisco."

"There was a practice when parties were there," Harriet later explained, "to go and put down the names. It was generally done by the ladies. Often they registered as from all kinds of places . . . We knew it wasn't necessary to register, but once in a while for fun we would give fictitious names and sometimes fictitious places . . . and so on this occasion I went to this book and put these names down."

Chester, of course, had once lived in San Francisco, a place that was a major topic of discussion since the earthquake that spring and Harriet probably thought it was a romantic place to be from.

After dinner, they sat on the piazza, took some more photos and talked for a while, but soon left on the trolley and parted back in Cortland in time for supper.

In contrast, Grace's Fourth was spent at home with her sisters and not in the celebrations and parades in the village, where nearly everyone else was celebrating with bands and music.

The next night, after everyone else in the house was in bed, Grace went downstairs, wrapped herself in a blanket and sat down at the kitchen table near the cast iron stove and wrote her

last and most touching letter to Chester; the letter that is never
forgotten by anyone who has read it:

Thursday night
My dear Chester - I am curled up by the kitchen fire and
you would shout if you could see me. Everyone else is in
bed. The girls came up and we shot the last firecrackers.
Our lawn looks as green as the Cortland House corner. I
will tell you all about my Fourth when I see you. I hope
you had a nice time.

This is the last letter I can write dear. I feel as though
you are not coming. Perhaps this is not right, but I cannot help feeling that I am never going to see you again.
How I wish this was Monday.

I am going down to stay with Maude next Sunday
night, dear, and then go to DeRuyter the next morning
and will get there about 10 o'clock. If you take the 9:45
train from the Lehigh there you will get there about
eleven.

I am sorry I could not go to Hamilton, dear, but
Mama and Papa did not want me to go and there are so
many things I have had to work hard for in the last two
weeks. They think I am just going out there to DeRuyter
for a visit.

Now, dear, when I get there I will go at once to the
hotel and I don't think I will see any of the people. If I
do and they ask me to come to the house I will say
something so they won't mistrust anything. Tell them I
have a friend coming from Cortland; that we are to meet
there to go to a funeral or a wedding in some town
farther on. Awfully sorry, but we were invited to come
and I had to cut my vacation a little short and go. Will
that be all O.K. dear? Maybe that won't be just what I
will say, but don't worry about anything for I shall
manage somehow.

Only I want you to come in the morning. I don't want
to wait there in the hotel all day, for if they should see
me there, and all day, they would think it funny I did not
go to the house. You must come in the morning for I
have had to make - you don't know how many plans to fit
your last letter - in order to meet you Monday. I dislike
waiting until Monday but now that I have I don't think

anything only fair that you should come Monday
morning. But, dear, you must see the necessity yourself of
getting there and not making me wait. If you dislike the
idea of coming Monday morning and can get a train up
there Sunday, you can come up Sunday night and be
there to meet me. Perhaps that would be the best way.
All I care is that I don't want to wait there all day or half
a day. I think there is a train that leaves the Lehigh at
six something Sunday night. I don't know what I would
do if you were not there or did not come. I am about
crazy now.

I have been bidding goodbye to some places today.
There are so many nooks, dear, and all of them so dear
to me. I have lived here nearly all of my life. First, I said
goodbye to the spring house with its great masses of
green moss; then the beehive, a cute little house in the
orchard, and, of course, all of the neighbors that have
mended my dresses from a little tot up to save me a
thrashing I really deserved.

Oh dear, you don't realize what all of this is to me. I
know I shall never see any of them again. And Mama!
Great heavens, how I do love Mama! I don't know what I
shall do without her. She is never cross and she always
helps me so much. Sometimes, I think if I could tell
Mama, but I can't. She has trouble enough as it is, and I
couldn't break her heart like that. If I come back dead,
perhaps, if she does not know, she won't be angry with
me. I will never be happy again, dear. I wish I could die.

I am going to bed now dear. Please come and don't let
me wait there. It is for both of us to be there. If you have
made some plans for something Sunday night you must
come Monday morning.

Please think, dear, that I had to give up a whole summer's pleasure and you will surely be brave enough to
give up one evening for me. I shall expect and look for
you Monday forenoon.

Heaven bless you until then.

Lovingly and with kisses, The Kid

I will go to the Tabor House and you come for me
there. I wish you would come up Sunday night, so as to
be there, and, sweetheart, I think it would be easier for
you. Please come up Sunday night, dear.

# CHAPTER FOUR

# *Grace Brown's Final Journey*

On the afternoon of Sunday, July 8, Chester Gillette returned from the Presbyterian Church, where he had attended services with his uncle, to his room at 17½ East Main Street to pack his bags for what everyone who knew him assumed was to be a one-week vacation.

He took his suitcase out from under the bed and filled it with most of his clothing. He included his Kodak, which still held the plates he had taken with Harriet Benedict four days before. After closing it, he stuck in between the straps his camera tripod, his umbrella and his tennis racket.

Among the things he left behind at the Crains' house were his bicycle, his trunk, his desk, the pictures on the walls, some of his clothing and Grace's letters. Most of her letters were left in his desk, but the one that had arrived only yesterday, the one in which she described all the places and people to whom she had said goodbye, he hid underneath his ties in a box on top of his dresser so the landlady would not find it.

There is no way to know what was going through his mind as he packed, why some things were taken and why other things were left behind, but the entire contents of his suitcase were analyzed in detail by others over the next few months.

He had talked about going on vacation even before Grace left, but he seems to have decided upon the Adirondacks as a destination only the day before he left. His friend, the factory superintendent Albert Gross, recalled speaking to Chester about the vacation:

> I had some talk with him about his going away three or
> four weeks before he went. There was nothing said as to
> where he was going. I think it was the first or second
> week in July that he wanted to go. At one time he spoke
> something about taking a trip to his sister's [Hazel, who
> was working in Connecticut], at vacation time. I asked
> him where he was going. He said he thought some of
> going to see his sister, but it was too expensive. I said to
> him that I knew he didn't receive much wages. If he
> wished to borrow any money I would be perfectly willing
> to loan him $20 or he could have $40 and pay it back
> when he wanted to. He said he owed enough money now,
> thanked me and declined to accept the amount.

During his last week at the factory, Chester called on his uncle at home one evening. N.H. said later that they discussed several places Chester might go.

"He said he wanted to go where it was not very expensive," N.H. recalled. Among the places Chester mentioned, he said, were the Adirondacks and the Thousand Islands.

On Saturday morning, just a few hours before he was to leave the factory for his vacation, Chester talked to several people about his plans. Neva Wilcox said Chester told her he would not be at work on Monday because he was going away to the North Woods.

"I asked him how long he was going to be gone," she said. "He said a week, two weeks, a month, six months. If his money held out he would be back in a week. If not, it would depend upon what position he got to earn his money coming back."

To Harold Gillette, N.H.'s son, Chester said that same Saturday morning that he planned to go the North Woods for a week. Before he left, he asked Ella Hoag, his friend and the company paymistress, if he could draw some of his pay in advance.

"He wanted to draw a week's pay with the week he had just worked," she said. "He said he was going on his vacation. I paid him for the week before that on Friday. I paid him that week $20. The last $10 would have been payable the next Friday after he went away." Chester said later that he had $28 in his wallet when he left Cortland.

That night, Chester went to visit his uncle and asked to borrow a mileage book for the New York Central Railroad. A mileage book was a convenient way of paying fares. It was purchased for a set price and the conductor marked it according to how many miles were travelled on the railroad. The fact that he wanted a New York Central book indicated that he planned to travel east or west, since that line did not go north and south through Cortland. He could take the New York Central from near Cortland to anywhere in the Adirondacks.

"I didn't have (a mileage book)," N.H. said later, "but I gave him the money to buy one. I told him to use what he wanted of it and he could pay me for what he used on his return."

At church the next day, Chester's last day in Cortland, he met his uncle again, but even at this point he did not know, or did not want to say where he was going. His uncle suggested Chautauqua, where N.H. had attended several conferences dating from the time he lived in New York City.

"He told me he didn't know whether he would go to the Thousand Islands or the Adirondacks or the North Woods," N.H. said. "At this time I suggested going to Chautauqua as the cheaper place."

Chester, never one for making decisions, seems to have put everything off to the last minute, not only about his destination, but also about what he would do when he got there. He must have spent a great deal of time during that last weekend in Cortland going over in his mind the possible alternatives.

One he must certainly have considered, given his past life history, was simply running away. He could have taken his salary, his advances, the little money he had saved and the money for N.H.'s mileage book and taken the train to anywhere in the country. He could have gone back to Chicago, to his parents in Denver or to some new place to start over. The problem with that solution, however, was that it would mean giving up what was certainly the best social and financial position he had ever had. The past year in Cortland must certainly have been one of the most enjoyable of his life and he did not want to give it up.

Another option was to marry Grace Brown. He must certainly have cared something for her, even at this point, but it would have been a social disaster. The Cortland Gillettes would certainly disown him and his new-found friends would no longer invite him to the Normal School parties, dances and outings.

His third option was to refuse to marry her and accept the consequences. He could have denied the relationship and blamed her pregnancy on someone else. But the factory workers, he knew, would be on Grace's side. Even if she brought a paternity suit she would have had difficulty proving him the father. But even if Chester could legally survive the suit, he would never live down the scandal of it. He would be in an even worse position than if he had chosen to marry her.

The final option, and one he must have thought about before this time, even if he had not already made up his mind, was to get Grace out of the picture permanently. Grace, in fact, may have first brought the idea into his head with all her talk in her letters about dying soon. Chester, reading those words, could not help but think how convenient that would be.

The newspapers of the day were full of stories of crimes of passion. Spurned girlfriends seemed, at least according to the stories, to seek their revenge in murder nearly every day and boyfriends did the same. Chester was always an avid reader of the popular press and he could not have missed those stories.

Grace's death, he must have thought, would solve both of their problems. Grace's honor would remain intact because no one would know of her condition and Chester would be free to live his life in Cortland as he chose.

The prosecution later claimed that Chester had decided on murder even before he left Cortland, but there is no real evidence of that and it would be out of character for him to make any extensive plans about anything. More likely, he was keeping all of his options, including the most drastic one, open.

Chester's story was that he left Cortland with vague plans of marrying Grace somewhere in the Adirondacks and never returning to Cortland. But that story is very unlikely and the best evidence is what he packed in his suitcase that day.

Always short of cash, it would not be like Chester to leave behind such valuable items as his bicycle and his desk when he could have sold them. He claimed, however, that selling them would have attracted too much attention and aroused suspicions. He didn't resign his job as Grace had done before she left and he didn't give up his room. He showed every intention of returning after a week.

But he also packed in his suitcase two of his tennis balls. The racket, he said later, he brought along so that people would think he was going on vacation. He could not explain later, however, why the tennis balls were packed inside the suitcase if he planned to run away to get married. That, as the prosecution pointed out later, was evidence that he planned to go to other places and do other things after he had done away with Grace Brown. He also packed a New York Central, Adirondack Division, travel folder that included a map of the Adirondacks. Chester denied, however, that he used the map to plot where to do away with Grace.

After he finished his packing, Chester took his russet-colored suitcase with the initials C.E.G. on the outside near the handle, and boarded the trolley car for the trip to the Lehigh Valley Railroad Station, just off Main Street on Railway Avenue. No one seems to have seen him leaving as he boarded the 6:35 train. He passed through East Homer, Truxton, Cuyler (the boyhood home of his benefactor, Lucien Warner) and finally arrived at the small village of DeRuyter, the station closest to South Otselic.

He arrived at the station about 7 p.m., but probably went to a restaurant for supper because he did not arrive at the hotel, the Tabor House, until about 8:30. Myra Coy, wife of John Coy the owner of the hotel, saw him come in about then with his suitcase with the tennis racket attached to it.

The hotel was a three-story wooden building at the main intersection of the village with shutters on the windows and a two-story high porch that overlooked the streets on two sides. Built in 1849, it was popular with fishermen who travelled from all over the state to fish for bass and pickerel in the nearby streams.

Ralph S. Weaver, the clerk on duty, said Chester registered about 10:50. But instead of his name, Chester wrote in the book,

"Charles George, N.Y."

Chester later explained that he used a false name to help protect Grace's reputation. She had relatives in DeRuyter who might have seen him with her later. From the time Grace left Cortland they seem to have agreed that their trip should be kept as quiet as possible.

But that hardly seems an adequate reason for the deception. More likely, as was suggested later, the false name was the first sign that Chester was planning a murder. It later became one of the main pieces of evidence used to prove that the murder had been planned in advance.

Chester, who had read many of the mystery stories of the day, knew that he would have to choose an alias that matched the initials on his suitcase. It was just the kind of thing that had led to murderers being caught by skillful detectives in the stories.

He was assigned Room 5 and left a note to be called at 7:30 the next morning.

Meanwhile, just 10 miles away, Grace Brown was spending her last evening in her home town with her friend and former teacher, Maude Crumb. Grace had packed her trunk on Sunday, the same day as Chester, but she packed different kinds of items. She brought nearly all her clothes, including the ones she had made especially for the trip. But she also brought her working clothes, the ones she wore in the factory, so that she would be ready if she found a job somewhere else. Also, wrapped in paper, were all the letters Chester had written to her, even those written nearly a year before.

She had told her father that she was going back to Cortland because her vacation was over. He loaded her trunk into the family buckboard and drove her into the village, where her trunk was left at the post office. She walked the few yards to Dr. Crumb's house. She must have had difficulty keeping her joy to herself as she talked to her old friend, for she must have believed she was very close to marriage after all this time.

Monday morning dawned gray and overcast. Grace awoke about 5 a.m., had breakfast with the Crumbs and walked back across the street, past the bandstand where she had listened to music since she was a child, and over to the post office where her trunk was waiting for her. She left the Crumb house about 6 a.m.

and boarded the stage for DeRuyter soon after, just as she had done many times in returning to Cortland from visits to her family. She arrived at DeRuyter just before nine and was let off at the Tabor House, just as she had arranged in her last letter.

According to one report, which was never verified, Grace met her cousin, Marcia Brown, just after getting out of the stage-coach.

"Why didn't you tell us you were coming to DeRuyter, Grace, and why didn't you come last night and stay with us?" Marcia is said to have asked. According to this story, Grace told her she planned to elope with Chester and they would be married later that day. It seems unlikely, however, that after keeping her marriage a secret from her family and best friend that she would tell her cousin. More likely, the story was exaggerated later out of a different conversation.

Better substantiated was her meeting, a few minutes later, with her uncle, Fred Brown, Marcia's father. He talked to her briefly in the sitting room of the Tabor House when she first came in, but she broke off the conversation quickly, obviously in a hurry to look for Chester.

There were apparently no witnesses to her meeting with him a few minutes later, but it must have been a tremendous relief to Grace to find him there, since she had had no verification that he had agreed to her plan. They spent a long time talking together in the sitting room.

Chester had been awake since 7:30 and had had breakfast in the hotel at about 8. He spent the next several hours in his room, reading a book, but had to leave when Mrs. Coy came in to clean the room.

Mrs. Coy knew Grace and recognized her when she went into the kitchen to get a drink of water at about 9:30. About a half hour later, Mrs. Coy came out of the kitchen and saw Grace and Chester still talking in the sitting room. Among the things they discussed was a destination for their trip, eventually deciding on Fourth Lake, a popular tourist spot in the Fulton Chain of Lakes in the Adirondacks.

"I saw her sitting in an arm chair and he stood in front of her," Mrs. Coy said, but she did not hear what they were talking about. A half hour later they were both gone. They had decided that since Grace knew so many people in DeRuyter it would be better for them to take separate routes to the train station and go to Canastota in different cars.

Chester walked to the station, along Main Street and Railroad Street, but if he thought that no one would notice him, he was mistaken. He must have been very surprised, after all the care he had taken to avoid detection, when he ran across Harold Williams, the 13-year-old son of his former Cortland landlady, Harriet Williams, at about 10:30.

Harold was in DeRuyter for the Fourth of July and was returning to Cortland. "Hello, Chester," Harold greeted him. Chester said hello. "Where are you going?" asked Harold, but Chester would only say he was going to Canastota.

After he made the turn into Railroad Street, Chester, carrying his umbrella because of the rain, tried to pass three girls who were also carrying an umbrella, and the two umbrellas locked.

The train was scheduled to arrive at 10:37 but was 20 minutes late. Grace had arrived at the station at about 10:20, checked her trunk and bought a ticket for Canastota. Morrell E. Tallett, the ticket agent who knew Grace, said she "was sitting in the waiting room most of the time. She came to the ticket window a second time after she bought her ticket to speak to me - something pleasant on the subject of her vacation or something."

Tallett said he first saw Chester at the end of the station just as the train pulled out.

"I saw him board the last passenger car on the train," he said. "He had a suitcase and umbrella. I thought something was attached to the suitcase like a tennis racket."

Once on the train, Chester walked from the back of the train towards the front and had an even greater surprise than when he met Harold Williams. There, sitting together in the middle of the car, were Josephine Patrick, the young woman who lived on his street and with whom he had attended parties, and Gladys Westcott, a friend from Truxton who also knew Chester. They were on their way to the Calavista Lodge on Seventh Lake in the Adirondacks for a vacation.

"He stood by our seat and conversed with us until we reached Canastota," Miss Patrick recalled. "I didn't see anyone else with him. He didn't say anything about anyone being with him." She said Chester told them he had got on the train at DeRuyter and that he was supposed to meet someone there, but had missed him, so he was going to the young man's home in Canastota. They were planning a trip to the North Woods, Chester explained.

"He said the young man had an uncle on Raquette Lake, I believe he said, he had a camp there and this young man had a canoe and he thought he would have a better time if he met this young man and went with him."

Chester, always the gentleman, offered to check their trunks for them at Canastota, but they said they had to purchase a mileage book in Canastota first, so declined the offer.

Chester, Miss Patrick said, told her that "he might be down through that way", that is to Seventh Lake, "the latter part of the week and would call at that camp. I think he said it would be either Thursday or Friday he would be there. I don't think it was definite."

Just before the train reached Canastota, Chester left the two young women and they did not see him again until later in the week. They took the next train for Utica, which left almost immediately. Chester and Grace, seeking to avoid them, waited an hour and a half for the next train, meaning they would miss their connection in Utica and would have to stay overnight in Utica before going to the Adirondacks.

At Canastota, Grace said she had seen Chester talking to the two young women and, according to Chester's later account, asked him where they were going. When he mentioned Seventh Lake, Grace said, "Well, let's not go to Fourth Lake then."

"Of course, I wanted to know why and I asked her," Chester said later. "She said she was afraid she would meet those girls and might meet some others. I told her they were not (going to be) on Fourth Lake. She said, 'Well, it is very close to that.' "

"Well, I don't care, where shall we go?" Chester said he asked.

"Let's go to Tupper Lake," she said.

They were looking at Chester's railroad folder and Grace pointed to Tupper Lake on the map.

"I asked her if she knew anything about Tupper Lake," he said. "She said no. It was down there in the folder. She supposed it was like any of the others. I said, all right, it would not make much difference."

From noon until about 1 p.m. they waited at the station and discussed their plans. On the train to Utica they sat together for the first time and arrived at the Utica station just after 3 p.m. They walked the three blocks from the station across John Street and over the Erie Canal bridge to the Hotel Martin, just off John Street on Bleecker Street, where the Boston Store parking garage is located today.

The hotel lobby was full of marble columns and the hotel itself was one of the largest in the city, with seven floors over an entire block. Charles H. Dube, a native of Florida who was the desk clerk, recalled that they arrived between 5 and 6 p.m. In the register Chester wrote "Charles Gordon and wife, N.Y." and Dube assigned them Room 32. A bellboy took them up the back stairs, since the front stairs were being repaired.

A few minutes later, William H. Martin, the owner of the hotel, saw Chester and Grace walking back down the stairs. He asked Chester if he was looking for the dining room and Martin showed him where it was.

They spent the night in the hotel together, probably the first time they had ever slept together. They certainly must have gone over their plans once again, although Chester never said what they talked about.

The next morning, another gray, sunless day, they went down to breakfast together and returned to their room. At this point according the Chester's later account, he asked her, "What shall we do now?" Grace asked him if he had any plans.

"No, nothing very definite," he said.

"I supposed we were going to the North Woods," she said.

"Well, we can" Chester said and added that he knew no reason why they could not.

"Well," Grace said, "then we might just as well do as we planned to do; we might just as well go there."

"All right," Chester said, "Only we can't stay very long unless I get some work there."

Then Chester took the two shirts he had worn on the two previous days and a handkerchief, put them into a bundle and took them around the corner of the hotel to Leahy's Laundry on John Street.

Guy Zimmerman, the clerk at the laundry, said Chester came

in about 8:30, gave him the laundry and asked that it be sent to Chester Gillette at Old Forge as soon as possible. For some reason that is not quite clear, Chester either forgot or intentionally did not use one of his aliases at the laundry and the package later served as a clue to his whereabouts just before his arrest. The prosecution later claimed that he used his real name because he knew that by the time the laundry arrived Grace would no longer be alive and he would not have to hide under a false name.

After returning to the hotel, Grace and Chester went for a walk through Utica. They walked out the front door of the hotel, down half a block on Bleecker Street to Genesee Street, the main intersection of town, called "the busy corner," a block away from the canal. They walked south on Genesee Street, the main street of the city lined with trees.

Chester never talked about what they said during that walk, but it would have been difficult to avoid the topic of marriage. Utica, a city of over 60,000 people at that time, was about six times the size of Cortland and was probably the largest city Grace had ever seen. But it was not very exceptional to Chester, who had been to Chicago and San Francisco.

They passed several tall office buildings, Grace Episcopal Church, the Butterfield Hotel and City Hall, where marriage licenses were issued. Then they walked past the gold dome of the Savings Bank of Utica, the impressive homes of the Fort Schuyler Club and the New Century Club, the newly built public library and the home of millionaire Thomas R. Proctor. Along the way they passed two florist shops, two jewelry stores and two churches, all associated with thoughts of marriage.

When they reached the parkway, which was then called Pleasant Street, they took a trolley car back down Genesee Street to John Street, and walked back to the railroad station.

Since they did not return to the hotel, Chester never paid the bill, which amounted to $1.50 for the room and their meals. Since he was using a false name, Chester apparently figured he could get away with the trick, the same one for which he was caught several years before in Savannah, Illinois.

They went to a restaurant near the station and ordered a light lunch which neither of them ate. Then they boarded the Adirondack Division of the New York Central for the trip north into the Adirondacks.

It was a wonderfully scenic ride, then considered one of the most beautiful in the state. Most of the track was laid through unbroken wilderness and passengers spent hours without seeing a road or a building. There were breathtaking views of mountains, lakes and streams and passengers could count on seeing deer and other animals from the windows.

Among the other passengers on the train was Royal K. Fuller, a reporter for the *New York Herald* who was on his vacation. He got on the train at Clearwater at about 2 p.m. and rode to Big Moose, just a few stops away. He sat two seats behind Chester and Grace and there was no one in the seat between to block his view of them.

"There were not 12 people in that car," he said later. "I think there were as many as that." Both Chester and Grace had taken off their straw hats, he recalled. Chester had taken off his coat and rolled up his sleeves and Grace had on a short-sleeved white blouse. Fuller said he thought they were a newlywed couple because they were "spooning."

Some three and a half hours later they arrived at Tupper Lake, a small village of about 3,500, and walked through the waiting room out onto the platform where there was a carriage waiting to take passengers to their destinations. They rode to the Alta Cliff Hotel, located just out of town at the west end of Park Street.

Meyer Neuman, the owner of the Alta Cliff, had lived in Tupper Lake for about four years but had only purchased the hotel a few months before and was not yet ready to accept guests. Grace and Chester arrived about 6:30, but Neuman was out, so Grace sat on a rocking chair on the veranda and Chester stood next to her, waiting for him to return. When Neuman arrived, a short time later and found the couple on his porch, he asked them who they were.

"Charles George," said Chester, holding out his hand.

"Mr. George," Neuman said, "you should have written to me before you came up here. People who come here usually write me first so I can prepare myself for them."

Chester lied that he had written a letter but Neuman must not have received it. Chester said it was raining too hard for them to go anywhere else and asked if he and "his wife" could stay for just one night. Neuman agreed and they were given a room.

At supper time, they came downstairs and Chester signed the register: "Charles George and wife, New York, N.Y." While they were eating their dinner some of their conversation was overheard by Clara Greenwood, a hotel employee. Chester seemed to be concerned that Grace was not eating enough and urged her to eat more but Grace said she was eating as much as she wanted, and that she was not very hungry. Later, Miss Greenwood saw them talking together on the veranda.

After supper, the rain cleared a bit and Chester and Grace went for a walk into the main part of the village and up onto a hill from which they could see the lake. Whether it was because of the rainy weather or some other reason, they decided they did not like the town and talked about going somewhere else. Chester said later that they were both disappointed with the place and they decided to leave the next morning.

A few minutes after they returned to the Alta Cliff, Chester came downstairs and asked Neuman about the scenery in the area and if there were any high mountains or scenic lakes. Neuman later testified:

> I told him there was none. I told him if he would go
> about 20 miles from here in most any direction he would
> see more scenery in a day than he would see here in a
> year. He then asked about Raquette Lake and I told him
> Raquette Lake was very nice. There is very nice scenery
> there. He asked if I did know of a hotel that is a kind of
> quiet place. I told him I didn't know of any or else I
> would be glad to recommend them to him.

Neuman suggested Lake Placid, farther north, as a possible place to go, but Chester said he and his wife had been in the mountain air for a few weeks and his wife was very tired. But, he said, they expected to spend another two weeks in the Adirondacks. Finally, he told Neuman, he decided that they would go to Raquette Lake the next day.

For the second night in a row, they slept together and woke about 6:30 to find that the weather had finally cleared. For the first time since their trip began the sky was clear and the sun was shining.

They came down to breakfast about 7 and, since the cook was not yet awake, Neuman made the breakfast himself. While they were eating, Neuman called Daniel J. McDonald, the wagon driver, to come to the hotel in time to take them to the station so they could catch the next train going south.

Grace was wearing her light green skirt and a white blouse and as she ate her breakfast she was crying, according to Clara Greenwood, who was not close enough to them to hear what the couple was saying.

Chester said later that they talked about where they would go. They said they hoped all the lakes were not like Tupper Lake. Chester said he asked her if she wanted to go back to Utica, but Grace said no. Then he asked her about Fourth Lake, their original destination. Grace said no, mentioning the girls from the train who would be near there, but eventually Chester persuaded her.

"All right," Chester said he told her, "I don't think we will see those girls or anybody else we know."

Before they left for the train, Grace put on her black silk jacket, but forgot her umbrella. Chester paid the bill and they left in the wagon.

They arrived at the Tupper Lake Junction station about 8:10 and took the train south, along the way they had come the day before. Grace's trunk was checked through to Old Forge, not to Fourth Lake, where they had talked about going.

According to Chester, he and Grace talked about where they would go while they were on the train. Chester's version of what they said was:

> I asked her how long we were going to be at Fulton
> Chain or at the Fulton Chain of Lakes and I said I didn't
> think we had better stay very long, that is, very many
> days, and she said, no, she didn't want to, and then she
> said, "Let's get off at Big Moose, go over there, and
> come back and go down Fourth Lake or Fulton Chain
> this afternoon. I told her - I asked her what was at Big
> Moose, if she knew anything about it. She said she did. I
> told her if I remembered the station I had seen the day
> before it didn't look very inviting . . . Well, she said,
> some friends of hers, Mary something, I don't know

whether she mentioned the name or not. She said she was
there last year, that is, the year before, and had spent
three or four days and had a very pleasant time, enjoyed
it ever so much. She said she thought it would be a pretty
place. She said she knew it would be better than Tupper
Lake. I said it would not have to be very good then."

Later, Grace and Chester spent their time writing postcards, a
popular activity in 1906 and a common sight among tourists on
trains. But what they wrote on the cards showed the opposite
things they were thinking about.

Grace's card had a small photo of Genesee Street in Utica on it
and she had probably bought it in the Utica station. Around the
photo she wrote: "Dear mother, Am having a lovely time. Don't
worry. Will write you more tonight about the trip. It was rather
unexpected but am glad we are here. Love to all the girls and
have them in school, Lovingly, Billy."

Since her parents said they thought she had returned to Cortland, it seems it would have been a great shock to tell them in
such a short note that she was really in the Adirondacks. She
knew, however, that she couldn't keep her parents from finding
out that she was not in Cortland and she didn't want her parents
to worry about her. The part about keeping the girls in school is
an indication that she planned to stay away a long time, since it
was July 11, and there was no school until September.

At the same time, Chester was addressing his card to Mrs. Ella
Hoag, Gillette Skirt Co., Cortland, N.Y. On it he wrote: "Please
send five dollars to Eagle Bay, N.Y. so that I can get it on
Friday."

The card was later used as evidence that Chester had by this
time planned the murder out in detail. He had found Eagle Bay
on the map, just south of Big Moose, and knew that he would be
there on Friday.

Chester gave his card to mail clerk Thomas E. DeDell on the
train but kept Grace's until they got off the train.

Big Moose station was several miles from the lake and was very
much out in the wilderness. There were only two or three houses
nearby and it was not a very inviting place to stop unless one was
looking for seclusion. They were met at the station by the local

UTICA RAILROAD STATION - *Where Grace and Chester got off the train on July 9, 1906 and boarded it again on July 10 for the Adirondacks.*

UTICA IN 1906 - *Part of the area in which they took their walk on the morning of July 10.*

*HOTEL MARTIN - Where Grace and Chester spent the night of July 9. Chester left without paying the bill.*

*TUPPER LAKE - Where Grace and Chester spent the night of July 10.*

*GLENMORE HOTEL - Where they arrived on July 11.*

*The marsh at Big Moose where Grace picked the pond lilies.*

CHESTER ESCAPES - An
artist's impression of Chester's
escape.

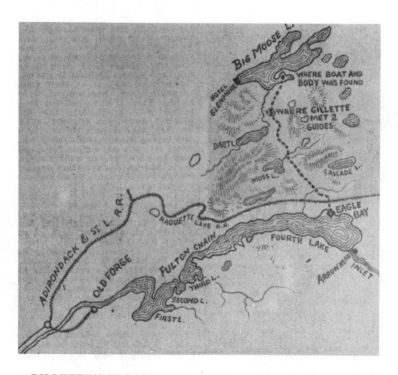

GILLETTE'S ESCAPE - A map showing Chester's route from
Big Moose to Eagle Bay.

*THE ARROWHEAD, INLET, N.Y. - Where Chester was arrested.*

*STEAMER* UNCAS - *The boat that brought Ward and Klock to arrest Chester and which later took them back to Old Forge.*

wagon driver, James A. McAllister just before 10 a.m. He asked them what hotel they wanted to go to.

"He said any old hotel would do that had small boats to rent and was near the lake," McAllister said. "I told him I would drive him to the Glenmore, as that was the nearest one, and he said he would go there."

Just before they started on the journey to the hotel, Chester gave McAllister Grace's postcard and the driver walked over to the station to mail it.

They were the only passengers in the wagon and Chester took his suitcase and boarded with Grace, who did not have her trunk because it had been checked through to Old Forge. When they were about a half mile down the road, Grace asked McAllister what train they could take to go south that night.

"I told her there were three trains," McAllister said. "One at 10:55, one at 11:15 and one at 12:48. She said she would take the 11:15 train. She said, 'Oh dear, I will be tired out before that time.' She said the 11:15 would be late enough for her."

When they reached the Glenmore, Grace told him, "Don't forget us tonight," and McAllister promised to take them back to the station then.

They arrived at the Glenmore about 10:30, got off at the entrance and walked up the front steps, from which they could see the steamer *Zilpha* waiting at the dock nearby. Chester went into the office to register while Grace waited outside on the veranda, admiring the view. The Glenmore, set at the extreme western end of Big Moose Lake had a view of nearly the entire lake. The hotel itself was constructed in a rustic style out of logs and stone and was set back into the birch and evergreen trees, which acted as a frame for the famous view.

Andrew Morrison, the clerk of the hotel, recalled seeing them walk up the hotel steps and Chester stepping right up to speak to him:

> I saw [him] write two names. He wrote 'Carl Grahm, Albany; Grace Brown, South Otselic' . . . The lady did not go to the desk with him. He told me that he wished to go through the lake on a steamboat and come back to the hotel for dinner and go out on the afternoon train. I

told him I had nothing to do with the steamboat. He
would have to go down and notify the captain or
engineer, who would, in turn, notify him when they
would leave the dock. He then went outside.

Chester walked down to the dock where the *Zilpha* was
waiting, about 150 feet from the hotel. According to Chester's account, he found the engineer, Frank Crabb, and spoke with him
about the boat:

> I asked him if we could go on the steamboat when they
> left. He said we could. I asked him when they left and he
> said in a short time and I then asked him if he would
> blow the whistle before they left, so that we would know
> when he was ready or when he went, and he said he
> would. Then I went back on the porch and talked with
> Grace and looked at a paper or a magazine that was
> found there on the porch. I then took off my coat and
> started to take it in the office and hang it up, and Grace
> took her hat and asked me to take that and put it in the
> office and I put her hat on the rack that was against the
> wall on one side of the office, and hung up my coat, and
> then stopped at the desk and started talking with Mr.
> Andrew Morrison.

Chester asked Morrison if there were any particular sights on
the lake that they might want to see on their trip. Morrison told
him about a wooden rustic foot bridge over the outlet of the lake
near the south shore, a boathouse near Higby's camp and several
other camps around the lake.

"I told him he would not have very much time to take the
steamboat trip and get back to the hotel for dinner," Morrison
said later, and suggested that they take a rowboat instead of the
steamer. "He said all right, he would take a rowboat. He wanted
to know where to get one. I said my father had the boats in
charge. He would have to go down to the boathouse and see him.
He then went to the door."

Out on the veranda, Chester told Grace about the change in
plans. Grace, who could not swim, probably would have pre-
ferred the steamboat, but the rowboat would give them a chance
to be alone, so she agreed. Chester said later:

> I went back to the office and told Mr. Morrison all
> right, I guessed we would take a rowboat, and then got
> my things that I had put in the office and took them. I
> had a suitcase and camera and coat. Strapped to the suit-
> case was a tennis racket and case and an umbrella. I had
> put those things in the office when I first went into the
> office. I took them and went out on the porch and gave
> Grace my coat and we went down to the boathouse near
> the dock. The boathouse was in front of the Glenmore."

Grace went directly to the boathouse, but Chester stopped off
at the steamboat dock to tell Frank Crabbe that they would not
be taking the steamboat after all. Robert Morrison, Andrew's
father, who was the boatkeeper, said he first saw Chester and
Grace at about 10:45. He spoke later about what happened:

> He asked me if he could get a boat. I told him yes. I
> pulled a boat out of the boathouse. They got into it and
> went up the lake. He had a dress suitcase with him . . .

The boat was a 17-foot long wooden rowboat called an "Adirondack skiff." Chester put the suitcase in the center of the boat
and Grace sat in the back of the boat on a detachable cloth-
covered seat that was more comfortable than the wooden slats on
the other seats. Chester sat near the front of the boat where he
could reach the oars in the metal oarlocks.

Left behind in the hotel was Grace's straw hat. Chester had
not picked it up when he brought his other luggage down to the
boat. Morrison said later he particularly remembered the suitcase because he had not seen one taken into one of his boats
before. Chester later said he took it because it had their lunch in
it - some fruit and some crackers they had bought in Utica. The
prosecution, however, would later claim that it was brought into
the boat so Chester could bring it with him on his escape after the
murder.

Chester and Grace floated south from the Glenmore dock,
along the southwest shore of the lake towards the picturesque
spots that Andrew Morrison had mentioned. They passed the
rustic bridge at the outlet of the lake and entered a smaller bay of
the lake called South Bay. They went as far east into the bay as

they could to a place far from any of the camps that lined the lake and far away from where the other boaters were rowing. It was a place where pond lilies grew in abundance and Grace picked some and put them into the pocket of her black silk jacket.

Then, according to Chester, they just floated for a long period of time, reading magazines and enjoying the sunshine. About 1 p.m. the sunshine got too hot so they moved closer to the shore and into the shade of the large evergreen trees that ringed South Bay. Edward O. Stanley, who owned a camp on the south shore, remembered seeing them at that time.

"There was a man and a woman in a boat," he said. "There was a suitcase in the boat just forward of the middle seat . . . When I saw the boat it was in front of our camp, 75 to 100 yards in the lake." As the boat travelled to the east, he said, he lost sight of it.

A few minutes later, according to Chester's account, they stopped the boat on the shore of the lake in a deserted area and got out to look for a place to have their lunch. He said:

> We went a short distance from shore, fifty feet, and sat down there. I asked her if she was not getting hungry. She said no, she didn't feel well. She didn't care for anything. I then went and got my suitcase, which was in the boat, took it out on shore where she was, and got some luncheon and then arranged the suitcase for her to sit on. It was kind of damp there. The grass was wet, so I fixed the suitcase near a tree.

Chester said he gave her his coat and they stayed there about an hour, eating and reading. But no evidence was ever found that they actually made this stop and the prosecution later claimed that it never took place. It was invented, the prosecution claimed, so that Chester would have a reason why his suitcase did not get wet. Chester claimed that when they returned to the boat, they left the suitcase behind, planning to pick it up there later.

Next, according to Chester's account, they went west, back the way they had come a few hours before, only this time they rowed along the north shore instead of the south shore. They went all the way out to Covey's Point, which divided South Bay from the rest of the lake.

They crossed the bay and rowed into the outlet of the lake they had passed before and under the rustic bridge into the outlet, called the Moose River. They rowed as far as they could go, to a dam with a road over it. There they got out and got a drink of water from a spring. When they returned into South Bay, they met another couple in a boat, Bernard Foster and his wife from Utica.

"They were just sort of drifting," Foster recalled. "They were going into the bay. The boat was right up close to the shore . . . I left that bay about a quarter of six, I should say. The man and the woman were in there then . . When we came out of Punkey Bay there were no other boats in there."

Foster was the last person other than Chester to see Grace Brown alive. After Foster's account, there is only Chester's version of what happened.

Chester said they went back to the eastern end of South Bay to pick more of the pond lilies, since the ones Grace had picked earlier had withered in the heat. She put most of the lilies inside the pocket of her coat, but pinned one to her lapel. For another few minutes they rowed and drifted into a small, deserted bay on the south shore.

Exactly what happened next will probably remain a mystery forever. The central event in the lives of both Grace and Chester is still not understood in any detail. Chester, the only one who knew what happened, never gave a satisfactory account of it. Instead, he told many stories. At first, he said it was an accident. Later, at the trial, he said Grace committed suicide. Still later, he is said to have confessed that he was responsible for her death, but a full account of how it happened wasn't included.

The facts that are known for certain are that Grace ended up at the bottom of the lake with a gash across her forehead and Chester ran away into the woods without telling anyone what happened. The boat was found floating upside down with Grace's black jacket on the keel. Nearby were Chester's straw hat and the magazine he had been reading.

There are many versions of how it happened, each of them explaining some facts, but leaving others unanswered. If it was an accident, as Chester first claimed, why didn't he go back and tell the authorities? Why did he later change his story and say that Grace had committed suicide?

The most complete, but least believable account is the one Chester used later on the witness stand. He said he and Grace got into a discussion of what they should do and Chester decided that they should go back and tell her father that she was pregnant. Grace said she could never do that and stood up in the boat and jumped out. Chester, trying to reach her, tipped the boat over and could not find her so he swam to shore.

But Chester's version fails to ring true and readers today find it as hard to believe as the spectators in the courthouse did in 1906. But there is certainly some evidence that Grace was suicidal. Her statements in her letters that she wanted to die, backed up by the statements she made during her last weeks in Cortland make it difficult to completely rule out suicide. She was sickly and weak and certainly had been through three very difficult and tiring days. Chester may have told her, finally, that he would never marry her and planned to leave her soon. He may even have suggested that it would be better for both of them if she killed herself. Since her life was ruined anyway, why ruin his as well?

The district attorney later gave two scenarios of how Grace's death occurred. First, he said, Chester hit Grace with his tennis racket while they were on the shore. He knocked her unconscious and took her out in the boat and threw her into the lake. Later, he revised the story so that Chester struck her while they were in the boat. Then he threw her into the lake, rowed back to shore, turned the boat over and pushed it back out into the lake.

The only evidence that Chester struck Grace was the mark on her head, which could have been caused by the pole that was used later in bringing her body up out of the water. There was never any evidence that the tennis racket produced the mark on Grace's face. It could just as easily have been caused by Chester using an oar or by a fall against the side of the boat.

When all the evidence that was known then and is known now is taken into account, it is very difficult to believe that Chester was not somehow responsible for Grace's death. He certainly had a sufficient motive and had much to gain by her death.

Whether he verbally abused her to the point that she jumped out of the boat or actually struck her or just threw her out of the boat and let her drown makes little difference morally. He was responsible for the death no matter how it occurred. But legally, the difference between letting her die and planning her death in detail was the difference between life in prison and the electric chair.

During the past 75 years, dozens of people have tried to find the piece of evidence that would prove once and for all how Grace Brown died that day, but so far the proof has eluded them.

Chester, by chance or design, reached the shore. He claimed that he swam to shore and went to get his suitcase so he could change into dry clothes.

Also, by chance or by design, he happened to be in the one part of the lake that was the most convenient for an escape to the south. That part of the lake, although deserted, was very close to the road, which Chester seems to have had no difficulty finding. He may have seen the road on one of the many maps of the lake that were in the Glenmore lobby or on the railroad map he had with him, although he later denied he had seen them.

He set off through the woods to the southwest, throwing away his collar and tie and putting the rest of his wet clothes in the suitcase. He put on a black slouch hat because his straw hat was left floating in the lake. After climbing a barbed wire fence he reached the road to Eagle Bay, where he had asked the day before that the $5 be sent.

But almost as soon as he reached the road he met several young men walking in the other direction. It was now 8 p.m., nearly dark, but the three remembered seeing him walking through the woods. They were Irving Crego, Harold Parker and James S. Hart. They were returning to Big Moose from an outing to Fourth Lake.

"He carried a dress suitcase in his hand," recalled Crego. "I didn't say anything to him." James Hart, who lagged behind the other two, said Chester seemed to be "walking very fast. I just passed him by."

After meeting the boys, Chester said he was having some difficulty carrying all the equipment he had with him. He adjusted the straps on his suitcase so that he could put his arms through them and carry it like a back pack. But this meant that he had to carry the tripod and the tennis racket, so he buried the tennis racket under a log near the road.

Chester walked the six miles to Eagle Bay, crossed over the railroad tracks and arrived at the station. He went down to the steamboat dock and waited about five to ten minutes before the boat arrived.

Albert J. Styles, the purser of the *Uncas*, recalled Chester was wearing "a gray suit, black slouch hat and canvas leggins and his shirt collar was turned up around his neck . . . He had on his shoulders a camera as I should judge from the looks of it."

Chester was on the steamboat for only a few minutes before getting off at the next stop, the Arrowhead Hotel at Inlet at the end of Fourth Lake. Albert G. Boshart, the hotel manager, said only one passenger got off the *Uncas* that night:

> He had a dress suitcase with him and a camera. He had on a dark suit of clothes and a black soft hat and had brown leggins on . . . After he came in he came up to the desk and asked me my rates at the hotel by the day or by the week and I told him what the rates were. I told him my rates ran from two to four dollars a day by the day and by the week from sixteen to twenty dollars. Says he 'I intend - I expect I have got some friends at Seventh Lake, and I am going up there in the morning, and if they are there I may stay with them. If not, I will come back and stay here.' He said, 'I want to stay tonight.' I said, 'All right sir.' I called the bellboy and assigned him room twenty-four and he went to bed . . . He wrote his name in the hotel register . . . He wrote Chester Gillette, Cortland, N.Y.

The bellboy, Everett H. Johnson, made a mistake and took Chester to room 23 instead of 24, so he had to come back a few minutes later and take him to the correct room.

"He asked me if he could get something to eat," Johnson said. "I told him it was too late for supper, but I could get him a lunch. I brought it back there . . . When I got there he was eating an orange."

The next morning, Thursday, July 12, Johnson remembered hearing Chester ask someone where the barber shop was. Later, after getting his hair cut, Chester walked over to the Inlet Post

Office and requested that his mail be forwarded from Eagle Bay to Inlet.

"He wanted to know if there was any mail there for Chester Gillette," said George F. Delmarsh the postmaster. "I looked it over and told him no, there was not. Then he says: 'I suppose I have some at Eagle Bay.' He wanted to know if I wouldn't send there and have it brought over. I told him, "drop them a card," and he says, 'I will,' and he laid down a penny and I handed him a postal card."

Leaving the post office, Chester headed for the Hotel Neodak, where canoes were available for rent. There he met LeRoy Rogers, the hotel boathouse superintendent, who recalled:

> It was 9 o'clock in the morning. He wanted to get a
> boat, a canoe, he said. He asked me the way to Seventh
> Lake and I told him, and I told him there was a carry,
> and I didn't see how he was going to carry the canoe.
> There wasn't any yoke. It was not a carrying canoe. I told
> him there was a guideboat of my own in the boathouse,
> but he preferred to take the canoe and he did take it and
> he went away. He said he wanted to go up to Seventh
> Lake to take pictures.

Chester paddled through Fifth Lake and carried the canoe over to Sixth Lake, then paddled through to Seventh Lake. He reached the Seventh Lake House at about noon. Frank A. Williams, manager of the Seventh Lake House, recalled meeting him:

> He said he wanted to take a little trip around the lake
> and get back for dinner. He wanted to know what time
> we served dinner and I told him half past twelve to two,
> but I requested that he be there about one o'clock . . .
> He left the office and I didn't see him again until one
> o'clock . . . He came in and registered and I seated him
> in the dining room. He wrote his name, "Chester Gillette,
> Cortland, N.Y."

After dinner, Chester asked Williams about Black Bear Mountain, a popular tourist attraction because of its spectacular view. Williams told him there were two trails to the top and went down to the dock with Chester to point him in the right direction. Chester hiked up the mountain by himself, took some pictures and returned to the Seventh Lake House at about 4 p.m. to pay for his dinner. Then Chester asked Williams about "a couple of ladies stopping on the lake somewhere." Chester did not mention their names and he had apparently forgotten where Miss Patrick and Miss Westcott had told him they were staying.

"I gave him the names of two public boarding camps on the lakes," Williams said, "and showed him where they both were, and he went away."

But Chester made no attempt to find the two women that evening and paddled his canoe back to the Arrowhead.

Over dinner that evening in the Arrowhead dining room, he met Minnie E. McDuffy, a resident of New York City who was spending her vacation in the Adirondacks.

"He said he had been taking a trip up the Chain of Lakes that day and up Black Bear Mountain," she said. "He said he had enjoyed it very much. It was beautiful country. He went alone and found a trail for himself." When the topic of conversation drifted to the singing and playing that was a tradition at Adirondack camps in the evening, she said, Chester told her that he neither played nor sang.

The next morning, Friday the 13th, Chester asked the hotel manager, Mr. Boshart, if he could have some laundry done. Boshart said he normally didn't do laundry for guests, but he made an exception for the pair of trousers Chester gave to him. Chester said later they were the ones he had on when the boat overturned.

At breakfast, Chester arranged with a group of other guests to lead an expedition up Black Bear Mountain. Among those in the group were the Rev. Delevan Dean of Lowville; his brother, Robert Dean; his sister, Gertrude M. Dean, and the Rev. Cuthbert F. Frost of Lowville. All were guests at the Arrowhead. Miss Dean said the trip had been arranged before but that Chester was added to the party at the last minute because he said he had been there the day before and would show them the way.

"My brother came to me and asked me if I objected to his going along," Miss Dean said. "My mother was there and she didn't mind, so I did not object." They left at about 10 a.m. and took a different route from the one Chester had taken the day before. On the way Chester snapped several pictures, including a group shot of the entire party at a rest stop on the way to the top.

"We had lunch up on the mountain," Miss Dean recalled. "We broiled steak and then we had fried cakes, cookies, tea and different things." Later, Chester carved his initials on a rock and the date, July 13, 1906.

During the trip, Chester told them his life story. When they were thirsty he told them how he had crossed the great western desert on the train. He told them he had been a railroad brakeman, that he had been to Oberlin College for two years and that he was employed at a skirt factory in Cortland.

After supper, back at the Arrowhead, Chester went over to the post office to inquire about his $5. It had not yet arrived, but while he was walking back, he met Edward E. Whitford, a teacher at the City College of New York, who mentioned that he was camping at Seventh Lake. When Chester asked about Josephine Patrick, Whitford said he knew her and that she was staying at the Calavista Lodge.

Chester said, "I guess if their plans are all arranged I won't butt in." But Whitford said, "You better come up and see them. They will be glad to see you."

Just a few minutes after he talked about the two women he had met on the train that Monday, he walked into a store and found Gladys Westcott buying some picture postcards.

"I talked with him a minute and then called Miss Patrick," Miss Westcott said. "She was on a seat a little ways from the store." Chester told them that he expected to be back in Cortland at the end of the week and they invited him to visit them at their lodge the next day.

"He said he would be glad to," said Miss Westcott, "that he would come in a boat in the morning and take the steamer or launch to our cottage . . . We arranged to meet him at 9 o'clock the next morning. I think we planned to go to Eighth Lake, but I am not sure."

After the young women left, Chester returned to the Arrowhead and found a party in progress on the veranda. Most of the guests were singing songs in the evening air. Chester didn't join in the singing but sat with them and listened for a while.

Later that night, after he had gone to bed, Rev. Frost came back downstairs to get a drink of water and heard some men playing cards in the office. Chester was there with Seward Miller and a Mr. Rowley. Frost heard some of the conversation.

"Did you fellows hear of the terrible tragedy at Big Moose?" Chester asked.

"What tragedy?" the two men asked.

"Why, they say some young girl met her death in the lake there," Chester explained. Mr. Frost went upstairs without hearing the rest of the conversation.

Chester went to bed around 9:30 that evening and got up early the next morning so he would spend the day, most likely his last in the Adirondacks before returning to Cortland, with his two Cortland friends.

He had just finished his breakfast and was returning to his room when he stopped suddenly at the foot of the stairs near the front desk.

Standing there in front of the desk was Albert Gross, his friend from the factory. With him were the undersheriff and district attorney of Herkimer County who said they wanted to ask him some questions.

# CHAPTER FIVE

# *The Chain*
# *Of Evidence*

H erkimer County District Attorney George Ward and his friend Undersheriff Austin B. Klock were at the Utica races, a horse racing track on Rutger Street on Friday evening, the 13th of July, when someone handed them a copy of that evening's *Utica Observer* folded over to the headline: "The Big Moose Tragedy."

They both had read the accounts of the drowning that morning in the *Utica Daily Press*, but there had not been anything in those early accounts to suggest that it had been anything other than an accident. Now, however, Herkimer County Coroner Isaac Coffin was quoted as saying he thought foul play was involved because the body of "Carl Grahm" had not been found and because there was a "slight contusion over the right eye and a bruise on the lower lip" of Grace Brown's body.

But even more interesting to the two Herkimer County lawmen was the evidence reported by C. Floyd Hopkins, the 27-year-old *Observer* police reporter. He had talked on the telephone to Coffin and newspaperman Royal B. Fuller at Big Moose earlier that day, but while reporters for other afternoon papers had been content with reporting that information, Hopkins had taken it a step further.

He had put in a call to the Gothic House hotel in South Otselic where, by chance, Frank Brown happened to be in town on an errand. This was the first Brown had heard about the incident at Big Moose and while he admitted that he had a daughter named Grace Brown, he was sure she was in Cortland and had no reason to go to the Adirondacks. When Hopkins mentioned "Carl Grahm's" name to him, however, he said he thought there might be someone with that name who Grace knew in Cortland.

Armed with that bit of information, Hopkins put in a call to the Gillette Skirt Factory, where he was informed that Grace Brown had not worked there in nearly a month and certainly had not returned to work there that week, as Frank Brown had said. No, he was told in answer to his next question, there was no one employed there named "Carl Grahm," but certainly he must mean "Chester Gillette," who had worked in the factory until the Saturday before and had "kept company" with Grace before she went away. As a matter of fact, Hopkins was told, Gillette had said something about going away to the Adirondacks on vacation that week.

Hopkins had the scoop of the year but, unfortunately for him, it came too late to make the headlines and was included at the very end of his earlier article about Big Moose. The importance of those details wasn't missed by Ward and Klock as they read the article. They knew they were looking at a murder case, so they left the races immediately and took a trolley to the Utica train station in time to meet the night train to the Adirondacks.

George Washington Ward, a native of Illinois, moved with his family to Herkimer County when he was a small boy and grew up on a farm in a tiny community called "Sprout Brook". After a few years of teaching school in Herkimer County he went west and was a reporter for the *Kansas City Star*. He returned to New York to study law at Cornell University and graduated in 1892. He set up his practice in Dolgeville, near the old family farm, and for a time was the village attorney. As his practice became more extensive he moved his office to Little Falls but maintained his residence in Dolgeville.

In 1903, at the age of 33, he was elected district attorney and in the summer of 1906 he was the Republican candidate for Herkimer County judge. It's impossible to guess how much his initial enthusiasm for prosecuting the Gillette case had to do with his campaign, but it must have been at least a contributing factor. Both he and Klock, who was the Republican candidate for sheriff, had reputations as dedicated public servants who would have done their duty in any case. Both of them, however, had much to gain from the publicity surrounding the prosecution of a sensational murder case.

From the very beginning, Ward's determination to send Chester to the electric chair was aided by a series of coincidences and lucky breaks without which Chester might have gone free. The first of the bad breaks for Chester was that Grace's death occurred in Herkimer County. Other sections of Big Moose Lake were in Hamilton County, a much more rural section of near wilderness area where the wheels of justice turned much more slowly. Herkimer County stretched nearly 100 miles from north to south. While the northern part around Big Moose was a virtual wilderness, the southern part was composed of a group of heavily-settled villages and industries and therefore possessed a much more complete police force.

The next bad break for Chester occurred on the platform of the Utica train station. Ward had called his office and he and Klock were met in Utica by Deputy Granville S. Ingraham, who brought the latest news from Coffin. The three of them were waiting on the platform at about 1 a.m. Saturday morning when they were approached by a man in a suit who asked them if they knew anything about Chester Gillette.

The man was Bert Gross, the superintendent of the skirt factory and Chester's friend. Gross showed the lawmen the card Chester had written to Mrs. Hoag asking for $5. After reading the accounts of Grace's death in the newspapers and hearing about the telephone call that day from Hopkins, Gross was concerned that his friend might be in serious trouble. He had set out to find him, armed only with the Eagle Bay address on the card. As the four of them travelled north through the trees in the darkness of early morning, he told them everything he knew about Chester and Grace, apparently without knowing he was helping them build a case against his friend.

At Remsen, not quite 45 minutes down the line from Utica, they found another important clue. The station baggage master, who had seen Chester's name in the *Utica Observer*, recalled seeing a package of laundry addressed to a Chester Gillette at Old Forge. About an hour later they reached Old Forge, at the west end of Fourth Lake, and Ingraham went to search for the laundry package. Ward, Klock and Gross continued on to Eagle Bay, where Chester had asked that the money be sent. At this point, they had no idea where Chester might be and they wanted to keep both stations covered.

Ingraham arrived at the Old Forge mail station at about 6 a.m. and, before going to breakfast, left word to be notified if anyone called for the laundry package. Only a few minutes later a messenger came into the restaurant to inform him that Captain Hoffman of the Chain Lakes mail boat had asked for the laundry. Hoffman told Ingraham that Chester Gillette, a guest at the Arrowhead Hotel at the other end of the lake, had asked that the package be delivered to him. Ingraham then took the package into custody and boarded the boat for the trip to Inlet and the Arrowhead.

Meanwhile, Ward, Klock and Gross had been informed at the Eagle Bay Post Office that Chester had sent a note there just the day before requesting that his mail be sent to the Arrowhead. Ward, in his eagerness to make sure Chester didn't slip through his fingers, seized a steam launch and they were quickly across the lake. They hurried up to the main desk, checked the register and found the name Chester Gillette and the date July 11. Boshart, the proprietor, told them that Chester had arrived there about 10 p.m. that night and added that Chester himself was in the dining room next door having his breakfast.

While they were speaking to Boshart, a young man came around the corner near the desk and started to climb the stairs. He was just five feet away when he saw the three men standing at the desk. His face lit up with recognition as he recognized Gross and he stepped forward to shake his hand.

"Hello Bert, what are you doing here?" he asked.

"Chester, do you know that Billy Brown was drowned over here at the lake?" Gross asked.

"My God, is that so?"

"Yes, and Chester, I thought you were under the water too!"

"I never heard of it," Chester said.

Ward then asked Chester if he could explain his whereabouts on Monday and Tuesday and Chester said he had been at a camp about 12 miles away at Raquette Lake.

"What camp?" Ward asked.

"I don't know the name," Chester said.

"That won't do," Ward said, "You know where you were and you must give a full account of your whereabouts."

Klock then placed him under arrest and ordered him to return to his room to get his things.

"If you want me, I suppose I'll have to go," Chester said.

The four of them then went to Chester's room and he put his clothes into his suitcase before they went down to the dock to wait for the *Clearwater* to take them back to the station at Old Forge. On the way back, they spotted Ingraham on the mail boat going the other way and he rejoined the group. They arrived at Old Forge about 10 a.m. and were greeted by a large number of people who had already heard that a murderer had been arrested.

At the Old Forge House, Chester was placed in a guarded room until the justice of the peace, James Higby, arrived. He was one of the men who had searched for Grace's body and the father of Roy Higby, who had first found the body. While they were waiting, Ward went to the station to get Grace's trunk, which had been checked through to Old Forge the day Grace died. Forcing the trunk open, Ward found the letters that Chester had written to her while she was in South Otselic.

Hopkins, the reporter who first linked the death with Chester's name, also arrived at Old Forge that morning and was there to record the events. He wrote that Chester spent most of the late morning and early afternoon laying crosswise on the bed in his room, rolling from one side to the other and then onto his back. He "appeared deep in thought," and kept telling stories to the police and then changing them to fit new facts. After insisting for a while that he knew nothing about what had happened at Big Moose and that he had not been there, he was now saying that there had been an accident, that the boat had tipped over and Grace drowned before he could save her. Few of those he talked to, however, were willing to believe anything he said.

At first, Chester said his suitcase had been in the boat when it tipped over, but after an examination of the suitcase showed that it had never been wet, he changed the story and said he had left it on shore before the boat tipped over.

"The point he has appeared the most intent to make," Hopkins wrote, "is an endeavor to make the officers and others believe that he is not at all worried over the situation."

From the moment he was arrested, Chester did not hesitate to talk freely about the case, but kept changing his mind about the story, getting himself deeper and deeper into trouble. First he said he was on vacation, but could not explain why he had so little money, not even enough, he admitted, to pay his bill at the Arrowhead. He said he had been intimate with Grace for over a year and that he had been aware since April that she was pregnant. He then said the trip to the woods was a wedding trip, but couldn't answer when Ward asked him where he planned to marry Grace.

When Ward asked him about the letters in Grace's trunk, Chester foolishly volunteered the information that the return letters, that Grace had written to him from South Otselic, were in his room in Cortland. So, casually, he gave away one of the most important pieces of evidence later used against him.

Later in the afternoon, Room 12 of the Old Forge House was transformed into a makeshift courtroom for Chester's arraignment. Hopkins said Chester appeared to be under severe mental strain when he was questioned, but pleaded innocent when he was officially charged with murder before Higby. Included among the witnesses at the arraignment were many of the people Chester probably remembered only vaguely, but who remembered him very well. There was Royal Fuller, the newspaperman who saw him with Grace on the train and Robert and Andrew Morrison from the Glenmore. All of them positively identified him as the man who had been with Grace Brown and who went under the name "Carl Grahm."

When the arraignment was completed, Ward sent an urgent message to Coffin. Ward realized right away that the results of an autopsy would be crucial evidence in proving that Grace had died by a deliberate action of Chester and not by accident.

The message he sent was: "Man caught. All points to murder.

Make most thorough autopsy. Be exact. Call in Drs. E. H. and
A. O. Douglas; Dr. Smith and Dr. Hays. (signed) Ward."

But the message arrived too late. Coffin had permitted the
undertaker to embalm the body before Coffin decided on his own
that an autopsy was necessary. Much of the evidence that could
have been obtained was destroyed by the embalming process.
When the message arrived, after Dr. Seymour Richards had
already started the autopsy, he seems to have stopped to follow
Ward's instructions to call in additional experts. The message
implies that Ward had doubts about Richards' ability to handle
the autopsy on his own. The doctors Ward mentioned were his
personal friends; people he knew he could count on. When the
autopsy was finally completed, later that evening, the doctors
agreed that no official statement would be given out about their
findings. But not all of them could resist answering the persistent
questions of reporters.

Two newspapers, both without identifying their source, said
the doctors had found air in Grace's lungs, an indication of death
by drowning, but that she had probably been unconscious before
she went into the water. It was believed, they said, that Chester
had struck her before she entered the water.

Frank Brown, who arrived in Frankfort after the autopsy that
evening with I. K. Woodsley, an undertaker from South Otselic,
was called into the back room to make a positive identification of
the body. When the sheet was pulled back and he looked at the
face, he exclaimed, "Oh Grace, Oh Grace, you poor child. You
don't look natural," and began to cry. Later, in an interview, he
said:

> It was Gillette all right who was with Grace up there.
> They have been keeping company for some time. Lately,
> however, I had noticed that she had acted rather cool
> towards Gillette, but I did not think anything of it
> because from what I could learn he was as attentive to
> her as ever. Why they should go up there I do not know.
> I cannot explain it.

Frank had probably just been told by the doctors of Grace's
"delicate condition," as the newspapers put it later, and had not
had time to put that together as a motive for the crime. The

reporters said Frank was very reserved and inclined not to speak ill of Chester, even though he was convinced that the police had arrested the murderer of his daughter.

Chester, meanwhile, was finding himself an instant celebrity. On the trip from Old Forge to Herkimer that evening there were crowds at every station lined up to see the murderer they had read about in the newspapers. Chester, dressed in a light coat, a white flannel shirt with a white four-in-hand tie, black trousers and shoes, leaned on the window of the train with his head in his hand. He sat in the inner seat while Klock, who had brought his handcuffs but felt they were not needed, sat in the outer seat. A Utica newsboy named Morris Vigours came through the car and Chester, always a reader, looked at three or four magazines before choosing *Pearsons* and was soon reading. He seems to have avoided, at this point at least, reading about himself in the newspapers.

When he saw the crowds at the stations, shouting his name and waving their fists, Chester asked Klock, "Sheriff, how do you suppose they found this out?" It was only then that Chester was told that the whole arrest and capture had been written up in the evening papers.

At Middleville, only a few miles from their destination, the members of a high school baseball team boarded the train and sang songs all the way to Herkimer. According to Klock, Chester forgot his predicament long enough to join in the singing with them.

The train arrived in Herkimer at about 7:30 p.m. and Klock got out his handcuffs and attached his left arm to Chester's right, probably because he was concerned that Chester might get away in the crowd that had gathered at the station. The horse-drawn bus that was used by the jail was pulled around to the far side of the train, opposite the platform. Then Klock, a big man who seemed even bigger when handcuffed to the diminutive Chester, quickly got off the train with his prisoner. Chester had turned his collar up and pulled his black slouch hat down over his ears, so most people did not get a good look at him as they boarded the bus and took the back streets the few blocks to the jail.

The Herkimer County Jail on North Main Street was an imposing old solid stone building. Chester entered through the front door, walked up the stone steps and under the coat of arms of two crossed keys set over the door. Across the street he probably noticed the tall steepled building with the wide steps; the county courthouse where his fate was soon to be decided. Inside, at the front desk of the jail, he handed over his silver, open-faced watch with its black silk fob, a card case and a brown wallet with $3 in it. After entering Chester's vital statistics in the jail log, Klock led him into one of the cells on the first floor. Through it all, Chester remained calm and reserved.

Just minutes after Chester was admitted to his cell, attorney Albert M. Mills arrived at the main entrance and demanded to see the new prisoner.

"I would like to have a talk with this boy," said Mills to Sheriff John R. Richard, "I have some telegrams . . ." Mills was admitted in to see the prisoner without showing the telegrams and he refused to tell the reporters outside who they were from. Two days later, however, he said he had been requested by Cortland attorney B. A. Benedict, Harriet's father, to see Chester and advise him about the preliminary legal details of his situation. Mills spoke with Chester only a few minutes and his entire message seems to have consisted of only four words: "Keep your mouth shut." He said a few days later that all Benedict had asked him to do was to brief Chester on his right to remain silent and not answer questions. He insisted that Benedict had not asked him to be Chester's lawyer.

On his way out of the jail, Mills also ordered that no newspapermen were to talk to Chester. Running the gauntlet of the press and the curious outside the jail, Mills was repeatedly asked about Chester, but he only smiled and said, "I think we will have rain tomorrow."

Albert M. Mills was born September 10, 1841, in the village of New Hartford, just south of Utica. He attended Fairfield Academy and Amherst College for two years before joining the 8th New York Cavalry in the Civil War. He was twice wounded and for the rest of his life his saber was among his most prized possessions. After the war he attended the University of Michigan Law School, graduating in 1867. He set up practice in Newport, New York, north of Herkimer, for several years and in Syracuse for a brief period before his election as Herkimer

County district attorney in 1870. In 1879 he was elected to a single term as state senator and ran for congress in 1892, but was defeated. Since then, he had made a reputation as an able trial lawyer and a staunch Democrat. That, of course, put him on the other side of the political fence from Republican George Ward.

While his first contact with Chester was as little more than a legal advisor, Mills could not have missed the political implications of the case. If Ward won a conviction he would be a local hero. It would take a good lawyer to get Chester off and spoil Ward's publicity.

By now, the newspaper reporters were climbing over each other for news about the sensational case and those involved began to make their first real reconstructions of how the crime had been committed.

"There is scarcely any doubt," said Coroner Coffin that day, "that Miss Brown was taken out on the lake and deliberately murdered. It appears that soon after their arrival at the Glenmore at Big Moose, Gillette was seen studying intently a map of the woods while Miss Brown paced to and fro on the balcony or veranda. Of course the girl had no idea of the fate in store for her . . . I have been unable up to the present time to determine as to whether the crime was committed on Wednesday or early Thursday morning and I may not be able to do so." He said the autopsy showed Grace had been badly beaten before being pushed into the lake, contradicting his earlier statement that the mark on her face had been only a slight injury.

"The lungs," he added, "when taken from their cavity were not filled entirely with water. There was still some air in them. We are unable to say positively whether death was caused by drowning or by the blows that had been administered."

Meanwhile, Ward and Ingraham were combing the Adirondacks for every clue they could find, acting as quickly as possible to gather the evidence and the witnesses. After spending the entire night on the train before Chester's arrest, they spent night and day talking with and taking statements from potential witnesses who saw Chester or Grace at the Glenmore, at the Arrowhead or at Big Moose. The newspapers were also uncovering pieces of evidence that helped to put the story together. One reporter found "Charles Gordon and wife, N.Y." on the register of the Hotel Martin and deduced that it had to be Chester and Grace. Their friends and fellow factory workers at Cortland were also telling what they knew.

Sherriff Richard went to Cortland on Saturday to talk to the people who had known them and searched Chester's room for the letters Chester had said could be found there. Chester's landlady, Lizzie Crain, let Richard and the Cortland chief of police into the room and they quickly found the letters in Chester's desk. They also found a letter asking Chester to teach a Sunday school class at the Presbyterian Church signed by the assistant superintendent of the Sunday school, and the note from Harriet Benedict asking about the poster. The one thing they didn't find was the last and most touching letter. That was not discovered until two weeks later when Mrs. Crain was cleaning up the room and found it in a box with Chester's ties and collars. She immediately sent it on to Ward, who must have found it very welcome reading, considering the effect it would have on a jury.

Richard, in discussing the letters with reporters said, "It was a good thing we started when we did. If it had been about three days later we probably never would have seen those letters," hinting that some of Chester's friends planned to take them before the sheriff arrived.

At 1 p.m. Sunday, July 15, Grace Brown's coffin was buried in Valley View Cemetery on a high bluff overlooking the village of South Otselic. It was just a few yards from the hotel where she had called Chester and from the post office where her letters had been posted. Also nearby was the home of her friend, Maude Crumb, where she had spent her last night in South Otselic. Attending the ceremony were her family and many of her childhood friends. The Reverend Mr. Whitney of the Baptist Church, in whose church she sang as a young girl, didn't mention the cause of death in his brief prayer. Instead he concentrated on giving comfort to the family. After the body was laid to rest, the family returned to a house filled with flowers sent by friends from throughout the area.

At the same time, Chester attended the Sunday jail service with several of the other prisoners. He is said to have taken an active part in the service, including the singing of some of the hymns.

Ward, who was still with Ingraham in the Adirondacks gathering evidence, made a brief statement which was printed in the Monday newspapers.

"This fellow is a degenerate," Ward said of Chester, "and all circumstances point to the belief that he knocked the girl senseless and threw her overboard. We found part of her hair fastened to an oarlock of the boat, which is evidence that the body was dumped overboard after she had been beaten into unconsciousness with either an oar or a slingshot (apparently meaning the tennis racket)."

During the next few days Chester amazed his jailors with his calm acceptance of the charges against him. He took books out of the prison library and spent most of his time reading, chatting with the other prisoners and walking up and down the inner corridors. The only thing that bothered him was staying indoors all day and all night. For years he had led an active life, squeezing as much as he could into a day. Now he found himself with nothing to occupy his time. He complained to the authorities that he wasn't getting enough exercise and that the lack of sunshine was making him pale. He slept so much better than the other prisoners, who were charged with much less serious crimes, that they all made fun of him and called him names like "sleepy head."

On Tuesday, Ward finally returned to Herkimer after spending 96 continuous hours in his detective work. On the way back he stopped off at the Hotel Martin to secure the hotel register that had been identified by the newspaper reporter. Klock had already called at the hotel the day before and told the manager that since the register would be needed as evidence that they should guard it carefully and not let anyone tamper with it. It was, therefore, quite a surprise to night desk clerk Egan when two rough-looking men walked in the door at 2 a.m. and demanded to see the register.

Egan asked them why they wanted it. Ward simply said he was looking for a friend as he examined the book, following with his finger down the list of names until he came to Charles Gordon. Egan, seeing the name they were pointing at, said that if that was the friend they were looking for the management would like to know about it, since Gordon had left without paying his bill. Ward then demanded that the page be torn out and given to him.

Egan, following orders, refused and threatened to call the manager. Ward offered Egan $5 to copy the names off the register onto a blank page so that Ward could take the original. When Egan refused a second time, Ward grabbed the register from the desk, tore out the page he wanted and a blank page from the back of the book. He pasted the blank sheet in the place where the page with the Gordon name had been and copied the names from the page onto it.

Egan meanwhile, had summoned manager Martin, who arrived a few minutes later and threatened to call the police. It was only at this point that Ward and Ingraham identified themselves and showed their identification to Martin, who finally permitted them to take the page after they promised to pay for the damages.

Later that morning, at an impromptu press conference, Ward and Ingraham told reporters that they had more than enough evidence to send Chester to the electric chair. "We have got this fellow pat so that he will not reach first base," is how Ingraham described it to a reporter for the *Utica Herald Dispatch*.

When he arrived in Herkimer later that day, Ward spent two hours in his office talking to Josephine Patrick and Gladys Westcott, who had been summoned to Herkimer with their fathers after returning from the Adirondacks. Ward had talked to them earlier at Seventh Lake, but he wanted to take full written statements because of their importance to the case. County Court stenographer Charles L. Earl was kept busy writing down their testimony. They told him about Chester's life in Cortland, his meeting them on the train and his actions after Grace's death.

By this time, Ward's collection of witnesses and evidence was just about complete. He had the body with the mark on the face, a motive any jury would understand and dozens of witnesses who were eager to testify about all the lies the prisoner had told. His only missing link was the lack of a murder weapon.

Ward felt certain that the missing tennis racket was what he needed. While Chester may have used his fists on the victim, Ward reasoned, there would be nothing to show the jury. If he could find the racket he could show the jury, with a dramatic swing, how the death blow was struck. Chester had told him at first that the racket was probably floating in the lake. Later, Shephard Hart of Oswego, one of the three boys who had seen Chester on the road from Big Moose, said he remembered Chester carrying it at that point. An extensive search of the road, however, had not turned up any trace of it.

Ward spent most of the rest of the day carefully tagging and storing the various pieces of evidence he had collected: the hotel registers with the false names in Chester's handwriting, the suitcase and the trunk, the umbrella, the camera, the letters and the two postcards that had been written on the train to Big Moose. All of them were wrapped up and locked in a cell near Chester's.

Among the pieces of evidence was one that was too large for Ward to bring with him: the boat where the death had occurred. It was shipped in the baggage car of a train and caused quite a bit of comment when it was brought through Utica on its way to Herkimer. It remained in Utica for several hours because it was too big to fit in the regular baggage car and had to wait for a larger car. Although the top of the boat was covered with canvas, a tag identified it as being sent by George Ward from Big Moose to Herkimer so everyone knew what it was. People at the station lifted up the cover to look inside.

Ward was faced with a personal problem, however, If he waited for the next regular court session in December, it would mean that the trial would probably extend past the expiration of his term in January. That would mean that the new district attorney would prosecute the case. As soon as he returned to Herkimer he set about the formal request for a special court term that would allow Chester to be tried earlier and allow him to prosecute the case himself.

The newspapers, meanwhile, were exploring other aspects of the case. The story of Chester's relationship with Harriet Benedict was slowly leaking out and the newspapers made much of it in headlines such as "Was Gillette Engaged to Another Girl?" in Thursday's *Utica Herald Dispatch*. In many of the first reports, Miss Benedict was not named, but was described as the daughter of a prominent lawyer.

Much was also made of the fact that Chester's relatives had not yet gone to see him and were not doing anything to help him. Before Chester's arrest, N. H. Gillette had told a reporter for the

*Syracuse Herald*, "Chester is not the boy to hide at such a time, and I know he would give an accounting of himself if he were alive." But when Chester was found alive, N. H. was shocked into silence and refused to give out any statements at all. According to several second-hand accounts, Mrs. Gillette had become ill when the first reports reached her and she had requested that the matter be kept from the family as much as possible.

Since subpoenas were being handed out for the coroner's inquest, many Cortland residents were nervous that they might have to testify. The fear of publicity seems to have terrorized the people of Cortland and many of the more respected citizens who knew Chester refused to discuss the matter in public at all. But in private it was a prime topic of discussion.

On Sunday afternoon, July 22, after more than a week in jail with little contact with the outside world, Chester had his first visitor. He had received some letters and packages from Cortland and had finally sent a telegram to Gross asking him if anyone in Cortland planned to help him. Gross telegraphed that he would send someone the next day to discuss the matter in private.

At 3 p.m. on Sunday, help arrived in the person of Fred Gillette, Chester's friend and cousin. With him was Rowland L. Davis, one of the most respected attorneys in Cortland. They spent 20 minutes alone with Chester discussing his case. There is no doubt that Davis had been sent by a small group of loyal friends including Fred Gillette, Ella Hoag, Albert Gross and possibly others. All evidence suggests that no member of N. H. Gillette's family or Harriet Benedicts' family were involved in helping Chester, even at this early stage.

Davis, interviewed after the meeting, said "there are many things in his case that can be construed in favor of this boy. The public has been given a lot of stuff that has created a prejudice against him." He said he believed N. H. Gillette would come to Chester's aid if he was satisfied the charges against Chester were false. But other members of the family, he said, did not want to get involved in the case and that had been the reason for the delay in sending help.

The jailors said later that Chester's attitude improved considerably after the meeting and he was encouraged that he would receive the best legal help and would soon be free.

GEORGE WARD - district attorney who arrested Chester.

ARROWHEAD HOTEL LOBBY — AT THE HEAD OF BEAUTIFUL FOURTH LAKE
CENTRAL ADIRONDACK MOUNTAINS, P.O. INLET, N. Y.

Hotel lobby at the Arrowhead near where Chester was arrested.

*The veranda at the Arrowhead, where Chester spent part of his last night of freedom.*

*Home of George Ward, Herkimer County District Attorney.*

Ward had planned to hold a formal coroner's inquest beginning on Monday, July 23, but for some reason the inquest was never begun. Instead, Ward spent the next few days in his office interviewing over 100 potential witnesses, taking their statements down in full to make sure they didn't forget important facts if they were called at the trial. The witnesses filled the local hotels and came, one by one, over to Ward's office in the courthouse to tell what they knew. When he was finished talking with them, each witness was led across the street to the jail so he could identify Chester. Ward knew that it was best to refresh the memories of his witnesses so there would be no embarassing moments when they were called to testify. A steady stream of witnesses walked across the street, up the jail stairs to the top floor, where Chester had been moved to a private cell away from the other prisoners.

One of the first to take the brief walk across the street to the jail was Frank Brown, who had seen Chester only once before, the previous December in Cortland. With his first look at Chester he screamed, "You villain, you killed my girl!" and rushed up to the bars and tried to grab Chester before Klock could pull him away.

When it was William H. Martin's turn, he told Chester that he still owed money for the Hotel Martin bill. Chester said he had made arrangements for the bill to be paid in a few days.

Also among the witnesses was Harold R. Gillette, N.H.'s son and Chester's cousin, who said his family had definitely decided not to help Chester. In fact, he said, they did not care to have their name mentioned in any manner concerning the case. Harold declined an offer to see Chester in the jail, saying he could think of nothing that could be done to help his cousin.

By Wednesday, crowds were standing in the street between the courthouse and the jail, looking at the witnesses as they were called into Ward's office and then brought over to see Chester. After over three dozen witnesses had been brought through to stare at him, Chester told Sheriff Richard, "I'm tired of this. If there are any more, let them come in and go out so I can be alone."

Richard, who had been bothered all day by the crowds and the reporters asking to see the murderer, took Chester at his literal word and went to the front door to announce that anyone who wished to see Chester could come in. There was a mad rush as the crowd formed a single file line up the stairs where they could take turns staring at the prisoner in his cage. Men, women and children all had their turns. Chester, who had been spending the time between visitors cleaning his cell, was wiping the cell bars with a rag, watching all the people pass by with their mouths open, looking at the murderer they had read about in the newspapers. Most of them stayed in the room only a few minutes and most didn't speak to him at all. Many of them remarked how terrible the cell was instead of saying anything about the prisoner.

With the rules changed to permit the admission of the general public, Richard could no longer keep the reporters out, and later that day they got their first chance for an interview. Chester stood in his cell with the door open and rubbed the bars with his rag as he talked. He was unshaven and wore a gray outing shirt and dark trousers.

Chester's new cell was large enough to seem almost luxurious compared to the tiny cages in other parts of the building. It had been built to house two prisoners in tiny cells at one end, but it also had a much larger outer room, about twelve feet by eight feet, containing the toilet and sink and designed to give the prisoners some walking space without letting them out from behind the bars. Chester was given this entire suite of three rooms. In one of the smaller cells he had his cot and a small dressing table. The other he used as a storeroom for his clothing.

"Well, I wish I could talk about the case, but I can't," he told the group of reporters. "I have been advised not to discuss the case in any manner whatever."

"How are you feeling?" he was asked.

"Very well," he said. "I am making the best of my surroundings. I am satisfied with my treatment and relish my meals. Of course, the time drags on very slowly."

He was then asked about the reports that he was engaged to a girl in Cortland and his mood changed quickly.

"There's no truth whatever in that statement," he said. "I want that story denied emphatically. Bring nobody else in. Don't mention any lady's name, please. You have not used any name yet, I see. Keep it out."

The reporters tried to get some idea of what defense he would use at his trial, but Chester refused to give them any hints.

The next day, Chester received a visitor who arrived unexpectedly on the afternoon train. It was his 18-year-old sister, Hazel, who had been working in Connecticut as a governess. When she had read about Chester's arrest in the newspapers, she told her employers she had to leave and took the train to Herkimer. She was crying when she arrived at the jail and the jailors quickly admitted her.

Chester saw her for only a few minutes and told her, "Don't feel bad. Go back to school. There's nothing to this anyway - nothing to cry about." He insisted, however, that she not tell their parents anything about what had happened. She said she planned to go back to Chicago and would probably visit their parents in Denver.

On Thursday, after interviewing the last of the witnesses, Ward issued a public statement about the status of the case:

> For over two weeks we have been hustling on this case
> and our work has been thorough and complete. The
> chain of evidence against Gillette cannot be broken or
> even weakened, no matter what kind of defense will be
> put up by attorneys for the young man. Gillette's
> character and standing in Cortland were of the best and
> it was to uphold his untarnished reputation that the
> crime was committed. The birth of an illegitimate child
> would put a dark blot on his life. This is the chief motive
> that has been established.

Ward also said he had developed the film from Chester's camera and had photographs showing Chester on his trip to Black Bear Mountain after Grace's death and several views of Big Moose Lake. He did not mention to the press that the photographs also included several made at Little York Lake of and by Harriet Benedict. Ward was attempting to keep the Benedicts out of the controversy and scandal surrounding the case.

The press was full of speculation as to who would defend Chester, for it was highly unusual that no one had been hired during the first weeks of the case. Most of the problem seems to have been centered in Cortland, where none of the rich relatives and friends were willing to foot the bill, and those who wanted to help could not afford to hire lawyers.

Chester had been encouraged at first that his uncle or Benedict would hire a lawyer to handle his case. But as time went on and Harriet's name began to be mentioned in the newspapers, Benedict abandoned Chester to protect his daughter. N. H. Gillette gave in to the wishes of the other members of the family and withdrew from the case.

Davis, interviewed in Cortland after talking to Chester, said Chester had asked him to be his attorney at the trial but Davis said he had not yet decided. Most of his indecision was probably based on the question of who would pay his bill. It was estimated that it would cost several thousand dollars to defend Chester, an amount of money that was probably well beyond the collective means of Bert Gross, Fred Gillette and Mrs. Hoag, the trio who seemed most interested in helping him.

Davis said Chester had impressed him as a hard-working industrious fellow who had not had a home training because he had to leave his family at the age of 16. He had endeavored to brave the struggle of the world single-handedly. At least, that was the beginning of a defense. But Davis, too, withdrew from the case and had nothing more to do with Chester.

With his uncle out of the picture, the only wealthy benefactor left to Chester was Warner. He was living in the Waldorf Astoria in New York City and could not have avoided reading about the case in the New York City newspapers. There is no evidence, however, that he made any attempt to contact Chester or that any attempt was made to contact him for assistance. Two weeks after the first articles about the case appeared in the newspapers the Warners left, on August 2, for a world tour. Mrs. Warner became seriously ill a few weeks later in Naples and spent two months recuperating in a Cairo, Egypt, hotel. She did not fully recover until almost a year later and did not return to New York until June 29, 1907.

In an interview with a reporter from the Herkimer paper, Chester mentioned that he had considered studying law and joked that considering his current situation it was a mistake that he had not. He said he was not worried about paying for his defense because he had rich relatives who were sure to help him.

By early August, however, it was pretty obvious that all those relatives had abandoned any thought of trying to help him. They were either so certain that he was guilty that they considered it a waste of money to defend him, or, more likely, the enormous flood of publicity made it impossible to get involved in the case without entirely surrendering their private lives to public scrutiny.

Picking up on those clues, the press began to report that Chester's relatives had deserted him. This infuriated Gross, Fred Gillette and Mrs. Hoag and prompted this notice, printed in the *Cortland Standard* of August 11 under the headline "Gillette Not Deserted":

> With reference to the assertion made in certain quarters that Chester Gillette has been deserted in his trouble by his relatives in Cortland and elsewhere, it may be stated with authority that this is not true. He has not been deserted. His relatives do not believe him guilty of the charge of murder and are in close touch with the case. Everything which they have done or have refrained from doing has been done under the advice of counsel. The young man understands the situation perfectly and is wisely keeping his mouth closed. There is no question but that he will have counsel to take up his case when the proper time comes and every effort will be made to see to it that he has a fair trial and a fair show. It is not necessary to say more at this time and the public is asked to suspend judgment for the present upon matters which they do not understand.

The notice was left unsigned, and many people probably thought it was written by N.H. Gillette. Just two days later, Gross visited Chester, brought him some clothes and books and then went to Little Falls to see Ward about the case.

Fred Gillette and Ella Hoag went to see Chester on August 20 and told him that they were having trouble finding an attorney. Later that same day they went to see Mills, who probably told them what his fees would be. He also may have mentioned the possibility of having Chester plead that he was impoverished, which would allow the court to pick up the costs for his defense.

The result of all this delay in selecting an attorney was that Ward had a tremendous head start in the collection of evidence. While Ward and the sheriff's department were spending nearly all their time tracking down witnesses, taking statements and issuing subpoenas for evidence, no one was doing the same thing for the defense. Ward's leaking of his evidence to the press was convincing the public that Chester was guilty and the fact that no one wanted to defend Chester left the impression that his case was hopeless.

Without a lawyer to advise him, Chester made some very poor deals with the sheriff's deputies. After repeated efforts to find the tennis racket failed, Klock went back to Chester and asked him about it one more time. Chester had been advised by Mills to keep quiet, but, one more time, he could not resist talking too much. According to some reports, he made a deal with Klock to get better treatment and better meals if he would tell where the racket was hidden, but there is no proof that any deal was actually struck.

In any case, Chester did tell Klock exactly where the racket was and Klock brought it back to Herkimer in early August. While he was in the Big Moose area, Klock picked a number of pond lilies, near the scene of Grace's death and identical to the ones that she had picked just a few hours before her death. Klock brought them back for Chester and despite having Klock tell him where they were from, Chester put them in a glass of water in his cell.

This and other such incidents, which were faithfully relayed to the press by Klock and the other deputies, were giving Chester a reputation as the oddest prisoner the area had ever seen. He did not act the least bit like a man about to be tried for a crime that could send him to the electric chair. Some even speculated that he was preparing for an insanity plea.

He slept in late in the morning, long after all the other prisoners had had breakfast, and then complained that he wasn't getting enough to eat and later complained about the quality of the food he did receive.

Later, however, the sheriff agreed to have food sent in to him from a restaurant and the sheriff's wife frequently cooked for him, a very unusual procedure. This may have been part of the agreement by which Chester told them where the tennis racket was located.

On July 31, Theresa Harnishfager, the former skirt factory forewoman who knew both Grace and Chester, was returning from Dolgeville to Syracuse with a friend named Sullivan and stopped to see Chester in his cell.

"He just laughed and joked and never even said he wished she were alive again," she said of the meeting. "He was completely blind to his position."

"Chester, I don't see how on earth you are going to defend yourself from this terrible charge," she told him.

"Don't you, Tessie?" is all she said Chester replied. "Well, I do. My plans are well laid."

In Albany on August 1, Gov. Frank Higgins, acting on Ward's request, ordered a special court term for Herkimer County and scheduled a special grand jury to meet August 20 to consider a formal indictment against Chester. At Ward's request, however, the reporting date was moved back to August 27.

On August 4, Chester received two letters from his parents, the first since he had been arrested. One was dated July 8, just a few days before Grace's death, and has not survived. The other, dated July 30, was written by his mother.

Chester's efforts to keep his parents from finding out about his troubles were also doomed to failure. Hazel, after seeing him, went to Denver, where the family had moved after parting with the Dowieites at Zion City because Frank Gillette could not find a job. While Hazel told her parents that Chester was in trouble, she could not bring herself to say just how bad the trouble was.

There are several interesting aspects to Louisa's July 30 letter. First, not knowing what crime he committed, she assumes it was robbery because of an unexplained theft she said occurred in the past. Second, although the letter was drawn up as an exhibit to be presented at the trial, it was never actually submitted.

4551 Blvd. F. Denver, Colo.    July 30

My dear darling boy . . .

The tears fall so fast I can hardly write, but I will control them and write to you now that I know where you are, though I do not know what you have done . . .

I suppose you have stolen money from Uncle Horace, and
that you are in jail in New York City but know nothing
. . . Oh, why did you do it, my dear, dear boy? I expect
you are asking yourself this question, over, and over
again now that your sin has found you out. The only
answer is 'sin, sin, sin, did it, and I did not control it.'

I have no inkling from Hazel's letter of the nature of
the sin, but I know your weak point, and know where you
have fallen so many times before, so I naturally jump to
the conclusion that is it. Oh, how could you steal from
Uncle Horace when he has been so kind to us always and
in every strait has offered money to help us? It is true
that Satan always strikes at our weakest point, and he
found yours . . .

It is our constant prayer that you may know Jesus. He
is the great burden bearer, and will carry yours now as
you are suffering for your wrong doing . . . God be with
you, and help you make all things right.

> Yours with an aching but loving heart
> Mother.

Two days later, Chester wrote his mother for the first time
since his arrest:

Aug. 6, 06

Dear Mother,

I am glad to know that you have heard something as I
have wanted to write for some time, but didn't want you
to know about me.

I have done what you think and please be careful what
you write as all my letters are opened by the jailor. I have
done several very bad things, but have not committed the
crime of which I am accused and for which I am to stand
trial sometime in Dec. It, of course, is a very serious
charge and is to be a hard fight for the lawyers but there
is no need to worry about it, although that is a useless
thing to tell you. I am sorry this had occurred for you
and uncle as it is very hard on both. I do not like the
confinement of course, but I am standing it very well.

I am glad you like it there [in Denver] and should like
it too as I always loved the mountains in the West. I hope
father can get plenty of work that he can do. I think

outdoor work is the best for him at present. Of course in
my present position I cannot send any money, although I
should like to. I have plans made for getting plenty of
money by next summer if I can get through the trial by
January.

I think it is best you do not write about this or me to
uncle as aunt is very justly very much worked up about it.
We, of course, have had no correspondence with each
other. If you are determined to write to anyone, which I
do not think best, you might write to Mrs. Ella Hoag,
Little York, N.Y. She is father's cousin and works in the
factory. Father can tell you about her . . .

Don't worry about me as it won't do any good now.
Write to me here at Herkimer, N.Y.

Love to all, your loving, but bad son,

Chester

I can't write to the children now, but send love to both
and tell Paul to be honest in everything.

Chester

Of course there is a girl mixed up in all this. Send me
some stationery please.

C. Herkimer, N.Y.

Chester wrote in vain, however, because the letter was intercepted and confiscated by the jailors, who gave it to Ward. He
may have planned to use it at the trial, but it was never entered
into evidence.

The letter reveals quite a bit about Chester's attitude at the
time. He certainly expected to be free within a few months and
was already dreaming up a new get-rich-quick scheme.

He could not quite bring himself to tell his mother that he had
been charged with murder, only that he had been "bad" and that
there was a "girl mixed up in all this." It shows how lightly he
took the death of his former lover.

His reference to his uncle shows that he was already aware of
the resistance that existed there to helping him. Although his
relatives and friends did what they could to stay out of the public
eye during the height of the publicity, Ward, a former reporter,
couldn't resist leaking out bits of the evidence he had collected in
the case. It wasn't long before the newspapers, armed with

Ward's stories about the other letters he had found in Gillette's room, were writing about Harriet Benedict as the "other woman" in Chester's life. Some reporters even went so far as to suggest they had been engaged.

B.A. Benedict was furious that his daughter's name and reputation were being damaged and called a group of reporters to his office on August 21 to issue a formal denial:

> While it is with much reluctance that I enter into a discussion of this affair, yet I do wish to correct some of the erroneous reports . . . In the first place, I wish to deny that any engagement existed between the two.
>
> Mr. Gillette has, it is true, taken my daughter to several entertainments and social functions. He, however, has never made evening calls upon my daughter, and, in fact, he never made but one formal call at the house, that being in the afternoon and of about one-half hour duration. My daughter has not or never had the slightest personal affection for Gillette, and while in the company of Gillette my daughter informs me that the subject of matrimony was never mentioned.
>
> There is likewise, no truth in the report that letters from my daughter were found in Gillette's rooms. She, I believe, wrote him one short note [Where oh where is my poster?], this being on a trivial subject. In summing up the affair I will say that the couple were ordinary friends, and I regret very much that any of these erroneous rumors have been circulated.

This put a stop, at least as far as the local papers were concerned, to reports about the engagement rumors, but the out-of-town papers, especially the yellow press from New York City, took it somewhat as an invitation. Benedict, they reasoned, was trying to cover up his daughter's relationship in the affair. Later, he had to publicly threaten to take the offending reporters to court in order to get them to stop. No evidence has ever been found to contradict Benedict's denial of any more meaningful relationship between the two, even though much was later made of it by Theodore Dreiser. It is possible, but unlikely, that there was a secret relationship that Benedict knew nothing about.

At 10:14 a.m. on August 31, the Herkimer County grand jury

handed up seven indictments to the Supreme Court of Herkimer County. One charged Chester Gillette with first-degree murder. Chester, brought into the courtroom from the jail across the street to hear the indictment, stood with his head bent low and spoke in a low tone of voice. He wore a natty gray suit, a white shirt with a turnover collar and a white four-in-hand tie. Observers said he was obviously nervous, although trying his best to look at ease.

After the indictment was read, Ward said, "Chester Gillette, the grand jury of Herkimer charges you with the crime of murder in the first degree committed on the 11th day of July, 1906, at the Town of Webb in the county of Herkimer, in killing Grace Brown. Have you counsel?"

"No sir," said Chester.

"Do you wish the court to assign counsel?"

"Yes, sir."

"How do you plead, guilty or not guilty?"

"Not guilty."

Judge Irving R. Devendorf then spoke to Chester from the bench in the front of the room.

"Gillette, the court is inclined to follow your wishes with reference to the employment of counsel, if the counsel selected by you are of sufficient ability. The court received a communication from you with reference to the selection of counsel. You haven't changed your mind with that regard have you?"

"No sir," said Chester.

Devendorf then said he had had a conversation with Mills and that Mills had suggested that another attorney, Charles D. Thomas also be assigned to the case. They were both summoned, but only Thomas, who had an office in Herkimer, was close enough to attend.

Thomas' first action, when he arrived a few minutes later, was to request that the trial be held the third week of December. Ward, of course, objected violently, saying he would be busy then, and suggested October as a better date. After considerable argument, Devendorf settled on Monday, November 12, a week after the elections.

With the question of Chester's defense counsel settled the next topic of speculation was what the line of defense would be.

Chester had already said that it had been an accident, but there were rumors that he would plead that Grace had committed suicide. There was also speculation that he might plead insanity.

The insanity defense was much in the public eye in 1906 because it had been the defense used in the other current murder case, that of Harry Thaw, who shot architect Sanford White in front of hundreds of people in Madison Square Garden and had hired the most expensive lawyers available to find him a way out of going to jail.

Mills and Thomas had just 10 weeks to gather evidence and witnesses before the trial was to start, little time to make up for the six weeks that Ward had already been working on it. There is much less information on how they went about gathering their own evidence. It is known that they visited Cortland at least once, on October 25, just a few weeks before the trial was to start, and talked to some of the workers at the factory. It is also known that one or the other went to Big Moose to examine the scene of the crime.

They also spent many evenings in Chester's cell, going over his story in detail, teaching him how to answer their questions on the stand and how to avoid giving out too much information when he was cross-examined by Ward.

Although the journalists of the era seem to have thought Chester's lawyers were doing all they could to help him, a letter that has since been discovered throws into doubt how dedicated the two lawyers were to the defense of their client. Dated October 12, just a month before the start of the trial, it is signed by Mills and addressed to Ward:

> My Dear Ward:
>   I have very reluctantly been looking into the case of the People vs. Gillette. I do not want to be in it and I hope something may yet happen to relieve me. I do not know as I can escape from the assignment of the Court, but will be glad to.
>   As far as I have examined the case it has occurred to me that the prisoner ought to have access to the articles which belonged to him and which were seized by the representatives of the law . . . I suppose the property is at Herkimer and it can easily be arranged that we may see it

all. I wish you would signify your disposition about it.

I am, Most sincerely yours.     A. M. Mills

At about the same time the letter was written, Mills told a reporter for the *Utica Herald Dispatch* that defending Chester was a nearly impossible job because of the way the case had been reported in the newspapers. He was, he said, considering resigning from the job because of that.

"To my mind the press has rendered it practically impossible for an impartial jury to be secured in this county," he said.

Late in October, a list of 150 jurors was selected, an unusually large number, reflecting the court's concern that it would be difficult to find a dozen residents who had open minds about the sensational case. Mills began drawing up the necessary papers to have the trial moved to another location because of the press coverage.

Between the visits of his lawyers, Chester settled into a dull routine of eating, reading and sleeping. He tried to keep himself in shape through a series of exercises. His routine was written in pencil on a piece of paper near the cell's only window. As an officially indicted prisoner of a capital crime, he found that there were even more stringent regulations that he had to abide by. His knife and fork were taken away in case he tried to commit suicide. He had to eat his meals "with what nature has provided him" - meaning his fingers - according to Ward.

Chester spent most of his time playing solitaire and reading books from the prison library, including *Ishmael, or In the Depths* by Emma D. E. N. Southworth, the story of a man born in poverty who managed to raise himself through suffering and toil to a famous career.

As the notoriety of the case spread, Chester began to receive a number of crank letters from strangers who urged him to confess his crime and repent his sins. Many included pages from hymn-books and prayers books.

Every few days, Chester received a package containing newspapers and magazines from a woman from Utica named "Marguerite" who was never identified.

With little else to spend his time on, Chester set about the interior decoration of his cell. When he first entered it, it was a dull place of bricks and stone with a simple cot, a toilet and a table. Over the bench that served as a dresser Chester stretched a line of string where he placed his collars and towels. A little gas stove was found for him and he was allowed to heat his food there. On his bench were spread out his letters, over 50 of them by the time his trial started.

But the oddest parts of his decorations were the photos and drawings, nearly 100 of them, that he cut out of magazines and pasted on the walls. There were many pictures of forests and outdoor scenes, but most of the pictures were of women. Many of them were famous actresses of the era, including Ethel Barrymore, Maude Adams, Florence Holmes, Julia Sanderson and Annie Russell. Some of the photographs and drawings were quite large and others were arranged around the larger ones to create an odd sort of portrait gallery.

Among the artwork he also posted a number of poems cut out of the magazines. Among the poems was one by Robert Gilbert Welsh about a scene in the woods by the water that several visitors thought was selected because of his predicament.

> While thus you woo the wayward breeze
> Beneath the moon of strawberries,
> Or hear autumnal voices croon
> Beneath the yellow harvest moon,
> New love you learn - oh you grow wise
> With wisdom of the earth and skies.

# CHAPTER SIX

# *On Trial*
# *For His Life*

At about 1:15 p.m. on November 12, 1906, Chester Ellsworth Gillette walked out the front door of the Herkimer County Jail and down the stone steps with the iron railing out onto Main Street for the short trip across the street to the Herkimer County Courthouse.

Accompanying the short, well-dressed prisoner was the much larger Sheriff-elect, Austin B. Klock, who had arrested Chester 120 days earlier, but who had grown to know him so well in the past four months that he saw no reason to shackle him.

Chester wore a derby hat, a black frock coat, gray-striped trousers, a white standing collar with the ends turned down in the latest fashion, a white tie, low black shoes and black stockings. He wore a heavy gold ring on the third finger of his left hand, a gift from Grace Brown in a time and place that now seemed far away.

There was a large crowd outside the courthouse, many of whom were potential jurors who had been called to serve during the trial. Some of them had spent the morning explaining to Judge Devendorf their excuses in an attempt to get out of doing their duty. But there was also a large crowd of curiosity seekers, attracted by the articles in the Sunday newspapers that had promised one of the most exciting trials in memory.

Those who saw Chester cross the street that day remarked later that he looked somewhat pale, but not at all nervous. And most remarkable, for a man walking to a trial that was to determine if he lived or died, the prisoner was chewing gum.

Klock led Chester to the side door of the courthouse to avoid the crowds on the front steps. They went up the inside stairs of the tall, red building with its church-like bell tower and the block letters above the double doors proclaiming "Court House" to the courtroom on the second floor.

The room was quite large, much larger than it is today, as part of it was later converted into offices. There were enough seats for nearly 1,000 spectators in the pew-like wooden benches on the main floor and in a gallery in the back of the room. The room was brightly lit on both sides by rows of tall windows, which ran from near the floor to the ceiling, some 24 feet above.

In front of the spectator benches, separated by an ornate wooden railing, was the judge's bench, set a few feet above the other seats in the room. To the right of the judge's stand was the stenographer's table and, at the extreme right, next to the wall, was the enclosed box with 12 chairs where the jury was to sit.

At the left, in front of the judge's bench, was a long table filled with nearly two dozen people, most of them with derby hats at their sides. Two, however, were women wearing elaborate hats complete with tall feathers and beads. This was the press table, filled with reporters from the wire services, the New York City newspapers and 10 local newspapers.

To the right of this table, nearly in front of the witness stand, was another table, running the long way from the judge's stand, back towards the spectators. At the end closest to the judge's bench was Ward, dressed in his business suit. At the other end were Chester's attorneys, Mills and Thomas, and it was to this end of the table that Klock escorted Chester.

Chester sat down in a plain wooden chair, with Thomas on his right and Mills on his left, around the corner at the end of the table. When Chester came in, everyone in the room watched him and continued to stare for nearly an hour. Spectators and jurors stood up trying to get a better look at the famous murderer.

Mills and Thomas had been in the courtroom since about 10 a.m., when the trial had formally begun with the reading of the list of potential jurors. This was a sort of roll call to make sure everyone who had been called was in the room and sitting in the special section that had been roped off for them. County Clerk Burney, after calling the list and finding two men dead and several sick, announced that the court would hear excuses of any who wished to be excused. At least half of them raised their hands, stood up and began to push forward.

"Stand back! Stand back of those tables," Burney had to shout to keep the men from crowding up to him. "The court says that only those with valid excuses will be allowed to go. So if you simply have the desire to get out of it, you might as well sit down."

But no one sat down and, one by one, the men (there were no women jurors then) listed their excuses. Firemen were excused as was a man who was 72 years old. But others, claiming they had broken their legs twice or who had rheumatism in their hands, were kept. Judge Devendorf ended up with 130 of the 150 after the excuses had been heard and adjourned the proceedings until 1:30 p.m.

The Honorable Irving Rosell Devendorf had been a justice of Supreme Court in Herkimer County only since the first of the year and the Gillette case was his first murder trial. He was a member of one of the oldest families in the county, tracing his ancestry back to the Palatine immigrants who first settled the Mohawk Valley. Born November 2, 1856, in the Town of Danube in Herkimer County, he studied law right out of high school in the offices of a judge and a lawyer and was admitted to the bar in 1880. During his studies, he slept on a cot in the law offices. In 1889 and 1894 he was elected district attorney on the Republican ticket. In 1895 he was elected county judge and surrogate.

A few minutes after Chester re-entered the room, Devendorf returned from his chambers behind the bench and the afternoon session began with the examination, one by one, of the jurors to find 12 acceptable to both the prosecution and the defense. It was a long, tedious process in most trials, but one made even more difficult in this case because the crime carried the death penalty and because it had received so much publicity in the newspapers.

The jurors were questioned, first by Ward, and then by either Mills or Thomas. Ward's main concern was to keep off the jury anyone who didn't believe in capital punishment. He dismissed several jurors who said they would never find someone guilty if it meant sending him to the electric chair. He also wanted to make sure that none of them had any qualms about deciding a case based only on circumstantial evidence.

Mills and Thomas wanted to make sure that the jurors had no preconceived notions of Chester's guilt. Since virtually all of the jurors admitted they had read at least some of the newspaper articles about the case, it was difficult for them to be sure on this point. They also tried to avoid jurors who had teenage daughters whom they might identify too closely with Grace Brown.

The selection process went on for the rest of the week, a somewhat boring process for those involved, and even more so for the spectators, who continued to pack the courthouse each day trying to get a look at Chester. The tedium was broken only when one of the jurors or one of the attorneys would make a funny or witty remark. Then all the spectators would break out in laughter, with Chester often joining in, until the heavily-bearded bailiff banged his six-foot wooden staff on the wooden floor, booming the room back into order.

For example, on Wednesday, a potential juror named C. M. Lindsey, a merchant from the town of Mannheim, was being questioned by Thomas.

"Have you had any relations with District Attorney Ward?" asked Thomas. "Has he ever done anything for you?"

"No," Lindsey said.

"Have you ever done anything for him?" Thomas asked.

"I voted for him this year."

Since everyone knew that Ward had been elected judge the week before by the slimmest of margins, this was a cause for laughter, and Chester joined in.

But most of the time, Chester sat all the way back in the wooden chair, his hips on the very front edge of the seat, his elbows resting on the arms and his hands clasped in his lap, or sometimes raised onto his chin. He watched the events calmly and showed little emotion, as if he were one of the spectators.

Towards the end of the week, the witnesses subpoenaed by Ward began to arrive in Herkimer and many of them did not hesitate to talk to the reporters who waited outside the courtroom. Since the court proceedings were not generating much in the way of interesting news, the kind their editors were demanding that they produce, it was a way for the reporters to find something to write about.

Among those willing to talk were Mr. and Mrs. Frank Brown and their daughters, Ada Hawley, Mary and Frances. While Frank Brown said little, his wife said she wanted to speak her mind.

"I think it would drive me mad if I had to sit and watch the man whom I know to be responsible for Grace's death," she told the *Utica Daily Press* reporter after her arrival in Herkimer on Tuesday. They had travelled in a horse-drawn wagon all the way from South Otselic.

"I never thought that I was a cruel woman before," Minerva said, "but I will be glad from the bottom of my heart to see the most punishment the law can give inflicted on him. We all know why he wanted to get rid of Grace. It was so he could marry Harriet Benedict, the Cortland girl with money and social position."

The idea that Grace may have committed suicide, she said, made no sense at all. If Grace had wanted to commit suicide, Mrs. Brown said, "Why should she have done it in this manner so that Gillette would have been blamed for it? She loved him too well for that."

Beginning on Wednesday, the Browns and their three daughters sat in the first row of the spectator section, as close to the jury as Ward could get them, and they remained there every day of the trial.

As the week wore on, more and more reporters gathered in Herkimer. Many of them skipped the first few days of the trial, knowing that jury selections always made dull reading. The Herkimer officials seem to have been somewhat unprepared for the onslaught, having little experience with sensational murder trials. The few hotels were already crowded with the 100 witnesses, most of whom were from outside the area, and many people had to find lodging at private homes.

The press corps took over an entire floor of the Palmer House, just down the street from the courthouse, and on many evenings they are said to have taken over the hotel bar as well. At the courthouse, a special telegraph station had to be set up in the basement to handle the thousands of words sent out each day. The reporters scribbled out their notes, most of them using short-hand at the table in the courtroom while runners, usually young boys, took their notes in batches downstairs to the telegraph operators, who sent them over the wire a few pages at a time.

Also in the courtroom were artists and photographers, whose job it was to capture Chester in a new pose each day and get shots of the various witnesses, especially the women who were testifying in the case. The photographers caused problems for Chester's lawyers throughout the trial, beginning on Thursday, November 15, when a photographer rushed up to Chester during a recess and flashed a great brilliance of flash powder. Thomas rushed up to him and told him to go away. This quickly developed into a game, with Chester spending much of his time with a newspaper in front of his face so no one could take his picture. Alternately, when he saw an artist sketching him, he turned away so his face could not be seen.

Thomas made a point of going over to the photographers and telling them that the photos were not permitted. On Thursday, Chester walked from the jail to the courtroom with a handkerchief over his face. Also that morning, for the first time, he was handcuffed to Klock. This was the direct result of a newspaper article published the day before. When court had adjourned on Wednesday, everyone in the courtroom got up to leave and Chester, seeking to avoid getting caught by the photographers, tried to beat them to the side door, used by the lawyers and jurors to avoid the crowds. Klock was talking to someone and wasn't paying attention when one of the spectators saw Chester and shouted, "Look!" thinking Chester was trying to escape. Klock, seeing him, shouted "Chester," and Chester stopped, leaned against a bench and picked up his derby hat and handed the other to Klock. They walked back to the jail together without thinking more of the incident. But the next day, the New York City newspapers ran headlines on the front page "Gillette Tries to Escape!" and Sheriff Richard ordered that Chester be hand-cuffed for the journey across the street each day.

But it may have been more than shyness that caused Chester to evade the photographers. He may have had a selfish motive. Just before the trial, Klock had taken Chester over to A.P. Zintmaster's studio, just down the street from the jail, to have a photograph taken for the record. This was a common procedure and would be used to identify a prisoner if he escaped. But with the arrival of the press, there was a great demand for a portrait of Chester. It was Klock, apparently, who suggested to Chester that he might want to sell copies of his photo to the press at a profit.

Several reliable accounts say the photo was for sale, but the price varies from article to article. According to the *Utica Herald Dispatch*, Chester first offered the photo for $10 and raised it to $20 after he had had a number of offers.

Klock, when asked by reporters about the propriety of selling the portrait, said, "I told him he might as well get something for it." When asked if the portrait didn't really belong to the county, rather than Chester, Klock offered to pay out of his own pocket, the cost of having it taken. The next day, however, Klock denied that he had anything to do with the attempts to sell the picture, probably after he had been severely lectured by Ward or Sheriff Richard.

Some of the surviving copies of Chester's portrait have a copyright marking saying they are the property of A.P. Zintmaster, the photographer, so it may have been Zintmaster, not Klock, who organized the sale. It is highly likely that Chester received some money from the sale and according to one reliable report, he used the money to buy the new suit he wore later in the trial.

By the time court adjourned on Thursday, all 150 names had been called and dismissed but there were only eight men in the jury box. All the others had been rejected by Ward or the defense attorneys as being unacceptable. That evening, 60 more names were selected to appear on Friday.

But there were heavy snowstorms Friday morning and many of those called from the rural parts of the county were late in arriving. The newspapermen filled the void during the delays with composing their speculations about the coming testimony. Most of it centered around the arrival of Harriet Benedict, whom they described as the "star witness." Some of the worst of the New York City papers contained heart-rending, and totally fictional accounts about a beautiful but pathetic damsel, crying in her room all day and, between sobs, screaming, "Chester, oh Chester."

But in reality, Harriet was calmly attending her sophomore classes at the Cortland Normal School and giving out numerous denials about any relationship with Chester. Her statements were printed, often in full, in the local newspapers, but ignored by the New York City press and the wire services.

In one of the statements she said, "I have never communicated with or received a word from him since his arrest. Neither myself nor either of my parents has ever visited him in jail, nor have I sent him flowers or candy, as has been reported in the papers . . . I have not been at the trial since its commencement and it is absolutely untrue that I sat in the courtroom by his lawyers, as has been reported. I call upon the newspapers to cease publication of these false stories circulated about me. I am advised to hold all newspapers in strict accountability for publishing any libelous articles concerning me."

When court adjourned on Friday, still without 12 jurors, Judge Devendorf ordered an unusual Saturday session. By the end of that day there were finally 12 men "good and true" seated and accepted in the box.

The 12 who were selected were certainly not an ideal jury for either the defense or for Ward. All 12 had admitted reading about the case in the newspapers and there was talk all week that Devendorf would eventually have to order a change of venue. But each had said he was ready to listen to the evidence with an open mind and decide based only on the facts presented in court.

Perhaps most unforutnate for Chester was the fact that a majority of them were farmers, some with teenage daughters, who could not help identifying with Frank Brown, seated in the front row before them, and thinking about their own daughters' fates at the hands of a city slicker like Gillette.

The 12 were Herbert T. Dodge, 49, a prosperous farmer from the Town of Schuyler with four children; Webster Kast, 43, a farmer from the Kast Bridge area of the Town of Herkimer with an 18-year-old son; Charles L. Edick, a blacksmith from the Town of German Flatts, just south of Ilion, a Methodist with two children; L. C. Barrigan, 31, a mail carrier in the Town of Columbia near the village of Salisbury, a Catholic with one child and a five-acre farm; Harvey Freeman, 38, a farmer, stone mason and father of three from the northern part of the Town of Columbia; C. E. Curtis, 32, a metal filer at the Remington Typewriter plant in Ilion, a Methodist with two children; Ralph Smyth, 32, a farmer from the Town of Columbia who was married but had no children; Willet L. Thayer, 62, a farmer from the Town of Russia who had two sons and was a member of the Prospect Congregational Church; Marshall Hatch, who was later elected foreman of the jury, 62, owner of a 244-acre farm in the Town of Columbia called "Pleasant View" and who had a 36-year-old daughter; James E. Dingman, 43, a cotton batting manufacturer from the city of Little Falls, a Methodist with one young child; James M. Petrie, 60, a farmer and Methodist from the Town of German Flatts with two married daughters, and Elvah S. Potter, 32, a farmer with 73 acres in a very rural area called Snells Bush who had three children.

At 11:07 on Saturday, November 17, just 22 minutes after the final juror had been seated and after a brief recess, the trial itself got under way. Two deputies brought in several maps of the Adirondacks and Big Moose Lake that Ward had had prepared and, together with some photographs of the area, they were placed behind the witness stand.

Then Ward rose from his chair at the end of the attorneys' table and began his opening address to the jury. He spoke rapidly but distinctly, and at times dramatically, using a wooden pointer to locate points on the maps. He began by explaining that he had taken such care in selecting the jurors because he wanted them to have "sufficient courage to stand up and face the facts as they are presented and enforce the law as it is written. Because a weak, feeble man . . . would not be apt to give a verdict or come to a conclusion that would be satisfactory."

He then went on to explain the differences between first and second degree murder, that murder in the first degree required "malice aforethought," or a deliberate plan rather than an act of emotion or passion.

Chester, he said, "took a human life, took the life of one Grace Brown with deliberation, with premeditation, in pursuance of a plan made and carried out weeks before the deed was done."

He then reviewed Grace's life in Cortland, where, Ward said, she "had to depend upon her own resources and her own skill in protecting and defending herself from the evils which surround every girl of that age." Chester, he said, was not a boy, as he had been called in the newspapers, but "a bearded man . . . He had all the intellectual advantages, and more experience in life than any man on this jury."

After the two met, Ward said, "there resulted to that unprotected girl what results to millions of girls in all times. She gave to him in the end all the treasures which she had. In the month of May of this year she found that she was about to become a mother."

But Chester, he said, had found his way into a different class of society. "The name of Gillette was a valuable asset in the social world where he lived, a different class from farmers' girls and others who worked in the mill. They began to reach out and invite him into their families, into their social affairs. He was becoming a friend and companion of girls in a different class of society. He found that that society had its doors open to him and that he had made a mistake in accepting and indulging in the companionship of the girls who worked for a living."

Chester, Ward said, ignored Grace's pleading for him to "protect and defend her, and stand sponsor for their unborn child. He refused to make good. By careful planning with the girl, he got her to leave Cortland and go to her father's house, telling her that he would come for her and take her away and marry her."

While at South Otselic, Ward said, Grace had her wedding garments made. Chester, meanwhile, "knew then, on the 8th of July, or a week previous, that he must seal that girl's lips; that if he did not succeed in so doing, she would come back to Cortland and blaze to the world the wrong he had done her and his relatives and sweethearts in the other class of society would know and understand what manner of man he was."

Then Ward detailed the events of Grace and Chester's journey, noting Chester's use of false names, the appointment he made and kept with Miss Patrick and Miss Westcott, Chester's sleeping "with the girl in his arms" for two nights and his use of his real name on the laundry package and at the Arrowhead, when he wanted to be known as Chester Gillette again.

"The People," Ward said, "contend that he was looking for such a place as he might kill and drown this girl and then go back to Fulton Chain, keep his engagement and get the goods (the laundry)."

Tupper Lake was ruled out as the site of the murder, Ward said, because there were too many people around. Big Moose was more isolated, so Chester took all his baggage there, leaving Grace's trunk behind and her hat in the hotel. And, Ward said, Chester purposely used Grace's real name at the Glenmore so that when her body was found she would be identified right away, which Ward said Chester hoped would prevent a full-scale inquiry into the matter.

He took her to South Bay, Ward said, because "it is the only secluded spot on the lake," and he wandered about the lake, waiting for the best moment to strike. The moment came at the supper hour, when the campers were in their homes and the lake was deserted.

"He expected to throw her into the water and drown her," Ward said, "but he found it more difficult than he had bargained for, and he was compelled and obliged to render her unconscious, to still her in the first place by striking her blows upon the head, and then, in his frenzy, having gone too far - when her last death cry rang out over the waters of the lake, there was a witness to that, and she will be here. Then, having accomplished his purpose, he threw her body into the water. He got on the land and slipped away."

Ward then described Chester's escape from Big Moose to Eagle Bay, where his postcard showed he knew he would be. He told about the hiding of the murder weapon and the numerous false stories he told after his arrest. He concluded by saying, "The only question you will have to decide, the only question that any honest or fair man has got to decide, is whether these witnesses whom you will hear tell the truth. There is no other question in the case."

Throughout Ward's speech Chester sat, unmoved, his face hidden behind his hand so no one would take his picture. Mrs.

Brown, however, sobbed audibly several times as Ward told her daughter's story.

The reporters were stunned by Ward's statement that he had found an eyewitness to the murder and they scrambled madly the rest of the weekend to find out who it was. The headlines in the Sunday papers boldly proclaimed that a witness would testify as to how the murder occurred. It must have been a terrible blow to Mills and Thomas as well, since it caught them entirely off guard. They must have spent a very concerned weekend, rethinking their line of defense to fit this new fact.

In reality, however, Ward had not found an eyewitness, but an "ear-witness" as the newspapers called her later. She was Mrs. Marjorie Carey of East Orange, New Jersey, who had been on a boat in Big Moose Lake at about the time the murder took place and who claimed to have heard a cry that sounded like a woman's.

When Ward concluded his opening remarks, Judge Devendorf announced that there would be no afternoon session and proposed an adjournment until 10 a.m. Monday. Mills, however, interrupted him by making a motion that the sensational stories about the case, many of them entirely untrue, being printed in the newspapers should be kept from the jury. This was not an automatic procedure in 1906 and Devendorf, trying his first important case, thought about it before ordering that the jury could read the newspapers only after all the stories about the case were cut out of them.

"Better order that they shall be burned," commented Thomas.

Ward spent the rest of the weekend at his home in Dolgeville, going over Grace Brown's letters, becoming familiar with them so that he would be able to read them later in the most effective manner. The defense attorneys, meanwhile, were somewhat confused by the eyewitness claim and spent a lot of time with Chester, going over his story yet again, deciding what to leave out and what to emphasize, probably asking him over and over if anyone could have seen him.

On Monday, November 19, just after 10 a.m., Frank B. Brown, the first witness, was sworn in and took his place on the witness stand. There were so many spectators in court that day, many more than the week before, that the gallery was opened for

*HERKIMER IN 1906 - Postcard views of how it looked during Chester's trial.*

Main Street, Herkimer, N. Y.

*HERKIMER COUNTY COURTHOUSE - As it looked around 1906.*

*HERKIMER COUNTY JAIL - As it looked around 1906. Chester's cell was the last window in the back on the third floor.*

*COURTHOUSE AND JAIL - 1981 photo showing how close they were to each other. Chester made the short walk back and forth each day for three weeks in November and December 1906.*

*HERKIMER TRAIN STATION - Station from which Chester left Herkimer for Auburn prison.*

*BROWN FAMILY PLOT -*
*Grace's father and mother*
*chose to be buried near her in*
*Valley View Cemetery, South*
*Otselic.*

the first time in 20 years. Nearly 1,000 spectators crowded into the room and many had to be sent away because there was no more room.

Among the exhibits in the front of the room were Grace's trunk and her portrait. On a table containing the evidence was a stack of letters, wrapped in a ribbon, but no one except Ward, Chester and his attorneys yet knew what they were.

Frank Brown described Grace's early life, her moving to Cortland and her three-week stay at home just before her death. He also identified Grace's trunk, her clothes and her portrait. Tears filled his eyes when he explained that he usually didn't refer to his daughter as Grace but as "Billy." This testimony, and much which was to come later, was objected to by Thomas as irrelevant to the case, but Devendorf permitted it to stand.

After Frank Brown's testimony, Ward began a step-by-step reconstruction of Grace and Chester's lives in Cortland, their activities in the skirt factory and finally their last trip together. A seemingly endless number of witnesses was called who saw them on virtually every stage of their trip from DeRuyter to Big Moose.

Many of the witnesses merely stated a series of facts which were not in dispute and many of these witnesses were not cross-examined. The skirt factory employees told about conversations that they had overheard and about their warnings to both of them that they should not meet alone. N.H. Gillette testified about Chester's background, as did his son, Harold R. Gillette. Lizzie Crain, Chester's landlady, told about Chester's comings and goings and described the finding of one of the letters. Carrie Wheeler, Grace's landlady, and her daughter, Olive, told about the late night meetings between Chester and Grace.

Mills and Thomas did not have much upon which to cross-examine until Albert Raymond, the proprietor of the Raymond House, was called. He testified that Chester and Grace had gone out on a boat ride from his place a few days before Grace went back to South Otselic. Raymond positively identified Chester, but he admitted under cross-examination that he was not sure about Grace and, when pushed by the defense attorneys, admitted that he was not even sure of the date.

The next day, Tuesday, November 20, was the one the spectators said later they recalled most vividly, even decades later. The crowd was so heavy that a constant attempt had to be made by court officials to keep the aisles clear of spectators. Many who couldn't get in stood on the stairs outside, hoping to hear, if not see, what was going on.

Ward called two witnesses, Grace's sister, Frances, and Grace's friend and teacher, Maude Crumb, who described what Grace had been like on her last visit to her family. Ward was using their testimony to set the scene for what was to follow.

After Maude stepped down, and with little warning, Ward asked Judge Devendorf to permit him to read the letters that had been referred to in the previous testimony. Mills immediately objected that it was improper, first because it was immaterial and second because the letters had been improperly obtained by searching Chester's room without a search warrant. Devendorf ruled that Ward could read the letters "but only for the purpose of showing how the defendant regarded his relations with the victim," and not for proving any statements of facts in the letters. This was a serious blow for the defense and both Mills and Thomas seem to have realized it from the beginning.

Ward walked over to the table on which the evidence was kept and untied the ribbon that had been wrapped around the letters. He read them in order, starting with the ones written in the fall of 1905 and April of 1906 and ending with the final ones written just days before Grace died.

He read them with all the emotion he could put into them and by the time he came to the last letter, the "bidding goodbye to some places today" letter, everyone in the courtroom was in tears. Even Ward, who had read the letters dozens of times before, had to wipe the tears from his eyes.

During the reading, the hundreds of people in the courtroom were nearly completely silent. The only sound was an occasional sob as the audience tried to hear every word. Some of the loudest sobs came from the Browns, who were probably hearing for the first time the words their daughter and sister had been writing those nights alone in her bedroom.

The reporters took down every word in shorthand, although several had apparently been given advance copies through Ward. Some of the reporters later recalled that although they were hardened by years of covering crimes and disasters, even the toughest of them were deeply affected by the letters. Beginning that evening, everyone in the country could read the letters and the case became even more celebrated than it had been.

The reporter for the *Utica Herald Dispatch* wrote that day: "There was a revulsion of feeling against the prisoner among many of those who had entertained feelings of sympathy for him and it was partly feared that some person's feelings might carry them to make a show of their anger against the prisoner." Extra precautions should be taken to protect him, he said.

In an editorial the next day, the *New York World* said, "There is nothing in "Tess" so appealing, so tearful as the pathetic letters written by Billy Brown to the youth who is on trial for her murder at the time when grief for her lost girlhood was mingled with fears of approaching disgrace."

The letters attracted so much attention that newspaper coverage was stepped up. Papers like the *New York Herald*, which had been using only brief summaries of the testimony, suddenly began to devote whole columns to the trial that was quickly becoming a national sensation. The yellow press journals, especially the two New York Hearst papers, sent even more people to Herkimer to provide drawings, photos and feature stories for the front pages of each day's papers.

All the reporters who were in the court that day wrote about a singular, curious fact: Chester Gillette was the only person in the room who didn't have tears in his eyes. Chester listened calmly with no reaction whatsoever to what was being read. As he did for the next two weeks, he never revealed the slightest hint of emotion, and many interpreted this as an attitude of indifference and even of inhumanity. Some described him as a foul monster completely devoid of feeling.

When Chester was asked, after the trial, about his composure, he said, "There wasn't a word said that I didn't wince as a horse does under the lash . . . If they had only known how I felt, well, I guess even those who judged most harshly would have been sorry for me . . . Nobody knew how I felt for I tried to conceal it, but I heard every word that was spoken during the trial and they all hurt me."

On Friday, November 24, the newspaper men and women were enjoying a bag of apples that had been brought in for them by

Sheriff Richard. One of the women reporters, during a break, walked over to Chester and gave him two of them, but he ignored her.

"Why don't you eat them?" she asked.

"I am afraid they will take me for a reporter," Chester said with bitterness and sarcasm.

A few minutes later, however, the reporters noticed that he was eating one of them. The reporters later signed a statement that Richard's apples "beat Adam out in a slow walk."

Whatever Chester's reasons for his attitude, it was certainly the worst one he could have taken and it's hard to understand why Mills or Thomas did not do something to change it, even if only superficially. Besides poisoning public opinion against the "callous, cold-hearted brute," as some papers called him, it certainly would have made a better impression on the jury. A few tears, a few sobs in the right places probably would have done more than any testimony to show that he was innocent, or at least sorry for what had happened. The fact that he seemed to care so little about Grace convinced many that day, and probably the jury as well, that he was a cold-blooded murderer.

Ward followed the reading of the letters with what many at the trial thought would be a one-two punch: he immediately called to the stand Harriet Benedict, the long-awaited "star witness" who the press had said would reveal her secret love affair with Chester. Her testimony, however, was not nearly as exciting as everyone had hoped. She said only that she had met Chester at a few parties and he had never been to her house except once to escort her to a party. She also told about going to Little York Lake with him on the 4th of July.

To avoid the crowds of reporters attempting to take her picture and to interview her, Harriet was permitted to wait in the judge's chambers in the rear of the courtroom and return there when she was finished. Other witnesses had to sit in the main courtroom. From the judge's chambers she was able to enter and exit without anyone seeing her.

During the rest of the second week of the trial, Ward called witness after witness who described every move Chester and Grace made since they left DeRuyter. Chester probably didn't even recognize the parade of ticket agents, hotel clerks, train passengers and people who walked by him in the street, but they all remembered him very well and recounted every detail. Chester's attorneys found little to dispute with these witnesses under cross-examination because their testimony did not conflict with the version Chester would tell on the stand later.

But to the jury and spectators it was a grand display of Ward's detective work. He appeared to be throwing a perfect net over the prisoner, showing every move he made, showing the hotel registers with the false names on them, making them see that the only reason he could have for hiding himself was that he was planning a murder. The dual names on the hotel registers also showed that Grace and Chester had shared a room together, perhaps as much a crime as murder to the rural residents of Herkimer County in 1906.

Most importantly for his case, however, Ward was demonstrating that Chester was not a man of his word; that he lied so casually and so frequently that no one could ever be sure he was telling the truth. Besides the false names, Ward had his witnesses describe in detail the elaborate stories Chester weaved, often for no apparent reason other than the sheer joy of making up tall tales.

Meyer Neuman, the Tupper Lake hotel keeper, for example, told how Chester had spoken of being in the Adirondacks for two weeks, the places he had been and where he planned to go. None of it, of course, was true.

There were other damaging facts as well. Andrew Morrison recalled that Chester had not asked the price of the rental boat, even though Chester was obviously short of money and had carefully asked the prices of other things he purchased on the trip. Ward would use this later to show that Chester didn't care about the rental fee because he never intended to bring the boat back.

Ward also produced a number of maps and photographs taken at the scene of Grace's death, with poles thrust into the water to show where the body had been found and where the boat had been found. Klock and Richard described searching the shore of the lake and the finding of the tennis racket, the lack of any place on the shore where Chester and Grace could have stopped for a picnic or where Chester could have left his suitcase. They also described the many conflicting stories Chester had told after his arrest.

Ward, who was present at the latter events but could not testify in his own case, had trouble at times getting Klock to say exactly what he wanted for the court record and would often coax and lead him, bringing loud objections from the defense attorneys.

The evidence table soon became overloaded with all the exhibits Ward presented. Besides Grace's trunk and Chester's suitcase, there were the hotel registers, the letters, the photographs Chester had taken and the ones taken at Big Moose later to identify the scene, a number of maps, locks of Grace Brown's hair taken from the boat, the clothing Grace was wearing when she died including a garter that was apparently torn in the struggle and finally the oars and the boat itself, which was used by Morrison in describing how the boat was found and how difficult it was to tip over.

Among the photographs on the table were the ones developed from the plates in Chester's Kodak. While he was in jail, Chester tried to prevent the plates from being developed and printed by telling his attorneys that there were no pictures on them. He was probably trying to protect Harriet Benedict, whose pictures were on the film from July 4 at Little York. But Ward had the plates printed, just in case, and discovered, besides the photos of Miss Benedict, scenes from Big Moose, taken the day Grace died, and photos of Chester with the group from the Arrowhead on their way to the top of Black Bear Mountain.

Ward thought it significant that although Chester had spent only a few hours with Harriet Benedict and three days with Grace, there were no pictures of Grace in the camera.

In all, Ward called 83 witnesses, some of them more than once as they were needed to clarify both earlier and later parts of the story. Josephine Patrick, for example, was called in the early part of the testimony to tell about her visit to the factory and later to tell about meeting Chester in the train and in Inlet just before Chester's arrest. Ward had obviously planned the testimony and the strategy out in detail to be able to allow the story to flow, without interruption from witness to witness.

But up until the end, he really had only a circumstantial case.

He proved that Chester was a pathological liar, that he had a motive to kill Grace and the opportunity to do it, that he had made many efforts to conceal himself and that he had run away from the scene of the crime. But Ward had no proof of what actually happened on the lake that day.

For that part of the case he called his last five witnesses, the medical examiners who had performed the autopsy. They testified over three days, Monday through Wednesday, November 26, 27 and 28.

The autopsy was absolutely essential to Ward's case because it was the only hard evidence that a crime had been committed. Mills and Thomas, of course, understood that and set out to show that the medical evidence was not as ironclad as Ward had hoped.

During this part of the trial, both sides relied on expert coaches who sat down at the attorneys' table with them and made notes and whispered comments during the testimony. Sitting with Ward and his assistant, attorney Charles Earl, was Dr. Crumb, Maude Crumb's husband from South Otselic, who suggested questions for Ward to ask while he was examining the witnesses.

At their end of the table, Mills and Thomas relied on Dr. A. Walter Suiter of Herkimer, a member of the State Board of Medical Examiners. It was probably Suiter who brought up most of the questions used in the cross-examination of the medical experts.

Ward knew that the autopsy was the weakest part of his case and he fought hard to preserve the integrity of the witnesses, despite the fact that the autopsy had been botched from the beginning, when the body was embalmed before the autopsy had been performed.

The first doctor, A.O. Douglas of Little Falls, seems not to have been prepared by Ward for the rigid cross-examination and he came close to breaking down on the witness stand under Mills' vicious questions. Douglas, 63, had been a coroner for five years but admitted that he was not an authority on post mortems.

Douglas testified that he had found blood clots on Grace's skull and that in his opinion these clots were caused by "external violence" before the body had been placed in the water. When

Ward picked up the tennis racket, showed it to the jury and let Douglas examine it, he said such an instrument could account for the marks he found. The report of the examination of the body, he said, showed there was no evidence that Grace had died by drowning.

Under Mills' cross-examination, however, Douglas admitted that he had not conducted an autopsy since medical school and had consulted no experts on the matter.

But his most startling admission was that there had been evidence of drowning found during the autopsy, but that it was left out of the official report. Mills, prompted no doubt by Suiter at his right hand, ticked off a whole series of evidences of drowning, and, one by one, Douglas had to admit that they were, indeed, evidences of drowning and that they had been found during the autopsy.

Asked why they were not in the report, Douglas said the physicians who had made the autopsy met on at least three separate occasions to go over their testimony to make sure they all told the same version. The most recent meeting, he said, was the day before he testified. The paper he had used on the witness stand to refresh his memory, he said, was given to him by Ward a few days after the autopsy and was not a copy of his own notes. Douglas seemed unaware of how close to perjury all of this looked.

Finally, Mills asked him if, considering all the evidence, he could state without reservation that the injuries were inflicted before the body was in the water. He admitted that he could not.

If Ward was concerned about these setbacks, he didn't show any sign of it, for he had, hidden under his table, one last trump card to play.

He played it during the testimony of the next doctor, E. H. Douglas, the brother of the first doctor. The second Douglas described the portion of the autopsy that involved an incision in Grace's lower abdomen and the removal of the fetus that would have become Grace and Chester's child. This had obviously been timed well, since Mr. and Mrs. Brown had not shown up for this portion of the testimony and did not return until it was over.

As Douglas described the fetus, Ward, reaching under his table, pulled out a large glass bottle, wrapped in brown paper.

Mills and Thomas, who seem to have been expecting this

tactic, objected strenuously that it was improper and immoral to bring such an exhibit into the case.

"It is done for purely spectacular purposes and to prejudice the minds of the jury," shouted Thomas. "The indictment does not permit the offering of any such evidence."

"Yes," said Devendorf, "I have thought that it would be well to keep this out of court. We talked about it but he (Ward) seems to think he wants to offer it and he has the right of trying his case as he sees fit."

While this conversation was taking place, Ward took the bottle to the witness stand and was peeling away the paper, a little bit at a time, so Douglas could identify its contents.

Mills then jumped up to join Thomas in shouting "Objection."

"Now one is enough," Ward shouted angrily, turning back to the attorneys' table. "One stump speech on this subject is about enough for one morning."

The spectators roared in laughter and the bailiffs had to pound their poles on the floor to regain order.

When quiet returned, Devendorf said, "If I could be sure that the defense would interpose no objection to the statement that the girl was pregnant, I should exclude this exhibit."

"Then," said Thomas, springing to his feet again, "I here pledge you that on my honor as a lawyer and a man."

"I think then I shall have to exclude it," the judge said.

Now Ward was angry. "The district attorney," he said, "is going to try this case as he sees fit and not the way you people want me to. That's as true as that you are alive. I want to have the doctor identify this. I demand every right to which the people are entitled. I have a right to bring the girl's whole body into court from the grave. When I offer this in exhibition, if I do, it will be time enough to object. I am only asking the doctor to identify it now."

Then Devendorf backed down. "Well," he said, "the people's rights must be preserved to them and I guess I shall have to admit it."

Now it was the defense's turn to be furious. "Give me an exception! Give me an exception!" shouted Thomas.

By this time, the attorneys' table looked more like a medical library with books on surgery and medicine spread out on both sides. Both Suiter and Crumb picked up book after book and quickly looked up references and scribbled notes, which they passed on to the lawyers to help in asking questions. Much of the testimony got so technical that it meant nothing to the jury, the judge or the spectators.

At one point, Chester, dressed now in a new gray suit that he probably had purchased for him with the money from selling his pictures, picked up one of the medical books and looked at it. Most of the time, however, he sat as he had the previous week, his hand on his chin, his elbow on the table, watching with interest, but without emotion, the witnesses in the front of the room.

The third doctor, George H. Smith of Little Falls, corroborated the previous testimony, but on cross-examination, Mills got him to say that he had lost his original notes from the autopsy, even though he knew he would be called to testify as to the results at the trial. The typed list he presented, he said, had been given to him by Ward and did not contain all the things that had been found during the autopsy. He confirmed that the doctors had met several times with Ward to discuss what they would say on the witness stand.

After that admission, Mills followed with, "Well now, isn't it a fact that you doctors, at this conference, sought to arrange your story so that it would indicate the girl was killed before being thrown into the water rather than that she died by accidental drowning?"

"We did," Smith said.

The doctors, therefore, did much to hurt Ward's case despite his best efforts to get them to show there was medical evidence for murder. The results of their testimony were, at best, inconclusive owing to the limits of forensic medicine in 1906 and the hasty and probably haphazard way the autopsy had been conducted.

Ward and the doctors tried to make up for this later by careful planning. Ward got them to say on the witness stand that the signs they had found were consistent with his version of how Grace was murdered. But under cross-examination, Mills got them to say that the facts were also consistent with other scenarios of how the death occurred.

While the doctors testified for Ward that there was evidence that a blow had been struck on Grace's head and that it was made before she fell into the water, they admitted on cross-examination that the blow could have come after she was in the water and that there were at least a few signs that drowning could have been a contributing factor in the death.

After eight and a half days of testimony, Ward entered some last minute pieces of evidence and at 10:40 Wednesday morning, November 28, he announced, "the people rest their case."

The defense seems to have thought that Ward would take at least the rest of the day and may not have been ready to open its case when court resumed that day after a brief recess. Mills had a reputation as an excellent orator and everyone assumed he would make the opening statement, so it came as a surprise when it was Thomas who got up to speak and delivered a very short address.

All of this may have been part of the strategy, however, because Thomas' brief statement meant that Ward had to cross-examine Chester before he was ready to do so and wasn't as prepared as he would have wanted to be.

Thomas told the jury that Ward's case was little more than a collection of circumstantial facts that, while complete, hardly added up to evidence that a murder had been committed.

"If you strip this case of its sentimental features," he said, "and the excessive imagination of this district attorney, you will find little in it that would lead any reasonable man to conclude that this charge is true."

Ward, he said, had not submitted any evidence that Chester and Grace's trip had been a wedding trip and said "it is idle to presume that a girl of the character of Grace Brown contemplated marriage with only that preparation."

What Ward had said was evidence of criminal preparation, he said, were only the actions of a pair of young lovers, faced with an impending birth.

"They were not experienced in the intrigues of life, nor was either a criminal," he said, "and neither did they seek aid from criminals, but they took the burden upon themselves, each carrying a share, and so the trip to the woods was planned. It was not planned hastily. It was not a secret trip. Both of them told their associates at the shop, the girl before she went home and the boy at the time of his departure, not that they were going together, but that she was going and he was going and they did."

Thomas and Mills always referred to Chester as a boy, while Ward was careful to refer to him as a man.

Finally, Thomas came to the main point of the defense. Chester, he said, was not guilty of murder but guilty of being a coward in a moment of crisis. He was guilty of a failure of character, not an act of murder.

"Now gentlemen, there are such things as moral cowards," he said. "There are men so constituted that in the presence of a great calamity they must loose themselves, and this boy, in my opinion, in that condition, wandered to the Arrowhead and registered under his own name. He didn't try to run away. He didn't try to conceal himself at all."

". . . I wish that there was power somewhere so that we might hear the pleading voice of Grace Brown, and I would take my chances that she would be pleading for Chester Gillette and absolving him from any charge or suggestion of guilt . . . You will hear clearly the evidence of the only person living who can give an accurate and truthful account of just how this thing occurred."

With that, he simply announced that he was calling as his first witness Chester Gillette.

# CHAPTER SEVEN

# *The*
# *Verdict*

When Chester's name was called to testify, reporters said they thought there was a slight nervousness in his manner as he got up from his chair next to Mills and walked to the front of the courtroom, seated himself in the big wooden chair and swore his oath on the Bible, as he had seen others do for the past week and a half.

He settled back into one corner of the large chair, partly facing the jury and partly facing the attorneys' table. He crossed his legs and looked out the window, waiting for the questions to begin.

For weeks, Mills and Thomas had been visiting Chester in his cell across the street, going over his story in great detail in preparation for this moment. He was obviously well-coached on what to say and what not to say and when it would be convenient for him not to remember some important detail.

The first part, he had been told, would be easy. Thomas would be asking him the questions and if he forgot something, Thomas would be able to prompt him to include it. Later, however, when he was cross-examined by Ward, he would have to be much more careful and was told to watch his lawyers to tell when he was drifting into dangerous territory.

At first, he spoke in a low voice that was difficult to hear, but it became more audible after Thomas told him to speak up. While he was speaking, Chester tilted his head all the way back so that it rested on the back of the chair. Later, he rested his right arm on the arm of the chair and used the left as a prop to hold up his head.

He started out by telling his life story, leaving out all references to the Salvation Army or Dowie and describing very briefly his relationship with Grace Brown in Cortland. Very quickly he got to the details of their trip together, the events at Big Moose and his escape to the Arrowhead.

Early in his testimony, after an objection by Ward, Devendorf ruled that Chester couldn't quote any conversations he had had with Grace. While this ruling was changed before Chester was finished with his story, it disrupted Chester's rehearsed story and led to more prompting by Thomas than would have otherwise been necessary. After the conversations were allowed into the story, he had to back track to tell what Grace had said to him.

Most of his version of the story merely backed up what Ward's dozens of witnesses had said, often adding a few details to explain why certain things had occurred. When he moved his story as far as Big Moose, he began to add much more detail. He used Ward's map and pointer as he described their movements on the lake that day.

"We started across toward this point," Chester said, pointing on the map, "where we left the suitcase, and then, instead of going straight across we went here, up toward the east end of South Bay to get some pond lilies. Those we had gotten in the morning were all withered and dried . . ."

"Then what?" asked Thomas.

"Rowed around or floated for a short time, well kind of drifted and then, well, Grace and I got to talking."

"Speak up so the jury can hear you," Thomas ordered.

"And we got to talking there about what we ought to do. I asked her what she thought we had better do. I said I didn't think we ought to or that we could keep on as we had been, keep on going as we had been, and thought we ought to do something.

"I asked her what she thought we had better do. She said,

'I don't know. We will go down to Fourth Lake tomorrow as planned, and then go back to Utica, or whatever you want to do.' "

"I told her I didn't think we ought to. I didn't think we had better. I finally said I thought the best thing we could do would be, well, to get her home and tell her father and mother just everything that had occurred, and then explain to her. I thought we might better do that than have them find it out, as they would find it out anyway. She said she couldn't tell her mother. Then she started to cry."

"She began to cry?" prompted Thomas.

"Yes sir. I spoke up. I said she would not have to. I would tell her father about it. I thought if I explained everything to him, why it would be all right. Then he would forgive us. Then she said, 'Well you don't know my father. You never could tell him.' "

"And then I said, 'Well what shall we do then? We can't keep up this way.' "

"Then she said, 'Well, I will end it here,' and she, well, jumped into the lake; stepped up onto the boat, kind of throwed herself in."

"What did you do?" asked Thomas.

"I tried to reach her," Chester said. "I leaned back in the seat in the other end, the bow seat, I guess. I tried to reach her and, well, I was not quick enough. I went in the lake, too. The boat tipped over as I started to get up. The boat went right over then. Of course, I went into the lake."

"Go on and describe what you did," prompted Thomas.

"Then I came up. I halloed, grabbed hold of the boat. Then, as soon as I could get the water out of my eyes and see, I got hold of the boat or got to the boat."

"Did you see her?" Asked Thomas.

"No, I stayed there at the boat but a minute or two. It seemed like a long time, anyway, and I didn't see her. Then I swam to shore."

Chester then described his escape through the woods and his stay at the Arrowhead and went back over his story to answer other questions which had been raised by prosecution witnesses, dealing mainly with minor points of the testimony.

When Thomas handed his client over to Ward with a "your witness," it was already late in the afternoon. Ward had certainly not expected to begin his cross-examination so soon, the same day he had concluded his case. Since the next day, November 29, was Thanksgiving, he had probably expected to have a whole day off to plan his attack. Now, however, he would have to begin his cross-examination, reveal his lines of questioning, and give Chester a day off to think up ways to answer his questions and study Ward's style.

Ward, who had been so orderly and logical in the presentation of his case, took a different tack with his cross-examination. He jumped from one item and one part of the story to another, rarely asking more than a few questions about a single subject before going to something new. He was hoping to catch Chester off guard so that he would reveal something that would incriminate him.

Among the first questions he asked was one about an alleged confession Chester was said to have made to his lawyers a few days before. This confession, supposedly overheard by one of the deputies in the jail, was printed in a number of newspapers. In it, Chester was said to have described striking Grace on the head with his tennis racket. But all involved denied any knowledge of it and it probably did not occur. Chester told Ward he had said nothing of the kind.

Then Ward went over Chester's story, examining large and small details and asking Chester to clarify them. Most of Chester's answers were evasive or non-committal. He answered many questions with "I don't recall" or said he was not sure. This infuriated Ward and he frequently became hostile during his questioning.

"Did Miss Harnishfager ever say to you that you ought not to be going with the girl, and did you say you were only having your fun?" Ward asked.

"No, sir," said Chester. "I didn't say that."

"Did she ever say that you ought not to be going with her while you had another girl?"

"Yes sir."

"What answer did you make?"

"I would rather not say," said Chester.

"I suppose you would," snapped back Ward, "but you are going to just the same."

"All right," Chester said, "I told her it was none of her business."

Ward also found ways to inject his own comments into his questions. Mills and Thomas always objected and it was usually ordered stricken from the record, but not from the minds of the jury.

"Had you ever gotten the best of the girl before you wrote her these letters in October, 1905?" asked Ward.

Mills objected to the words, "gotten the best of" and Devendorf ordered that they be stricken from the record, so Ward rephrased the question.

"When you wrote these letters, exhibits 5, 6 and 7, had you ever had improper relations with her?"

Again the same objection and the same ruling. Ward rephrased again.

"Had you ever had sexual intercourse with this girl at the time you wrote the letters, exhibits 6, 7 and 8?" This question was allowed to stand and Chester answered "I can't say positively."

Ward then got Chester to admit that Grace had resisted him many times and forced him to stop his seductions many times before finally giving in to him.

Chester made the somewhat contradictory statements that he and Grace had never spoken about marriage but that he intended to marry her during the trip to the Adirondacks. When Ward asked where they planned to be married, Chester said he couldn't say.

Chester further admitted that he had in his possession during the trip a timetable which contained a map showing the location of the road from Big Moose to Eagle Bay. Ward said this showed he could have planned his escape route even before he arrived at Big Moose. Chester, however, said he had not noticed the road when he looked at the map.

When asked to explain why he told Grace he was going away with her forever when he told people in Cortland he was only going on vacation, Chester said the people in Cortland would have asked too many questions if he told them the truth.

At times, when he seemed to be getting into trouble with

Ward's questions, Chester looked beyond his inquisitor to his attorneys. This irritated Ward and he demanded that Chester look at the jury. Thomas objected that Chester could look anywhere he wanted and did not have to follow Ward's orders.

"The witness is not subject to the directions of the district attorney," Thomas pleaded to the bench.

"No, he has no right to look at his counsel," Ward replied.

"I was not," Chester said to Ward. "'I was looking at you. It is necessary to keep an eye on you, I think." Laughter filled the room.

Next, Ward focused on Chester's finances, seeking to show that Chester had nowhere near enough money to finance an extended stay in the Adirondacks unless he got a job, something he showed no interest in doing. Chester said he had about $32 when he left Cortland, but by the time he reached the Arrowhead he didn't have enough to pay the bill.

Ward also focused on all the times Chester had not told the truth: when he told Miss Patrick and Miss Westcott where he was going when he met them on the train, when he told Gross he knew nothing about what had happened to Grace just before he was arrested and many times, of course, to Klock and Ward.

"What did you tell that lie for?" Ward asked of the latter incident.

"Well, I didn't want to tell the facts of the case then," Chester said.

"You didn't want to tell the truth?"

"No."

"When did you get a disposition to tell the truth, which you claim to have?" Mills objected to this question, but was overruled.

"Why, I don't know," Chester finally replied.

"Did you get it before you talked with your attorneys?"

"Yes, I think I did."

Chester's cross-examination took a total of 11 hours, spread out over two days, with the Thanksgiving recess in between. On his day off from the testimony, he was up at 8 a.m. and spent his time reading magazines in his cell. His dinner, sent from one of the hotels, consisted of roast turkey with dressing and cranberry sauce, mashed potatoes, coffee and pie.

*FRANK BROWN'S REACTION* - Frank Brown, Grace's father, has to be restrained from attacking Gillette in his cell in Herkimer (from a contemporary drawing).

*GILLETTE INTERVIEWED* - During one of the few times reporters were allowed to talk to Chester, he spent the time cleaning the bars of his cell with a rag while he talked.

*HERKIMER COUNTY JAIL - A 1981 view of the jail, which is now an office building.*

*CELL DECORATIONS - During his time in jail Chester covered his walls with over 100 photos clipped from magazines - mostly actresses and woodland scenes.*

*CHESTER'S ESCORT - Chester, left, wearing his derby, is escorted from the Courthouse to the jail by Austin B. Klock.*

*District Attorney George W. Ward.*

*PHOTO OF THE CROWDS - Taken outside the front of the courthouse before the trial.*

*TRIAL SCENE - A photo taken at the trial, probably on the first day. The black X is over Chester's head. Mills is on his right and Thomas on his left. Ward is talking to a potential juror.*

*THE JURY - The 12 men who found Chester guilty of murder, plus two guards.*

*Judge Irving R. Devendorf*

*Charles D. Thomas*

*Albert M. Mills*

*The Browns sat in the front row all during the trial.*

*CHESTER'S POSE - This is Gillette's expression and posture during most of the prosecution's testimony.*

In the afternoon, he had a long conference with Mills, going over new tactics to cope with the cross-examination, which had not been going very well. Later, barber John Frank came in, as he did each day, and shaved Chester while he read his mail.

The jury, meanwhile, was having its own Thanksgiving dinner in the dining room of the Palmer House. Some of the jurors said later that this was the worst day of the trial for them, a time they would rather have spent with their families than with 11 men they knew only slightly.

The family of Marshall Hatch, the foreman of the jury, forced to spend the holiday without him, got together around the dining room table and wrote him a poem, each penning a few verses and signing their names. The verses, full of family customs, friends and memories from past Thanksgivings, must have made it all the worse for Hatch.

At 3:15 the day after Thanksgiving, Ward concluded his cross-examination and Mills and Thomas were free to call the other defense witnesses. The remaining witnesses were all from Cortland and were all, more or less, character witnesses.

The sole exception was George Steele of Herkimer, a bank teller who was called because he was a tennis expert. He said that when a tennis racket gets wet, the strings tend to snap. Thus, he said, it would be expected that a racket buried in the woods for several weeks would tend to snap its strings. The broken strings of Chester's racket were, therefore, not necessarily caused by a blow.

Other witnesses, William Steinberg, Elda Hoag, Maggie McMahon and Neva Wilcox, were employees of the skirt factory. They said they had seen Grace crying during her final days there and that she had said she wanted to die.

Otis Patrick, Cortland County Clerk and Josephine's father, said Chester had been to his house on several occasions and that he went in the best society. On cross-examination, however, Ward got him to admit that he did not consider Chester a "top-notcher."

Later witnesses included some of Chester's personal friends: Fred Tyler, Fred Crook, the Rev. Robert Clements of the Presbyterian Church and Charles B. Robertson. All of them said they knew Chester, had been to affairs with him, and always found his character to be of the best. On cross-examination however, they all said they had never heard of Grace Brown before reading of her death in the newspapers in July and that Chester had been out with other women when they saw him.

After the dozens of witnesses called by Ward, it must have seemed to many a flimsy case for the defense when all of Chester's witnesses were called and testified in a little more than an hour. In reality, however, there were not many other people they could have called. Mills and Thomas had been hampered by a lack of time and funds. Chester's most effective character witness, his mother, was in Denver and Chester had insisted that she not be called.

At 4:45, Mills announced that the defense rested its case. Ward immediately called Chester back to the stand for further cross-examination.

Ward asked him to recall sitting on the veranda at the Arrowhead the night before he was arrested.

"Did a man ask what you knew about the Big Moose drowning?"

"Yes," Chester said.

"What did you say?"

"I asked what it was."

"Why did you ask when you were the only living man who knew? Did you want to mislead them?"

"No, I don't know as I did."

"What was said?"

"They were talking about it and finally one of them asked, 'Have you heard anything about the drowning at Big Moose?' "

"Did he ask it of you?"

"Not exactly."

"What made you answer?"

"He looked at me."

"You hadn't heard anything about it had you?"

"Yes."

Ward then recalled Ingraham, Robert Morrison, Klock and Thomas Barrett, the man who had seen Chester at Big Moose just before the boat tipped over. All of them gave additional details contradicting points Chester had made in his testimony.

More important however, was a new witness that Ward either

had not found before or who had recently agreed to testify. He was John Coy, proprietor of the Tabor House in DeRuyter, where Chester had stayed the night before he met Grace and went on the trip to the Adirondacks.

Coy told the story that Chester had gone out to the barn the night he arrived and asked about hiring a horse to go to South Otselic that night. Chester had already denied, during the cross-examination, that he tried to go to South Otselic that night. Coy said all his horses had been out that day and none was rested enough to go out, so he told Chester he could not help him.

It is difficult to see how going to South Otselic that night would have fit in with Grace and Chester's plans. Grace wasn't even home that night. She was staying with Maude Crumb and certainly would not have been able to sneak away. Ward later said that it was an attempt to set up a "straw man" who would later be charged with the murder. Hubert Whaley, an employee of Coy's, was called later to back up the story.

When court adjourned at noon on Saturday, there were still several witnesses to be called and they were heard on Monday morning. This included additional testimony by Silas Feeter, the surveyor who made the maps. He also introduced several final exhibits.

When Ward was finished, Devendorf called both Ward and Mills to the bench to ask them if they wanted to set a time limit on their summing up speeches, which in those days sometimes lasted several days. Apparently no limits were set since the speeches went on for hours.

Mills was the first to speak. With his reputation as an orator, many in the courtroom were expecting a fiery and colorful speech and Mills didn't disappoint them. The opinion of the journalists and spectators was that the evidence and testimony had gone against Chester up to this point and his only hope was Mills' speech.

Almost immediately, Mills made personal attacks on Ward, Sheriff Richard, the deputies and the press for what he said was a shameful, all-out campaign to convict an innocent man.

"Since the 14th Day of July last, he has been the object of the pursuit of almost an irresistible power," Mills said of his client. "There has been arrayed against him the learned district attorney with all his zeal and power and ability, which, it is not too much to say, is greater than that of any other gentleman who has been the district attorney of this county." Mills, as everyone knew, once held the job himself.

In contrast, he said, Chester was "this young man, scarcely out of his teens, a mere boy in fact," who had not yet had "a fair and impartial consideration of his case and his rights."

Richard, he said, had done no other work since July other than hunt up evidence against Chester. The sheriff's office, "and all the tentacles of influence and ability that he controls and directs" helped to gather evidence against Chester while the prisoner was "incarcerated in a narrow cell." The deputies, Mills said, improperly interrogated Chester in a successful attempt to get him to say things that would be used against him. Chester had had no money and no lawyer to help him until a recent date.

But worst of all, Mills said, was the fact that for four months Chester had been the victim of "the yelping cry of this rabid, public press." From the very first day, he said, the press persecuted Chester. In particular there was one paper, which he did not identify, "whose stories have been so false and so foul and fearful that it and its authors have earned a place over in one of the cells in the jail across the way." This was certainly a reference to the *New York Journal*, which had made up countless fictions about the trial.

Mills motioned over to the reporters' table as he made his comments and they all waited breathlessly to see if he would name the paper he was referring to.

From the beginning of the trial, Mills said, he was concerned that it would be impossible to find a jury that was not contaminated by the articles written about the case. ". . . One of the causes of apprehension that has stirred the soul of my associate and myself is lest this tide of malediction and prejudice which has swept over the county since this occurrence should have found some lodgment in the mind of the jury and should operate to the prejudice and injury of this boy on this trial."

During all this, Chester settled down in his chair next to Thomas, where he had an excellent view of Mills in action. Chester's back was, as usual, to the audience but to make sure no one could see him, he held his hand in front of his face. He didn't change his expression, at least as could be seen, even during the next part of Mills' speech, in which he described, as graphically as he could, what it was like to die in the electric chair.

Mills started out by telling the jury that mistakes had been made in the past in capital cases and began to describe some of them in detail, but Ward objected and Devendorf told Mills to stick to the case in question.

Mills continued, "after putting into the law the proposition that you may take irons red hot with electricity and apply them to the body of a man, until his flesh will burn and the odor arise to heaven, reeking with inhumanity of man to man, do you mean to tell me that a jury shall not consider and remember that as they proceed and be thereby increased in their caution and care in consideration of this evidence and in the consideration of any inferences that may be drawn from it? That they shall not consider the consequences, and such the consequence, of this verdict?"

Mills asked the jury to consider carefully Chester's background before they made their decision. In Cortland, he said, Chester lived for a year and a half, "a perfectly upright life, moving in good society, they say, with no bad habits, no kind of indulgence in the things that destroy a man's life . . . who has never associated with the criminal class."

His relations in Cortland with Grace Brown, although they may be considered improper by society, were not a crime, he said. "It occurs among young men and women thousands and thousands of times but it is not a crime and he cannot be punished for it."

The evidence collected by Ward, he said, was all circumstantial and proved nothing. "As you expect to sleep in peace in the future," he said, "I beseech of you to see to it that no mistake be made upon mere circumstantial evidence in a case of this character," because, "if a mistake is made in such a case it is absolutely beyond any power on the face of the earth to remedy or in the least degree ameliorate it."

There was, in fact, no motive for Chester to kill Grace, he said. Faced with the impending pregnancy, Chester could have made other choices. "It would have been the simplest and wisest way to have gotten rid of Grace Brown, if he wanted to, to simply have taken his valise and walked out of the State of New York. That would have ended it."

The trip to the Adirondacks, he said, was planned by Grace Brown and she urged Chester in her letters to take her on the trip. In mentioning the letters, Mills cautioned the jury about their impact "and the very touching and eloquent manner in which the district attorney, in his opening, read them." Ward's purpose, Mills said, "was to arouse within our hearts a feeling of sympathy, of pathos, a pathetic sympathy for her. And, of course, there always exists in such cases, no matter what the real facts be, a prejudice, a corresponding prejudice against the man in the case. Yet your experience of men and women and your knowledge of the character of the two sexes teaches you that in those relations between men and women it is not always the man who is to blame. He is not entitled to and does not deserve all the blame."

Mills then poked holes in parts of Ward's version of what had occurred at Big Moose on July 11. Ward had produced no eyewitnesses as he said he would, had not proved that there was a contract of marriage between Grace and Chester and had not proved that the clothes in her trunk had been intended as her wedding clothes.

He belittled the testimony of Albert Raymond that he had seen Chester and maybe Grace at Little York. With a man's life at stake, Mills said, a jury cannot take the word of an old man who may have seen something on a dimly lighted evening.

The idea that Chester was searching for a boat in which to kill Grace that night, was an absurd fabrication, Mills said. "I say it illustrates the extraordinary and unparalleled effort that has been made to distort every fact that can possibly be seized upon and every suggestion that can be made by any man, old or young, interested or not, to, if possible, build up a case against this boy upon the charge contained in the indictment."

If Chester had really been planning a murder from the time he left Cortland, Mills said, he would have done many things differently. He would not have used Grace's name on the Glenmore register, he would not have been willing to take the steamboat instead of the rowboat at Big Moose. "Did he intend to kill her on the steamboat, in the presence of the crew of that boat and all the passengers that were around?"

Chester knew nothing about Big Moose Lake when he arrived there, Mills said. He had never been there before, so it would hardly be a place for him to plan a murder.

There was absolutely no evidence that the tennis racket was a murder weapon. "Call it a weapon! It is not designed to be a weapon and it cannot be made to serve that purpose even in the vivid imagination of the district attorney with any success."

In all the testimony about the location of the boat and the body, Mills said, there was nothing that conflicted with Chester's version of it and Ward produced no evidence to contradict the story.

"No one except the all-seeing eye that presides over us knows for an absolute certainty what happened between those two young people there on that lake except the defendant himself," Mills said, "and I say there is no fact brought here to contradict him. There certainly is no connection or chain of facts and circumstances which can satisfy you gentlemen to the extent of declaring a sentence of death that the story which he tells is not true."

Faced with the situation following Grace's suicide, Mills said, Chester's actions may not have been praiseworthy, but they were certainly understandable. He did not inform the authorities because he was afraid the whole story would come out. He ran away because he was afraid. He went to Fourth Lake and tried to forget about his problems and enjoy himself. He lied when he was arrested because he was confused and had not had a chance to talk to an attorney. They were the actions of a frightened boy, not the actions of a murderer, he said.

"Murderers conceal things," he said in a series of statements that came back to haunt him when Ward got his turn. "Murderers hide things which are against them. Instead of telling these officers readily and willingly where those letters were, he could have had them destroyed and out of the way where their pathetic story could not have been read to the jury . . ."

Mills then discussed the results of the autopsy, which he said did not show for certain what caused the marks on the body. They could just as easily have been caused by transporting the body over the rough roads at Big Moose or by hitting the boat in a fall as by a tennis racket. The autopsy, he said, was bungled from the beginning because it was done after the body was embalmed. But worst of all, he said, the results were edited to help Ward's case.

"That post-mortem has got to be considered for a few moments because I say here, and I charge boldly that the post-mortem examination, however it may have been conducted, is not brought here in a fair and truthful manner, in fairness and integrity to this young boy, the defendant . . . If ever in the history of this county the graft that is going on here is investigated, some of the doctors of this county will figure in the investigation largely. They are paid large fees . . . I charge that they did not bring here all the facts that were found in the investigation of that body."

It would be wrong, Mills said, to send Chester to the electric chair based on the evidence of a bungled autopsy. "I should think these doctors would be ashamed, and I am ashamed for them."

Mills, expecting the line that Ward would follow in summation for the prosecution, began to read passages from Grace's letters. His tactic was to weave a web of pity around her, as Ward would do, but he then expanded it so that it would include Chester as well. He took out his own copy of the letters, which had been sold by newsboys outside the courtroom for 15 cents. He had underlined and annotated them so that he could read the numerous parts that hinted that Grace was suicidal, the many times she said she hoped she would die soon.

"She wrote in those tones of pathos in her humble home at Otselic," he said, "and when, on the waters of Big Moose Lake, there appeared to be no other alternative, no way except to go home and tell that dear, loving mama the awful disgrace that was upon her, she could not face that, as she says in her letter, and she jumped from the boat into the depths of Moose Lake . . . hoping, as she says here, that perhaps when she is dead her mother would not know."

Finally, as the courtroom clock reached 5 p.m., Mills concluded his statement by saying that Chester and Grace were only one couple out of thousands who had found themselves in a similar situation. Many of them, he said, rather than suffer from the publicity and disgrace, committed suicide. He also made one last appeal that the jury be certain before it sentenced a man to death:

> Gentlemen of the jury, I come back to the crux of the case, to the simple and single question - after passing through the pathos and sentiment and prejudice that there is in this case - that presents itself to you and to all of us, and that is the question: Is it proved beyond all doubt that the manner of the death which this defendant states of Grace Brown is or is not true?
> Is it proved beyond all doubt, so that when you go home and lie in your beds at night and you read in the public press that this boy has been electrocuted and his soul sent to his maker, that you can say with confidence and without misgiving whatsoever that you know beyond all doubt and question that you are absolutely right?
> If you cannot bring your verdict to that test and cannot say to yourselves and to your own satisfaction that there is no doubt about this matter, no unsolved mystery about it, then your verdict must be - and any other verdict would be infamous in the sight of heaven - your verdict must be not guilty!

Although it was 5 p.m. when Mills finally sat down, Devendorf decided not to adjourn right away and asked Ward to begin his summing-up speech, even though he would be interrupted in an hour.

Ward used most of that hour to defend himself, the sheriff's department and the doctors against Mills' attacks and charges of prejudice and graft:

> When the learned counsel made this address to you in a despairing effort to withdraw from the clutches of the law a man whom he knows and whom I know and whom you all know that this evidence condemns beyond all question, when he stands up here and says that all five of these doctors, men who enter your houses day after day and have the lives and the lives of your families in their hands, are perjurers and wanton liars, it ought not to be necessary to make an argument against such a statement as that.

Mills knew the statements were false, Ward said, but used them because he had no other way to offset the evidence Ward had presented.

"That soft voice of his, and those eloquent gestures have got many a criminal out from under the lash of the law. That influence, that suggestion has let many a guilty man escape in triumph."

If Mills had had any serious disagreements about the medical testimony, Ward said, he could have put his own doctor on the stand. Dr. Suiter was right in the courtroom and could have testified, but, Ward said, he would not have been able to contradict the five doctors.

The doctors did not keep their original notes, he said, because it was more convenient to keep the typed copy. Of course they left things out, he said, in the interest of making the information as compact as possible. What they left out, he said, were only immaterial things. He then went on to read the entire autopsy report, line by line, commenting on the implications of each item.

In answer to Mills' charges that he and the deputies were going to unusual lengths to persecute Chester because of the publicity involved, Ward said there were only two people interested in the jury's decision. Snapping his fingers, he said he didn't care that much what the verdict was for himself. The people were interested, he said, and Chester's attorneys were interested.

If Mills and Thomas could get Chester off, he said, despite all the evidence against him, it meant that they would achieve:

> . . . a remarkable triumph and that is the incentive to
> the great effort which the counsel has just made - because
> it is great. It is great in its slyness. It is great in its skill
> and it is great in its boldness. It is great in the boldness
> with which he has misquoted the testimony. It is great in
> the boldness with which he has tried to convince you that
> this poor, little, innocent boy came down here from Cort-
> land County and fell among thieves, which was too bad.
> It is great in the boldness with which he tried to make
> you think that all the force of the law and all the doctors
> and all the sheriffs and all the judges (and, after this case
> is over I think he will say all the jurymen,) were in a

conspiracy to deprive him of his liberty and to inflict
punishment upon him, while he was the only honest man
in the county!

Ward had only just begun his prepared speech when he was
handed a note by the bailiff and he agreed to the proposal for an
adjournment until the next morning. That night, instead of
returning to Dolgeville, he went to his nearby rented room and
went over his notes and especially Grace's letters. The original
letters, along with the rest of the court exhibits, were locked up
in the courthouse overnight, but Ward had one of the booklets
that had been sold outside the courtroom for 15 cents. The
booklet still exists among his papers and it shows how he selected
the parts he wanted to read the next day. Next to some of the
passages he wrote "suicide?", showing that Grace was too op-
timistic and too full of the joy of life to be planning such an
action. He also obtained a transcript of Mills' remarks to be used
in his response, particularly Mills' references to Chester as a
helpless boy and Mills' definition of a murderer.

But the next day, Mills was not present at the start of Ward's
statement. The weather was bitterly cold and the trolley cars
weren't running, so Mills had no way of getting to the courthouse. For the first time since the beginning of the trial, there
were no large crowds of spectators outside the courthouse. They
showed up only after the doors opened so they would not have to
wait in the sub-zero temperatures.

Thomas was with Chester when he walked into the room just
before the trial resumed at 9:45. Chester sat down deeply in his
chair and covered his face with his hand in his usual posture, but
once Ward began to speak, Chester followed him like a magnet
as the district attorney paced across the front of the courtroom.

Mills had tended to stay pretty much in one place when he
made his speech. He had stood near the jury and directed his
comments to them. Ward, however, walked all over the front of
the room. At times, he walked right over to Chester's seat and
shook his finger at him for long periods as he spoke about his
definition of a murderer in general and Chester in particular:

He is bloodthirsty and brutal. He is a blunderer. He
does not reason on the lines that any one of us do. He

reasons on different lines. Everything looks red before
him. There is nothing but one object that he is going to
grasp, and that is his personal safety, his personal well-
being, the possibility of an arrest. He sees nothing else.
He cares for nothing else. He casts all these things behind
him and says "I can do this slyly. I can get the girl on
the bottom of the lake. I can do it secretly. I can do it
carefully. I stand well in Cortland. I go to church. They
think I am a paragon of virtue, a decent man, when in
reality I am a ravisher. What I do in secret will be
unknown. I can take her out there and leave her body in
the lake, leave the name of an unknown man there in the
hotel, and all the world will say "Why, this girl was one
of lewd character. She went away with a strange man."
After that I can go and scratch my name on the rock up
there in the woods and I will go back to polite society all
free and clear.

Ward's speech turned into a seven-hour tongue lashing that
spectators said caused his words to burn with the intensity of his
feeling. He used scorn, condescension and satire and described
Chester as a "rat," a "slinking wolf," and a "snake."

He walked back over to Chester and told the jury that instead
on an "inexperienced boy" as Mills had called him, Chester "is
slick and smooth every minute and relied upon it. He relies on it
that his mind is quicker and smoother and more cunning than
you or I. He has more stability of purpose, more determination,
more cunning than a wolf has got."

> . . . and when a pretty flower had come down from the
> hills he scented her out as the instrument of his lust,
> plucked the petals one by one and threw them under his
> feet.
>
> Night after night he spent under the humble roof that
> sheltered that girl. Day after day he left his place of
> employment in the factory and went down to her table
> and engaged her attention and engaged her eye and
> engaged her heart. He ran the venomous coils of the
> serpent around her until the day or evening came that he
> could go into that house and smother her screams and
> hold her arms and overcome by force her struggles and
> resistance until he had taken her virginity. He, the

"inexperienced boy!" He, the friend of the minister, the county clerk, the college professor, and I don't know how many others. The "inexperienced boy!"

If any of Chester's friends, relatives or employers had known about where he went on those evenings, he said, they would have rejected and scorned him, so he had to keep it a secret. Faced with her pregnancy and the choice between marrying her and running away, he said, he found that he could not leave.

> He wanted to stay there among those good people,
> those poor, blind deluded poeple who liked him so well:
> the minister and the professor and the men of wealth and
> companionship and the dames of society. He wanted to
> wear his full dress suit. He wanted to go about to evening
> parties where the great dames and men who occupied
> prominent positions were. He wanted to go with them as
> their peer and equal.

By that time, Ward said, Chester had made up his mind that he had to get rid of Grace Brown. Reading from the letters, Ward compared her pleadings for him to come to Chester's callous answers.

While Grace took her working clothes on the journey, he said, Chester took his tennis racket and the tennis balls in his suitcase.

> He went with the tennis racket, he says, to make them
> believe that he was going on a vacation. And the tennis
> balls . . . hidden in his grip, did he take those along to
> play tennis with society ladies, or did he hide them in his
> grip so that people looking through his grip would see
> them there and think he had gone on vacation? Just
> another little lie . . . Mark how small a thing will put a
> liar down. Those two little balls convicted him of a
> monstrous lie there. See what little thing it takes to show
> the perjurer?

Then Ward turned around Mills' definition of a murderer that was used the day before so Ward could show that Chester had all the signs that his own attorney described:

The counsel said to you that murderers conceal, they flee, they hide things. Those were his words, and as he uttered them I thought how true they were! Murderers conceal. They conceal their plans and they conceal their purposes. They flee. They leave the body of their victims . . . Did he do that? They hide things. Did he hide anything? Did he hide the weapon that caused her death in the depth of the wilderness under the dirt? I think the providence of God guided his tongue when he described to you what a murderer did, because it fitted as no other description could fit this defendant. They conceal. They conceal their names. They conceal their identity.

It was absurd, Ward said, that Chester and Grace, after travelling all those miles through the Adirondacks, would suddenly decide that evening on Big Moose that Chester wanted her to go back and tell her father.

"He had the idea of getting rid of her by an accident on a lake when he took her over to Raymond's," Ward said. "He wanted to go out there - but he lost his nerve that night - and get rid of her by an accident."

Chester chose a lake for the scene of his crime, Ward said, because boating was his favorite sport. A man who owns firearms kills by shooting, a butcher uses a knife, but a man who uses canoes thinks of murdering in the water, he said.

But Chester had to do more than just get rid of Grace, Ward said, because too many people knew about their relationship. If she suddenly disappeared, the first question people would ask was who her boyfriend was and the finger would be pointed at him. Therefore, Ward said, Chester had to invent another boyfriend for Grace.

He thought that he could manufacture a straw man, a man who didn't exist, and that he could put the girl in company of that unknown man on a deep Adirondack lake and that he could leave her to die there and leave an unnamed hat floating on the water and an unknown name upon the register.

That was why, Ward said, Chester went to the stable in DeRuyter the night before he met Grace, to ask to borrow a

*FRANK BROWN WEEPS* - *After identifying Grace's clothes from her trunk, her father takes out his handerkerchief to wipe away his tears.*

*The doctors who testified at the trial.*

*Spectators at the trial examining the boat and suitcase used as evidence.*

*Grace Hill, a witness at the trial.*

*WITNESSES AT THE TRIAL - First Row, L-R: Chief E. E. Barnes, Cortland; Tessie Dillon of the factory; Ralph Weaver, hotel clerk, DeRuyter. 2nd Row, L-R: Theresa Harnishfager, Gillette factory supervisor; Minnie Hogan of the Gillette factory; Charles H. Dube, hotel clerk.*

*Chester on the witness stand.*

*Chester on the witness stand identifying Grace's portrait.*

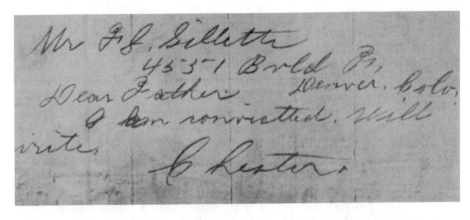

*Copy of the note Chester wrote to his father telling of his conviction.*

*The Browns thanking the jury for convicting Chester.*

horse and buggy. People there would remember that a strange man had asked to go and visit her there.

Grace's family, on being informed what had happened and fearing a scandal, would want to keep the entire episode quiet to protect the family's name for the sake of the other daughters.

"And he thought that Chester Gillette would return to Cortland and gossip with the other people in the factory about how funny it was that Grace Brown had gone away with a strange man, and he would have said as cooly as any of them, 'I never thought that of her, did you?' "

The journey was planned in detail before Chester even left Cortland, Ward said. He had studied the map and knew the lakes along the route. Tupper Lake turned out to be unacceptable so he looked for another lake on the map, somewhere where there were fewer people but close to Seventh Lake where his friends were, and near to a road on which he could escape. Big Moose was just what he was looking for, Ward said. His alibi was that he had been to Raquette Lake and he waited at Eagle Bay for the train to come in, the train from Raquette Lake, so people would think he got off of it.

"The plan was perfect," Ward said. "It was well made and cunningly and shrewdly devised." The plan, he added, was the reason he wanted Grace's postcard mailed at Big Moose, not on the train where his was mailed. His would not show where he had been. When Grace wrote on that card to her mother that she would write that evening, Ward said, Chester knew he would have to act right away. The words on Grace's card, he said, "sealed her doom."

He took all of his things into the boat, but made sure to leave some of hers behind. He found a secluded spot and kept returning to it, instead of visiting other, more beautiful places on the lake. Chester waited, in "that swamp" until it was dinner time and he was sure no one would be watching before he made his move.

> And I say to you that there is no question of doubt but
> then and there he tried to put this girl in the water, but
> meeting the same spirit that you saw in some of her
> letters when she knows she is being put upon, that he was

false, she put up a fight for her life. He didn't intend to strike her. He didn't intend to beat her. But when she realized his purpose, that scream went out over the waters and Mrs. Carey heard it.

And then, when he realized that he had gone so far and that the girl would not tamely submit, I say he struck her down in the boat. Not on the shore, but in the boat. And then to complete his devilish work he grabbed the tennis racket and brought it down on her skull, so she was stunned with a blow that went right to her brain. When that blow went into her brain it settled her; ended her. He threw her body over there just where it was found.

Chester dropped her body overboard, catching some of her hair on the oarlock, Ward said, and then went back to the shore. He had never had the suitcase out of the boat for a minute. He pushed the overturned boat back out into the lake, but not before he discovered that he still had her black cape. He threw that over the keel of the boat, just before shoving it away.

"Gentlemen, there is a God in heaven that manages sometimes the affairs of men. That is what left that cloak in the tiny ripples on the bosom of the lake," to be found the next day.

In conclusion, Ward said he thought the jury should take only 15 minutes to read a guilty verdict.

Men cannot go about this country and kill people, get maidens out of the way and seal their lips so easily and so handily as the narrow mind of a criminal might think. Why, gentlemen, if there should be a miscarriage of justice in this case, with this most outrageous crime, with this clear and convincing proof, I don't know what ideas it might put into the minds of men like this.

He represents a type . . . this type of man would not hesitate to seal a girl's lips in death when the occasion demands it and the only thing they fear is exposure by the authorities.

Then Ward went back to describe the crime once more, in even greater detail and drama:

Oh, the fierceness and animosity of the attack - the

determination that 'here and now I will seal your lips
forever,' and when she resisted his efforts to throw her
overboard, I have no doubt he said to her: 'you wanted to
die and here is where you die. Get over.' The man that
could sit here day after day and show no more feeling or
emotion or sensibility than he showed on the witness
stand is capable of any deed. The man that could ravish
that little girl with her bright mind and her sensitive
nature by force could kill her in a minute to protect
himself, because it was a lesser wrong.

No verdict will be acceptable, he said, except guilty as charged.

Ward was exhausted when he finished his remarks and offered
no resistance when Thomas, joined after lunch now by Mills,
offered a list of 20 objections to Ward's statements. Most of them
were for prejudicial language and the statements that Chester
forced Grace into sexual intercourse. Devendorf, seeing no
resistance from Ward, ordered that all 20 remarks be stricken
from the record, even a reference Ward had made to Shake-
spear's *Macbeth*.

At 4:40 p.m. Devendorf announced that the trial was closed
and he delivered an hour and forty minutes of instructions to the
jury. Reading from a prepared text, he was careful to use the
simplest of language, free of legal terms, so the jurors would be
sure to understand. Mills made notes on the remarks, but Ward
just listened and watched the jury intently for some sign of their
reactions. Chester watched Devendorf.

The jurors were told that the case was of great importance. For
the defendant, his life and liberty hung in the balance. For the
people, it was necessary to determine if a crime had been committed, and if so, that the defendant be punished.

"You are answerable to your conscience as well as your oath,"
he told the jurors. "I feel you will endeavor to do your whole
duty. You have no right to be controlled by anything but the
evidence."

He then carefully explained the differences between first and
second degree murder. First degree required evidence of premeditation. He also explained the difference between first and
second degree manslaughter. He cautioned them not to let the
penalties involved interfere with their decision. There were two

questions the jurors had to decide, he said. First, was a crime committed at Big Moose on July 11? Second, if Grace Brown was the victim of a homicide, was it murder or manslaughter and in what degree?

"If you find that Grace Brown came to her death by the hand of Chester Gillette," he said, "it matters not that the evidence was circumstantial."

At 5:58 the jurors filed out of their seats and were led by the bailiffs into a room just behind the jury box. The yellow door to the room was closed and locked behind them and a bailiff was sent out to bring their dinners from the Palmer House. Many of the spectators remained in the courtroom during the dinner hour, but were chased out at about 6:30 when one of the deputies said the jury wanted to eat their dinners in the courtroom instead of the jury room. The bailiff, however, pointed out that it would take an order from Devendorf to open the door once it was locked, so the jury had their dinners in the deliberation room and the spectators were allowed back into the courtroom.

Devendorf and Thomas, who both lived nearby, went home for dinner and stayed there waiting for the news of the verdict. Mills went to the Palmer House and had a leisurely dinner. Ward went immediately to the room at the Palmer House where he had been staying throughout the trial. After the exhausting emotional speech he gave that day he was very tired and left a message at the desk that he was to be sent for when the jury was ready. Then he went to his room and took a nap.

Chester, back in his cell across the street, had his dinner as usual and did not talk about the case to anyone. He read magazines and waited for the word that the jury was ready.

As soon as the members of the jury were finished with their dinners, they took a first vote on whether or not a crime had been committed. All 12 votes came back yes. Then Foreman Hatch told the others that it would not seem right if they voted to convict Chester too quickly, because some might say they had acted without proper consideration of all the facts.

With that understanding, they took four more ballots on the question of whether Chester was guilty of murder in the first degree. According to one version, several of the jurors handed in blank ballots for these votes. According to another version, one juror voted to acquit Chester with the understanding that he was casting his ballot that way only to prolong the deliberations.

When Hatch was ready for the sixth vote, however, he told the jurors it would be the last and all 12 ballots came back marked the same way.

Meanwhile, just outside the door, about 200 spectators waited in the courtroom. There was a buzz of conversation, a lot of looking at the clock and an air of expectancy. One reporter said it was like a theater lobby between acts, with the final act quickly approaching.

Some of the spectators made trips to the water fountain, which was in the corner of the room, right next to the yellow door, and tried to hear what was going on just beyond. At the back of the room, some little boys knocked on the benches and giggled when everyone in the room was suddenly silent, thinking they had heard the knock from the other side of the jury's door.

Many of the spectators grew tired of the wait and had left before 10 p.m. Among those who remained was Fred Brown, Grace's uncle from DeRuyter, who had agreed to wait and send word to the other members of the Brown family, who were resting at their boarding house on Prospect Street.

The technicians from the two telegraph companies were also busy getting ready for the climax of the trial that they had been involved with for nearly four weeks. They had a bet going as to which would be the first to send out the official word of the verdict.

The Postal Company, which had its offices in the courthouse basement, rigged up two wires which were brought up the stairs to the courtroom door. The other ends were attached to a buzzer near the keyboard operators. A code was set up. One buzz meant conviction in the first degree, two buzzes meant second degree and three buzzes for manslaughter. (There was, apparently, no code for not guilty.)

The Western Union Company, which had its offices in the Surrogate Court's chambers, made a human chain of men who would relay word to the telegraph operators to send the word across the country.

Mills was in the middle of an impromptu news conference, a rare thing for him, at 10:55 in the Palmer House lobby.

"Every hour gives us greater hope," he said while looking at the clock. "The longer the jury remains at its task, the more reason we have to look for something better than a first degree verdict. But it's all speculation. No person can do better than to venture a guess on the outcome."

He looked at the clock and another reporter began to ask him a question when a messenger came in with a one-word message.

"Verdict," was all the boy said.

The newspapermen disappeared in a second, followed by a group of people waiting in the lobby. Mills, however, knowing that he would get there in plenty of time, was in no hurry.

"That settles it," he said to one of the few reporters still there. He looked down at the ground and didn't look up until after the jury had made its report a few minutes later.

Inside the courtroom there had been four firm knocks at the yellow door and people who had been sitting down on the benches suddenly stood up. There was a rush to get the better seats in the front of the room and the bailiffs, who had not had an easy time all evening, had to pound their poles on the floor to keep order.

Deputy Delos Haller unlocked the door to the jurors room and Hatch was heard to say, "We are ready."

Fred Brown left to summon the other members of the Brown family and messengers were sent out to find Ward and the defense attorneys and to the jail across the street.

As soon as Chester heard that the messenger had arrived, he told Klock that the early verdict meant that he had been found guilty. After combing his hair and putting his jacket back on, Chester accompanied Klock back across the street. It was a trip they had made nearly 100 times in the past four weeks, counting recesses and lunch breaks.

"Now, Chester, hold yourself together," Klock told him on the way across the street. "It may - it is probably a verdict in the first degree when they are coming in so soon."

"I know it," was all Chester said.

They arrived in the courtroom at 11:08 and just before he sat down next to Mills and Thomas, Chester reached into his pocket and pulled out his package of gum. He offered some to Klock and then put the last piece in his mouth.

Ward appeared at about the same time. His hair had been

combed quickly and was not as orderly as it usually was. He was seen wiping sleep from his eyes.

Devendorf entered in his black gown at 11:15 and court was rapped into session. The jurors were asked to enter the room and they came in one by one, the object of everyone's attention, especially Chester's. Mills, however, looked down at the table.

"Gentlemen of the jury, have you reached your verdict and who shall speak for you?" asked County Clerk Burney.

"We have," answered Hatch. "We find the defendant guilty as charged in the indictment."

The wires closed at the courthouse door with one long buzz downstairs and the message "Gillette guilty in first degree" clicked out on teletypes throughout the country.

In the courtroom, all eyes were on Chester to see if his nerve would finally be broken. He kept on chewing his gum without missing a stroke. He blinked his eyes once or twice and waited to see what would happen next.

"Is that," asked Burney, "the verdict of each of you?"

"It is," the jurors responded in unison.

Mills, speaking for the first time, asked that the jury be polled. On Burney's order, each of the 12 rose when his name was called and said, "I find the defendant guilty as charged in the indictment."

Chester whispered to Thomas and took out a pencil to scribble a message on a piece of paper: "Dear Father, I am convicted, Will write. Chester."

Mills, meanwhile, was requesting that the sentencing be postponed until he had time to prepare motions to have the verdict set aside. Devendorf agreed.

Just as Court Crier Harter was announcing the adjournment, Chester reached over, as he had done so many times before, and picked up the two derby hats, handing one to Klock. Klock then put on the handcuffs and they walked back down the rear stairs over to the jail. Klock told him that under the rules a man convicted of a capital offense had to be guarded day and night, so a guard would be kept just outside his door. Chester nodded that he understood.

About 15 minutes after he had closed the door of Chester's cell, Klock and Richard went back to speak to Chester, but found him already in bed.

"What, are you in bed already?" asked Klock.

"Yes, and almost asleep," said the convicted murderer. A few minutes later the guards heard him snoring.

# CHAPTER EIGHT

# 'A Mother's
# Plea For Her Son'

Just before 10 p.m. on Sunday, December 9, a gray-haired, gray-eyed woman in her late 40s, wearing a gray suit and carrying a brown suitcase stepped off train No. 28 at the New York Central Railway Station in Herkimer. She walked up the street to the Waverly House Hotel, which had several vacant rooms now that most of the witnesses from the Gillette trial had left town. She asked for a room and signed the register "Mrs. L.M. Gillette."

"Are you Chester Gillette's mother?" asked the manager, a Mr. Baker.

"Yes," she said, smiling even though she was obviously weary from her long trip. She sighed as if she knew she was making an admission that she would make for the rest of her life, "I am the mother of Chester Gillette."

She asked Baker if it was too late to visit the jail and was told that the jail was closed. She then asked if she could send a telegram and he directed her back to the railroad station.

On her way back she met a reporter from the *Utica Daily Press*. The reporter, probably William E. Wolcott, the reporter who covered the trial, said he was absolutely astounded when she told him she could not answer any of his questions because she was employed as a reporter herself for the *New York Evening Journal* and the *Denver Times*. She was there, she said, to cover her son's sentence to death in the electric chair.

Wolcott rushed over to the jail to break the news to the deputies and guards there. Klock, who was on duty that night, didn't believe Wolcott's story at first for it sounded very much like the kinds of pranks the press had been playing for weeks trying to stir up interesting copy. Klock took a letter from Louisa, that had been received at the jail, over to the Waverly House register and compared the signatures before he was convinced. Klock told Baker that Louisa could come to the jail right away, even though it was late, but by that time Louisa had retired for the night.

Klock returned to tell Chester, who was playing cards with his guards and cooking a late meal on his gas store.

Louisa's journey had taken some 60 hours on the train by way of Chicago. Before she left Denver on Friday morning, she had received the news of her son's conviction and also the erroneous news reports that Chester had confessed to the crime. She had sent a telegram to him demanding that he repent his sin, but she left before Chester's answer, "Don't believe the newspapers," was received.

Despite their son's growing reputation, the Gillettes in Denver had enjoyed almost total freedom from notoriety. Once they found out the real nature of Chester's crime, they followed the news reports daily and some of their letters got through the embargo set up at the jail. Chester had insisted in his letters that he was innocent and begged his parents not to come to Herkimer for the trial.

At first, not even the Gillettes' neighbors and friends in Denver seem to have known that they were the parents of the famous prisoner in Herkimer. But all of that changed on December 2, just two days before Chester's conviction, when one of the Denver newspapers tracked them down and a reporter arrived to interview them at their house. His article was sent over the news wires and reprinted in newspapers across the country. Frank was described as "weak-looking in physique, his eyes wandering, with thin-drawn cheeks and heavily bearded." But most of the attention was focused on Louisa, the more talkative of the two. Surprisingly, she didn't even insist that her son was innocent.

"I have no opinion to express to the papers about whether or not Chester is guilty," she said. "I would tell what I think only to members of my own family, and we never discuss the case with outsiders. Of course, the state has made a very strong case against my son."

Frank said, "There was never anything in Chester's nature that I ever knew of that would lead him to do such a thing. He was never of a brutal character and was always lovable and kind. Of course, we knew very little of him for years. He has not been home except for occasional visits since he was 14 years old. A boy's nature may change as he grows older, but this is so different from anything that might be expected."

For readers hearing about Chester's family for the first time, this created the impression that he was a good boy who had been abandoned by his family, an impression Louisa spent much time trying to correct later.

Once they were found by the press, however, there was no peace for the Gillettes. Every new development in the case was brought to them for comment and they seem to have resigned themselves early to their new-found celebrity status.

When the newspaper boys screamed out the latest headline on December 5, "Gillette Will Die in the Chair," 14-year-old Paul came running home to his mother crying. Louisa had to explain to him that it wasn't true. He had been found guilty, but there was always hope for an appeal, she told him.

It is not known which newspaper editor had the original idea to send Louisa as a reporter to her own son's sentencing, but it was the kind of sensational hoopla that was all the rage in the era of yellow journalism. She was not a total stranger to the field, having been a correspondent for the Salvation Army's *War Cry* and other Christian publications over the years. The arrangements must have been made quickly, however, sometime between December 2, when she was first located and December 6, when the transportation agreements were made.

The *Denver Times*, where the original deal was made, contacted the *New York Journal*, William Randolph Hearst's flag-ship paper in New York City and together they agreed to share the costs of sending Louisa to Herkimer in exchange for her articles.

Several people recognized her on the train to Herkimer and many told her of their sympathy for her. One woman on the train told her a story about a man named Jack Marion of Beatrice, Nebraska, who was hung for murder when his friend disappeared. A few years after the execution, the supposed murder victim showed up, explaining that he had gone to South America and had not told anyone. Louisa was thankful for this story of the mistaken execution of an innocent man and used it many times trying to gain support for her son in the next year.

Louisa had not seen her son for two and a half years when she prepared to meet him in the jail cell the morning after her arrival in Herkimer. On her way to the jail a reporter walked with her.

"I have come here to urge my son, if he has been guilty, to make a confession," she said. "I have come to tell him to tell his story, whether or not he is guilty, just as it is."

It was 8:15 when she entered the jail office and introduced herself to Klock, saying she had arrived last night but was afraid the jail was closed.

"Mrs. Gillette," Klock said, "if you had come after 12 o'clock after coming the distance you travelled, and under the circumstances, you could have visited your son." He explained that the rules did not permit them to meet alone, but he promised to make it as private as he could. Two chairs were set up in the corridor outside Chester's cell so the two would not have to meet behind bars. Chester was brought out into one of the chairs and Louisa arrived a few minutes later.

Louisa burst into tears when she saw him. He stood up and she threw her arms around him.

"Oh my God! My boy! My son," she said when she saw him. Chester patted her on the shoulder and said, "There, there, mother. Don't take on so. Don't cry."

Then they both sat down on the chairs to talk. Klock sat in a far corner of the room so he could not hear what they said. Louisa frequently had to stop speaking because she was overcome with emotion, and when this happened Chester would pat her on the shoulder again. After a few minutes a messenger brought in a telegram from the *New York Journal*, reminding her that the editors were waiting for her articles. Louisa reached into her bag and took out a pencil and her notebook and began asking her son questions.

During this interview, Chester was shaved and he got his clothes ready for what was to be his final day in court. She left a short time later so that he could get dressed, but promised to be near him in the courtroom when the sentence was passed.

She arrived at the courthouse at 9:45 and sat near the end of the attorney's table. Immediately she became the center of attention as hundreds of spectators came up to her. A reporter for the *Utica Herald Dispatch* described her this way:

> She is a woman who makes a good impression. The
> black and white hat she wore was becoming. Her dress of
> brown and gray mixture had lapels with velvet trimmings
> and large ornaments. She is apparently under 50 years of
> age and appears from a distance well on the sunny side of
> that age. Determination seems to be the strongest char-
> acteristic that a student of physiognomy would find
> evidenced in her face. Her hair is quite gray at the sides,
> but in the back it retained most of its color and is of a
> dark reddish-brown. Mrs. Gillete is rather short of
> stature and is inclined to be fleshy.

A few minutes later, Klock brought Chester into the court-room for the last time. He sat down in a seat just in front of Louisa and next to Thomas. Chester talked with Louisa for a few minutes before the court was called into session.

Ward began by moving that the sentence be passed immedi-ately, but Thomas was on his feet before Ward could finish with an appeal that the verdict be set aside because Chester's rights were prejudiced and that there were errors of procedure. Deven-dorf denied Thomas' motions without hesitation.

Next, Thomas protested that the trial had no jurisdiction since the special term of the court had not been called by the Court of Appeals, but by the governor. He read a signed affidavit from Mills, who was out of town, enlarging on those objections, but Devendorf again dismissed the motions.

Then County Clerk Burney asked that Chester approach the

bench for sentencing. Chester got up and walked to the desk and was sworn in with his hand on the Bible. He gave his name, age and address but hesitated when it came time to give his occupation.

"Why, I worked in the factory there," he said.

"Factory employee?" suggested Burney.

"No, make it stock clerk," Chester said.

"Have you anything to say why the sentence of the court should not be pronounced at this time?" Burney asked.

"I have," said Chester, turning to Devendorf. "I desire to state that I am innocent of this crime and therefore ought not to be punished. I think that is all."

Devendorf, who had been sitting at his desk with one arm on the desk and a look of interest, stood up and, taking a piece of paper, began to read the death sentence.

Years later, Devendorf said it was one of the most difficult tasks of his life. "I can still see the faces of the defendants who appeared before me in cases of murder, first degree," he said in a speech, "those I sentenced to die in the electric chair. I have presided over many murder cases, but it is only the defendants I sentenced to the chair that I can remember."

But at this, his first death sentence since becoming a judge, Devendorf kept all evidence of emotion to himself as he read:

> You have been convicted of murder in the first degree.
> The sentence of the court is that you be taken by the
> sheriff of Herkimer County and delivered by him within
> 10 days to the warden of the state prison in Auburn,
> known as Auburn Prison, and that you there remain in
> confinement until the week beginning January 28, when
> you shall be visited with the penalty of death in the mode
> and manner and means prescribed by law.

Chester, as usual displaying no emotion, returned to the attorneys' table, sat down at his usual chair and took a sip of water. He whispered a few words with Thomas, probably an assurance by Thomas that the January 28 date would be postponed as soon as the appeal was filed.

The sentence was passed at 10:27 and Chester was back in his cell at 10:45. Louisa, however, was mobbed by reporters asking all kinds of questions. At first, she said she could say nothing, but later gave in. She was now confident that her son was innocent, she said, there was no more doubt in her mind.

While she was speaking, a woman took her hand and said how sympathetic she was for her and Louisa thanked the woman. Many more women, however, simply stared at her. The reporters suggested they go into the judge's room where the spectators could not see them. She cried briefly, the tears she had hidden while the court was in session, and wiped them away with a hand-kerchief.

"I want you reporters to give me a fair chance," she said. "Do not be too severe with my boy. I do not consider he has been treated fairly by the newspapers and you know the public press has wide influence." She said she expected Chester would get a new trial soon. A photographer took her picture and she excused herself, saying she had to file her own report.

Her resulting article must have been very disappointing to the editors who paid for her to be there. Instead of the heart-rending description of agony they must have been expecting, she gave them a facts-only account that anyone could have written.

"I am here and I was present in court when my son was sentenced," she wrote. "Chester bore up bravely and God gave me strength to control myself with the eyes of the curious throng upon me." But most of the article was a description of her journey to Herkimer and the people she had met on the train. She wrote the story of Jack Marion and how a man could be sentenced to die and the mistake learned only when it was too late. The *New York Journal* ran the story under the headline, "Gillette's Mother's Own Story of Visit to Condemned Son" even though Louisa included nothing of her intimate conversation with Chester in the article.

That afternoon, several reporters came to the jail asking to see Chester. Since Louisa was a journalist and had been able to talk to him as a reporter, why were they being denied? Sheriff Richard finally decided that the members of the press could choose two reporters who would be admitted with the understanding that the two would share their notes with everyone.

The reporters agreed to the arrangement and appointed Edith Cornwall of the *Syracuse Herald*, well-known for the outrageous hats she had worn during the trial, and William Wolcott of the *Utica Daily Press*.

When the reporters arrived, Chester was seated in his large outer cell, with a large board on his lap, playing Seven Up with William Syllabach, one of his guards.

"Will you have a game?" Chester asked the two journalists when they entered. He was described as looking very young, almost childish, as he demonstrated some of the variations on the game of Solitaire that he had designed so that he could win more often.

"Many lawyers seem to think you will get a new trial," said Cornwall.

"Yes, I understand they do," said Chester. "Lots of evidence was admitted that shouldn't have been and the district attorney's opening address and summing up were certainly calculated to inflame the minds of the jury, now, weren't they?"

Chester smiled and continued, "But there was one thing he forgot to account for and take into consideration and that is if I had killed Grace and left Cortland meaning to kill her, I would have destroyed those letters. He would have had no case without them and he must have known it."

"Were you glad to see your mother?" he was asked.

"Glad to see her, yes," Chester said, "Glad to see her here, no. I tell you it's pretty hard for a fellow to have his mother find him in this shape."

"Your mother has everyone's sympathy," he was told.

"I hope so," Chester said. "She is deserving of it in every way, poor mother. She is out now, trying to find a boarding place. She does not like stopping at the hotel. She feels as if everyone was looking at her and she's placed in a pretty tough position. I'm glad she wasn't here at the trial. It would have half killed her to hear the things they said about me."

Chester then was asked about his remarkable self-control in the courtroom.

"I listened to every word," he said, "and there was not one word that did not hurt me. No one knows how deeply I felt everything, for I nerved myself and tried not to show my feelings."

Wolcott asked if it was his idea or his lawyers' that he testify on the witness stand.

"I cannot say as to that," he said.

When Wolcott noted that that was the same answer he had used many times when he was cross-examined by Ward, Chester only laughed.

"I felt that my lawyers were doing everything that men could do to give me a fair show," he said, "but the district attorney was determined that I should not have it, and honestly, I don't think I got it. I listened to it all. I wanted to explain a hundred things, but I have no gift for talking any more than I have of writing. I couldn't write a decent letter to save my life. I guess I couldn't tell a story so that anyone could take stock in it."

Asked about how he felt about the death penalty, Chester said, "Of course, a man must die sometime, and I don't suppose it matters much whether it's in 10 days, 10 months or 10 years, but I'd like to die a different way on account of other people."

He objected, he said, to the way his attitude toward Grace was put forward at the trial.

"There has been every effort during the trial to make out that I never cared for Grace and that I wanted to get rid of her," he said. "I don't think they proved it. She never felt that way, but, I guess, well, there's no use talking about it."

Chester then took the reporters on a tour of his cell, showing them the pictures he had cut out and his attempts to make the cell more homelike.

Two days later, the reporters had another chance to interview him as he waited at the Herkimer station for the train that was to take him to Auburn Prison. The date and time of the transfer had not been announced, but the news travelled quickly and there were about 200 people at the station before the train arrived.

Louisa had visited him several times in the past two days and had had breakfast with him that morning, December 12, exactly five months after the day the body had been found at Big Moose. She stayed with him until he left the jail at about 11 a.m. Klock, Deputy Firth and Police Chief Manion escorted Chester to the station in the Palmer House wagon. Chester walked quickly, as he always did to avoid the crowds. He wasn't handcuffed, but his arms were interlocked with those of Klock and Firth and the small man dragged along the two larger men in his effort to get through the people.

Chester had on a light gray raincoat, loaned to him by one of the deputies and under his arm he carried a shoe box, neatly wrapped in white tissue paper, in which Sheriff Richard's wife had packed a lunch for him.

After they sat down on the bench in the station, Chester looked over at Klock and asked, "Have you got the ticket? Unless you have a ticket for me I'm not going." Everyone laughed and Chester seemed to have been in an unusually talkative and festive mood, the reporters noticed, especially for someone on his way to the electric chair.

It was the first time in four months he had been able to get away from Herkimer and he was probably thankful for the chance to go anywhere.

Klock asked the reporters if one of them had a cigar.

"I've got one," Chester announced, pulling a Havana from his pocket and showing it to the deputy.

"Keep it yourself," Klock said. One of the spectators then gave Chester another cigar, which he accepted and lighted. Chester gave the cigar band back to the donor, who had asked if he could keep it as a souvenir.

Chester enjoyed being the center of attention. He made a show of flicking the cigar ashes and leaning back and closing his eyes partially, tipping his derby forward.

During an interview with the reporters he said that he had been well treated by everyone in the jail and would miss them.

"Tell them about the roses," suggested Klock.

"Mrs. Richard wouldn't want me to," said Chester.

"Why not?" asked Klock.

"Well," Chester began, "there were some roses and I gave them to her (Mrs. Richard) as I came away." The roses had been given to his mother by a friend. "Mother brought some of them to me. I have had them in my cell and as I came away I gave them to Mrs. Richard as a sort of remembrance for favors I have received in the jail."

Chester then complained to the reporters that the newspapers had not told the truth when reporting the trial.

"Not by me," one of the reporters said.

"What?" Chester asked, "A reporter who tells nothing but the truth? I don't think a reporter could hold his job for a week if he did that."

When everyone finished laughing, Chester said he was angered that the newspapers had made him appear heartless.

"Why, just because a man doesn't break down in court and cry doesn't mean that he has no feeling and no heart," Chester said.

Someone mentioned that it was near lunch time and that they were hungry.

"I'm watching that dinner box," Chester said, looking at Klock, who was somewhat portly and had a reputation for being fond of food. "I've had my eye on that dinner box and I notice Klock has got it under his arm."

One of the reporters asked if he could have one of the pictures on Chester's cell wall. Chester said he hadn't brought any of them with him and he didn't want them.

When the train arrived, Firth, Klock and Chester went to a parlor car and Manion returned to the police station. Chester removed his coat, placed the lunch box on the shelf over his head and sat down in one of the comfortable chairs with Klock next to him. The reporters filled the seats nearby and for the next several hours the car became a travelling party with jokes and much story swapping by Chester and the reporters.

When the train reached Utica a few minutes later, a small crowd was there to meet him, even though there had been no advance notice. A reporter for the *Utica Observer* watched Chester carefully to see if Chester would recall that the station was the one where he got off the train with Grace during the first day of their trip and where they left the next day for the Adirondacks. But Chester showed no signs of recalling it and didn't mention anything about it, even though for the next hour or so the route would be the same, only reversed, as they had taken that first day from Canastota.

During the conversation, Chester asked Klock to be with him if he was executed in the electric chair.

"If the worst comes," Chester said, "I wish you would be with me in the end." Klock said he had no desire to see someone executed, unless it was an urgent personal request.

"Well, that's what it is," Chester said.

When the train stopped in Rome, many of the passengers on the train looked out at the ruins of Tony Ferlo's Saloon, which

*LOUISA GILLETTE - Chester's mother.*

*Chester being sentenced to death.*

*Auburn Prison.*

*The South Wall of Auburn Prison, near where death row was located.*

The electric chair in which Chester died.

GEORGE BENHAM - Warden
of Auburn Prison.

had been wrecked on November 4 when a switch engine jumped the track and ran into it.

"It looks like someone was pretty anxious to get a drink," one of the reporters said, and everyone laughed.

When the train left Rome, Klock pronounced it lunch time. Chester said he was not very hungry, but when Klock said he knew that Mrs. Richard had packed fried chicken, Chester said, "I had better get busy."

Inside the box was a note from Mrs. Richard, which Chester read and put aside. Under that were two pink carnations. Chester handed one to Klock and they both put them in their lapels.

The reporters, guards and the prisoner joined in eating drumsticks, rolls and cake. Chester even told the porter that he could have "the leavin's". At the bottom of the box were some nuts and crackers, which Chester passed around, putting the rest in his pocket. The talk was dinner table talk, about sports, the theater and the news of the day.

When one of the reporters said he was from Cortland, Chester asked about mutual acquaintences. One of the women mentioned was, Chester said, "a dandy dancer."

The train arrived at Syracuse at 1:55 and, unlike the previous stops, there was a large crowd there to meet him. Since the prisoner and his escorts would have to change trains there for Auburn, the crowd expected to see him. The reporters estimated that there were several thousand people there, but that seems unlikely. To avoid the crowd, the train officials allowed Chester and his entourage to move to another car on the same train that could be switched to the Auburn track so no one would have to get out.

The new car contained the entire troupe of a vaudeville show called "The Runaways," made up mostly of burlesque dancers. When the reporters told the girls who Chester was, they came over to the famous murderer and talked with him.

Chester tore up scraps of paper and wrote his name on them after the girls asked for his autograph. Later, he signed an entire deck of cards for the girls to keep as souvenirs.

"You have a comfortable chair there, Chester," one of the girls said.

'Yes,'' Chester added quickly, "but they have a more comfortable one awaiting me in Auburn.'' Everyone laughed and remarked how whimsically the murderer could talk about his own death.

While Chester was entertaining the showgirls, the jail officials at Auburn were worried about the crowds of people at the Auburn station and at the front gate of the prison. A plan was set up to get Chester past the crowd and details were wired ahead to the train.

Just after 2 p.m., the prison gates opened and two sets of guards came out. One group of four was sent with the regular prison wagon to the railroad station. But this was a decoy. The other group, in Prison Warden George Benham's personal coach, drove outside the city limits to a crossing where the train was to make a special stop that day. At 2:58, Chester, arm-in-arm with Klock and Firth, was escorted from the rear of one of the cars and into the coach. Some of the reporters went with them and the curtains were drawn so no one could see who was inside.

The coach was driven down State Street to the large horse gate, around the corner from the main gate where the crowds were waiting. Some people saw the coach coming and yelled, "There comes Gillette!" But before they could reach the coach it had passed through the gate and the door closed with a bang behind it.

Inside the gate was a large courtyard made up of the prison's exercise yards and the prison gardens. The coach pulled up to the rear of the administration building. Klock left the wagon first, followed by Chester, who jumped out lightly, grasping his overcoat with his left hand while pulling on his derby. He took in what was probably his first view of the prison, unless he managed to peek through the curtains along the walls as he went down State Street.

The prison was built like a medieval fortress. It dated back to 1816 and was built on an old Indian graveyard along the bank of the Owasco Outlet, a small stream leading from Owasco Lake just to the south of the city. The brown and gray stone walls were several feet thick. Throughout its history it had become a dreaded place by all sorts of criminals and little boys in Central New

York were warned against mischief by being told about it and the people kept there.

One of its most distinguishing features was the elaborate turret on top of the administration building. At the very peak of the metal scrollwork was the statue of a soldier, painted in the buff and blue of a Revolutionary War Continental Army soldier. No one knew why the soldier had been placed there, but legends had grown up about it from the long hours the prisoners spent looking at it from the prison yard.

The prisoners called it "Copper John" because it was made of copper. Since it faced outward, the soldier's face could not be seen from the prison yard. Prisoners spoke of looking forward to the day they could "look Copper John in the eye again," when they were outside. Chester may not have seen Copper John at all during his brief stay in the prison yard, but even he must have been familiar with the legends surrounding the Auburn electric chair.

Auburn had been the focus of world attention on August 6, 1890 when William Kemmler became the first man in history to be executed in such a chair. It was a particularly unpleasant way to die, many people thought, without the dignity that went with hanging. Most of the details of the operation of the chair were never made public, so legends flourished. It was rumored that a person glowed like an electric light bulb, that the victim's mouth opened and words came out and that all control was lost of urinary and digestive functions. None of this was true, but Chester must have heard these stories. He showed no signs of thinking about them that gray December day as he was taken up the back stairs to the head keeper's office.

Klock signed the papers in the office that officially turned over the prisoner to his new keepers and Chester took off his derby and placed it beneath his chair. He laid his overcoat over the arm of the chair and sat down. One of the prison guards then searched him. Out of his pockets they took a watch and chain, two apples, a magazine, his collar pins and his cufflinks. They removed most of his clothing and searched it for weapons. Chester put his clothes back on and was hurried down to the bath room where he was given a shower and issued a suit of dark prison clothing. He had his hair cut and finally, just before he was taken to his cell, he said goodbye to Klock.

"You have been a good friend to me," Chester said to the man who had arrested him five months before. "If I get the chair, I want you to come to the affair."

Not much is known about Murderers Row, the section of the prison to which Chester was taken. Located along the south wall of the prison, it contained five cells for condemned men and was designed to keep them separated from the other prisoners. There was a corridor with three cells on one side, two on the other and at the end of the corridor there was a large metal door. Behind this, Chester was soon to learn, was the chamber that contained the chair from which none of them would ever return.

The four other cells were all occupied when Chester was brought in. Three of the murderers were identified only as "Italians," but the other condemned man was William Brasch of Rochester, who had been convicted of drowning his wife on June 14. He was 23, the same age as Chester.

Chester's cell, although somewhat larger than his cell in Herkimer, was much less comfortable. For one thing, there was no window, only electric lights, which burned day and night. He was not permitted to have such direct contact with his guards, so instead of playing Seven Up, he had to content himself with playing solitaire. He was permitted to speak to the other prisoners and the first thing he must have asked was about the metal door at the end of the corridor.

His contact with the outside world was also limited. Visits were permitted only once a week and only close relatives, lawyers and spiritual advisers were permitted. No food could be brought in from outside and reading matter had to be approved by the prison chaplain. Even his letters, both incoming and outgoing, had to be examined by the warden.

The next day, Louisa left Herkimer to visit her son at Auburn. On her way through Utica she was met by a reporter who recognized her. To him she said:

> There is one thing I am very anxious to do, and feel I
> must do if the spirit continues to prompt me as it
> prompts me now, and that is to go to DeRuyter and see
> Grace Brown's mother. I have felt all along as though

that were something I ought to do. Of course, I shall not
intrude myself if I am certain that the sight of me would
be hateful to her, but I shall certainly write her a letter of
loving sympathy and tell her how greatly I long to speak
to her in person. If my letter is ignored or answered in a
harsh manner, of course, I shall not force myself. But I
hope that it may be different.

Louisa received no answer to her request and there is no
evidence that the two mothers ever met.

When she arrived in the warden's office she brought a potted
plant for her son's cell and she attempted to give him a letter
from a former girl friend, but the keeper would not permit it so
she read it to him instead.

From this point onward, Louisa and her children became the
only link between Chester and the outside world. Reporters were
not permitted into the prison, of course, and his letters, those
which managed to make it through the censors, were never made
public and are not known to exist. Mills and Thomas were working on Chester's appeal, but neither of them made any comments
about the case or about Chester.

Mills, who had been in Syracuse the day of the sentencing,
said to a reporter, "What Gillette does, what he says, what he
writes, what his people do or anything else in this line does not
interest me in the least. I will leave nothing undone to secure a
reversal of the verdict but, further than that, Chester Gillette is
outside my consideration."

Louisa and Chester seem to have had little doubt during this
period that there would be a new trial and that it would be
handled differently. Louisa seems to have spent part of her first
weeks in New York doing her own detective work. She went to
Cortland and talked to people in the factory and probably went
to see N. H. Gillette as well.

With Chester out of the public eye, Louisa, to some extent at
least, took over his role as the celebrity, keeping interest in his
case high and swallowing her fears of drawing attention to herself
for the sake of her son. She gave interviews wherever she went
and handed out written statements. She even gave up her job
with the newspapers because she said it was making unnecessary
demands of her.

That left her without a visible means of income and she seems to have supported herself solely through donations from sympathetic observers. She stayed in the homes of people who believed in her work, usually Salvation Army people. It's doubtful, given his financial condition, that Frank could have sent her much from Denver.

She spent her time talking to anyone who would listen to her, knocking on the doors of community leaders, lawyers, influential people and philanthropists throughout Central New York and was rewarded when many said they would help. In an interview during this time she said:

> We are proud and poor, but the case has reached such
> a stage now that I would not refuse any offer of
> assistance . . . I shall remain here until the Court of
> Appeals decides the case and even should it go adversely,
> there is still the governor, you know. My boy shall not go
> to the electric chair.

Reporters asked her about Chester's high spirits and joking attitude during the train ride to Auburn:

> I suppose that the feeling that he was out among
> people - young people - once more would have made him
> almost wild with excitement and pleasure. Chester always
> was that way. He resembles me in being able to live for
> the moment.
> My poor little daughter (Hazel, who now lived with
> Louisa in Auburn), is not like that. She suffers keenly.
> She cannot talk to people about her troubles and she can-
> not forget them or let go of them for a minute. I have
> never known of any girl who had such a capacity for
> suffering.

Asked about the publication of Grace's letters, she said:

> I am very glad they were published in that way. They
> were wonderfully sweet and beautiful letters and anyone
> must have been the better for reading them. I must not
> tell you of the emotion they caused in our family when
> they were read there. Hazel broke down utterly and kept

sobbing, "Oh Mamma, Oh Chester! The poor girl, how
she must have suffered." That night I wrote my son a
letter and told him that in his folly he had cast from him
such a love as few men are lucky enough to win.

But it is the wrong and sorrowful way of the world that
when a woman has once sacrificed her whole self for love,
she is met with ingratitude and change from the person
for whom she has made the sacrifice.

Each day the mail brought letters from people all over the
nation expressing sympathy for her and these made Louisa hopeful that there would be a public outcry for a new trial. The paper
she had worked for in Denver, the *Times*, set up a fund to raise
money for the appeal.

On December 18, she met with Mills and Thomas in Thomas's
office in Herkimer to go over plans for the appeal. They told her
there were certainly valid grounds for an appeal, but that the
process would be expensive, since the court would not pay for an
appeal, as it had for the trial. It would cost several thousand
dollars at a minimum.

Louisa told them she had no money and knew of no way to get
the money. It was at this meeting, or soon after, however that she
began to talk about a way to earn the money herself. It is not
known who first suggested that she set up a speaking tour, but it
was likely her own idea. She had a good speaking voice and had
used it for years in organizing revival meetings. The irony of it
probably appealed to her as well. She was going to use the notoriety that had been heaped upon Chester to raise the money to help
set him free. Immediately after speaking with the two lawyers,
she made her intentions known:

I am firmly of the belief in the innocence of my son,
but, as I am without funds, I have determined to go
before the public and endeavor to obtain means to be
used in the defense. I have received hundreds of letters
and telegrams from people in various parts of the state
who declare their belief in Chester's not being guilty of
murder. . . . From the kindly messages I have received I
cannot help but feel that public opinion has undergone a
material change since the verdict was announced and I

am convinced that there is now a well-defined sentiment
in favor of Chester.

She then listed the places she intended to speak, including
Carnegie Hall in New York City, Buffalo, Rochester, Albany,
Brooklyn, Troy, Poughkeepsie, Oswego and Binghamton, as well
as the places near the trial. At the end of the interview, at her request, all the reporters knelt and said a prayer to ask for Divine
guidance in her endeavor.

But from the very beginning, things did not go according to
her plans. Several newspapermen tried to help her at first, but
they later quit and she had to set up the lectures herself. Since
she had no money to rent the halls, she tried to talk pastors into
letting her use their church halls. The ministers were uncomfort-
able with such a use and nearly all of them turned her down. The
Salvation Army offered their halls, but these were usually too
small for the size audience she needed to attract.

Finally, after weeks of working behind the scenes, her first
lecture was arranged for Wednesday, January 16, 1907, at the
Majestic Theater in Utica. She never talked about how this was
set up, but apparently she was loaned enough money to pay for
the large theater, which was just finishing up a series of perfor-
mances by the Lipzin Yiddish Company of "The Stranger" and
had an open day before the next attraction, kinetograph pictures
of the Thanksgiving prize fight between Philadelphia Jack
O'Brien and Tommy Burns.

It was obvious that a lot of planning had gone into that first
lecture because so much depended on its being a success. The
profits from the first lecture would be used to finance the ones
that followed. It was modeled on a revival meeting because that
was the only kind of meeting with which she had had any experience.

Tickets went on sale at 9 a.m. the day of the lecture, which had
been given the title: "Chester Gillette - Guilty or Not Guilty - A
Mother's Plea for her Son." At first the tickets sold well, but
later in the day the weather took a turn for the worse. Temperatures fell to around zero and there was a brisk wind. Sales fell off
and State Senator James Ackroyd, who had agreed to introduce
Mrs. Gillette at the beginning of the lecture, telephoned to say he

was sick in bed with a cold and could not make it.

About 1,200 people were in the audience when Louisa, Hazel and their guests mounted the platform. With them were James Cowdre of the Utica Rescue Mission and Adjutant Young of the Salvation Army. They sat down and a quartet of members of the Utica Male Chorus opened the performance with "Lead Kindly Light" and "Jesus Savior Pilot Me."

Cowdre, after thanking the audience for attending, said the topic was love and that a mother's love was second only to God's love.

"Mothers who are present here tonight," he said, "if it were your boy, what would you do? My heart goes out tonight to our sister and her daughter who are here with us." He then led a brief prayer and introduced Louisa.

Louisa said she had tried to judge her son as an outsider might do. He had denied that he was guilty, she said, and asked them to pray for him. Then she told them the story of Chester's life beginning with his birth in Montana, through Spokane and her involvement with the Salvation Army.

"Chester should be judged as a merry, careless, thoughtless boy," she said, "one who went in for all the fun there was without intending harm. In the skirt factory he met girls who were different from those with whom he had been accustomed to associate. I do not mean by this to say anything against factory girls. A factory girl, if she is a good girl, is as good as any in the land."

She then talked about the mistakes that had been made in executions in the past, using the story of Jack Marion again and adding stories about people who had confessed to murders only after someone else had been executed by mistake.

> The newspapers have told many lies and have prejudiced many people. It has been said that the newspapers judged the case before it came to the jury.
> . . . The letters of Grace Brown, I think, influenced the jury more than anything else. The girl probably loved him. She gave him her purity, but that is not always a test of love. That girl was no more a pure girl than my boy was a pure boy. I do not know who was to blame. As a mother of two girls I say it is not just that this girl, who is dead, should not bear any of the blame, while my boy,

who is in prison, should bear it all. It is right that he should stand his share of the blame, but not her share. I feel it is not right if a girl puts temptation in a boy's path and leads him to the brink of a precipice, that he should bear all the blame. If Chester had shunned temptation he would not be where he is today. I say this girl placed temptation in my boy's way.

A girl in Cortland told me Grace Brown said she was going to win Chester Gillette by fair means or foul. I am not going to say anything about the influences in Grace Brown's life, but I wish that you knew them. There is so much good in the worst of us and so much of the bad in the best of us that it ill behooves us to judge others. If Grace Brown had lived she would have been blamed. Grace Brown planned the trip. I do not feel that Chester gave to her the love of his life. If he wronged her he should have married her. He went out with her because she wanted him to go. The letters show these things . . .

Whatever she had heard in Cortland about Grace, Louisa never made public.

At the conclusion, after Louisa had spoken nearly an hour and a half, she said she was convinced that her son was not guilty and that the trial had not been conducted fairly. She offered a prayer and the quartet returned to sing "Where is My Wandering Boy Tonight?" When the meeting was over, several people went up on the stage and shook her hand and told her that they thought her son was innocent. Louisa and the members of the audience agreed that it had been a financial and ideological success.

Two nights later, she held her second lecture in Herkimer. Although the crowds were not as large, the audience, she said later, was much more sympathetic. Many of the spectators had probably attended the trial and understood when she talked about how unfair the newspaper reports had been.

Instead of a quartet, this time the lecture featured a "recitation" by Hazel, who had stood on the stage in Utica but hadn't spoken. The topic of her recitation was not recorded in any of the reports, but she wore a black skirt and white blouse and the spectators commented on how shy she seemed.

In her second lecture, Louisa spoke at greater length about her experiences with condemned prisoners when she was in the

Salvation Army, and she talked about "bringing them to Christ." She also went even further in her criticism of Grace Brown as the person who should share the guilt and hinted that Grace Brown's reputation in Cortland was not as good as it had been made out to be.

"I never thought at the time," she said, "that I should be pleading as I am tonight for my boy. These experiences have done much toward broadening my sympathies and my charity."

Louisa said Chester had refused to tell her any of the details of his relationship with Grace in Cortland. Chester, she said, didn't feel it was right to talk about her when she wasn't there to defend herself.

After the first two lectures, Louisa's audiences grew smaller. The next night, at Little Falls, there was only a handful of people. Louisa read some of the letters of support from all over the country and from people who had attended the previous lectures. She said she seemed to be gaining confidence on the stage, but she was also having trouble renting halls in the larger cities.

The next week she spoke in Ilion and Frankfort, again to small audiences, and it was after the Frankfort lecture on January 19 that she found out that she had not changed public opinion as much as she had thought.

The Frankfort correspondent of the *Utica Daily Press*, instead of describing the lecture yet again, wrote a stinging attack of Louisa for her slander of Grace Brown and the Herkimer County doctors who had performed the autopsy. The article was reprinted in several other newspapers with comments that showed it reflected the attitudes of many in the area:

> Here in Frankfort, where the autopsy of Grace Brown's body was performed, there is no disposition to question the testimony of the Frankfort physicians who made the autopsy. No sentiment and no person will be able to convince people in this vicinity that the doctors who for years ministered to the sick and suffering of this community, who have stood by the death beds of loved ones, went to Herkimer last summer and deliberately swore to lies knowing that the life of another human being depended on their testimony.

Although there were many who felt sorry for Louisa, the article said, most felt even more sympathy for Mrs. Brown. And as for Gillette, he said, it hardly mattered how he killed Grace Brown, since he had already murdered her innocence.

> Whether Chester Gillette struck the cruel blow which killed the girl who loved and trusted him, or whether he overturned the boat with the purpose of drowning her, or whether, according to his own statement, he drove her to suicide by refusing her the only reparation in his power and then cold-bloodedly left her to drown without making one attempt to save her, makes little difference in the essential fact that he was morally her murderer.

It was difficult for most people to understand how even his mother could feel he was innocent, the correspondent said. Grace Brown may have shared some of the blame in the beginning, but she paid for it with her death and deserves no more of the blame.

"Should he be regarded as a hero or a martyr because people are sorry for his mother and sister?" asked the correspondent. "It would be folly to let Chester Gillette go free because of sympathy for his mother."

Louisa didn't comment directly on the essay, other than to say the report "from Frankfort" was "unfair". But it was obvious to her within a few days that the sentiments were shared by many people. Within a week she was already talking about giving up her lecture tour and returning to her family. Mills assured her that there was not much more she could do to help in the area.

On February 7, the day after the Little Falls lecture, she met with Ward, whose office was on the same block as the Opera House in which she spoke. Ward told her he was convinced that the Court of Appeals would not overturn the conviction or set a new trial. Before she left, he gave her a piece of advice.

"Don't cast any further aspersions on the character of Grace Brown," he told her. Nevertheless, Louisa described the meeting as cordial.

Meanwhile, a groundswell of opinion was building against her. The *Daily Press*, following the correspondent's attack, said in an editorial that there was "a revulsion on the part of the public, who regard the author of the famous letters with a deep feeling of admiration." People who talked with Louisa, the editorial said, did not publicly say so to her, but they chose to make their feelings known at the box office.

When she spoke in Auburn on February 19, less than 100 people were present. By this time Louisa was attempting to blame herself for the faults of her son by spending much time discussing "prenatal influences":

> People have said that even if Chester was not guilty of Grace Brown's death, he was morally responsible. A great deal rests with Chester. A great deal rests on the parents of both. The prenatal influence on my boy's life was not what it should have been. I have looked back over my life to see if I was responsible for my boy's years of sin. I looked back over those months and then I realized that I did not practice the self control I should have.
>
> . . . When I was angry, I said my thoughts. When I was hurt, I cried. So I brought into the world a son not as self controlled as he ought to have been . . . I felt also that the mother and father of Grace Brown can blame themselves . . . but I must not judge them. If it were not for this first sin, Chester would not be behind bars today.

It was obvious by now that the lectures were a failure and were not raising enough money to help Chester in any significant way. Two weeks after the Auburn lecture she was on her way back to Denver.

In an interview in Auburn, after visiting Chester for the last time, she said she was more convinced than ever that her son was innocent and would be found so at a new trial.

"He is very cheerful," she said, "and says that as I have given up my lectures he is glad to have me return home where I can be of service to the children and my invalid husband there."

Her lectures, she said, had not been a total failure "because I have obtained many facts through them that will be useful for the new trial . . . Through the lectures I met many warm friends so that I leave this part of the country with regret."

Hazel, however, remained in Auburn where she was permitted to visit Chester once a week. She lived with the local Salvation

Army director, but lived for the one day a week she could see her brother for a few hours. Then she had to run the gauntlet of newspaper reporters waiting for her, Chester's only contact with the outside world.

# CHAPTER NINE

# 'No Legal Mistake'

C hester spent his 16 months at Auburn Prison virtually cut off from the outside world. He could read only books from the prison library and was permitted no visitors other than close relatives and then only once a week. For most of that time, his only visitor was his sister, Hazel, who had moved to Auburn to be with him.

For someone as fond of companionship and the outdoors as Chester, it's not surprising that this close confinement began to have an effect on his personality and his outlook on life in general. Unfortunately, there is no first hand description of how those changes took place, since the only information that came out of the prison was through his relatives or from prison guards.

It is known that Chester made great use of the prison library, reading books on world travel, history, literature and even philosophy and religion. He resumed the correspondence course in engineering that he had begun in Cortland, but since he could not pay the tuition, he reached an agreement whereby he would pay the school back if he were ever set free.

There was every indication that, given all the time he had to think about his life and the mistakes he had made, he had come to some firm resolutions to change for the better.

He became a close friend of William Brasch, another convicted murderer who was the same age and had arrived in Auburn only a few weeks before Chester. They spent their days and nights telling the stories of their lives through the bars of the cells, although Chester didn't talk much about the circumstances surrounding his own conviction.

Brasch and Chester played checkers using a system they devised because they could not see each other. They each had a board and a set of men and assigned a number to each square so moves could be made by calling out the numbers.

Chester was confident he would soon be back in court at a new trial, that he would be found innocent and set free. Throughout 1907, he never seems to have doubted that somehow something would happen to prevent his execution. The guards were impressed with Chester's unusual gratitude for little kindnesses. Most prisoners, the guards said, were not very grateful when fruits, flowers and vegetables were smuggled in for them from friends outside, but Chester always thanked them for their help.

To his mother he wrote, "I am happy even here and I think I am gaining more than I am losing in my stay here in prison. I begin to wonder, too, if I haven't some talent this way in some place that might be used later. I am going to try it once, at any rate."

In another letter, he said, "I am very grateful that I am not affected by the hard times or the cold weather. We still receive three meals a day, which is more than I eat. Two meals are more than enough."

Still later, he said, "I am reading a book on travel and also another one on what one should do. I have been around the world twice since coming here. It certainly is interesting. The books I have read have been almost an education in themselves."

But the most remarkable change in Chester's life was brought about by the Rev. Henry MacIlravy of Little Falls. He was a wandering preacher who had travelled throughout New York State, conducting services from fence posts, stumps and horse blocks. When he could find an abandoned rural church with windows boarded up and the roof threatening to fall down, he pried open the doors and conducted his fiery services, which were very successful in attracting the type of people who usually didn't go to church.

He had settled in Little Falls in 1904 and set up regular services in the South Side Church. A thin man of 22 with close-cropped hair and broad shoulders, he had a face that reflected his dedication to his vocation. He often had a fierce look on his face and seldom smiled, a characteristic he was said to have developed when as a teenager he was very sick and almost died. By 1907, his church had become a mecca for the evangelistic poor of the area.

MacIlravy first met Louisa Gillette in February 1907, when Louisa was looking for a church in which to conduct one of her lectures. MacIlravy and Louisa shared many of the same ideas about religion and he was impressed with the mother of the convicted murderer, but he declined to let her use his church. He promised her, however, that he would visit her son in Auburn.

At this time, evangelists were very interested in the conversion of convicts. Louisa herself had been involved in such activity when she was with the Salvation Army. Convicts were publicly proclaimed sinners and as such were perfect targets for conversion. A crusader could measure his or her ability against such a criminal, and Chester's fame made him a perfect target. He received numerous letters from such people while he was in Herkimer. A man from Stone Arabia in Montgomery County, known as the Reverend Mr. Gramps, talked to him in Herkimer and later, in Auburn, he said he had been given an urgent message from God that Chester was to be converted to Christianity.

Chester rejected all those efforts with the same attitude that he had adopted many years before with regard to his parents' fundamentalism and involvement with Dowie. He went his own way.

It was no surprise, then, that Chester refused to see MacIlravy. The young minister was admitted only after he promised to talk about things other than religion. Chester, who called him "Mac", seems to have liked him right away and MacIlravy came to visit him every two weeks. Eventually, of course, the topic did turn to religion and MacIlravy did what Chester's own parents and their friends could not do - converted him into a full-fledged,

born-again Christian. This seems not to have happened overnight in a flash of revelation, but came gradually during the year
Chester saw no one but his sister and MacIlravy. Perhaps it was
the closeness of their ages plus the fact that MacIlravy had no
competition from Chester's other interests: the outdoors and
women. Chester added the Bible to his small library of books and
even a self-help book MacIlravy had given him called *A Young
Man's Questions*. Gradually, Biblical language began to enter
his letters. His parents, of course, could not have been more
pleased.

Things were not going well for the Gillettes in Denver,
however. It was all they could do to provide for themselves, much
less come up with the additional funds needed for the appeal.
Frank and 14-year-old Paul were working in a lumber mill and
Hazel worked there briefly after her return from Auburn. Louisa
wrote some newspaper articles and did odd jobs. Lucille went to
Auburn in July to replace her sister and stayed at the Salvation
Army barracks while taking a stenography course at a local college. She visited Chester every Wednesday. Paul also helped the
family by herding sheep for $30 a month and worked as an office
boy. Frank at one time had a job washing dishes for $7 a week.

Meanwhile, the wheels of justice were turning slowly in
Herkimer and Albany. After several delays requested by Mills
and Thomas so they could gather more evidence, the appeal
papers were finally put in order at 1 a.m. July 25, 1907. The official record of the case was 3,000 pages long and was printed in
three volumes. It took a week and a half just to type it before it
could be submitted to the Court of Appeals, the state's highest
court.

It was six more months before the Court of Appeals opened its
formal hearing on the request for a new trial. Newspaper reports
said the documents submitted for the appeal were the bulkiest
ever presented to the court, and the justices spent much of the six
months reading the trial transcript and the papers submitted by
Ward on one side and Mills and Thomas on the other.

Mills brought his case to the court on January 9, 1908. He
presented a long list of irregularities that he said showed the trial
had not been conducted fairly. Only circumstantial evidence was
presented, he said. Much of the testimony was hearsay and not

based on facts. The photographs of the scene of the incident on Big Moose were taken in such a way as to confuse the jury. The testimony of Albert Raymond and Marjorie Carey should not have been admitted. The sample of Grace Brown's hair should not have been admitted and the fetus should not have been admitted. There were also a number of technical points.

But his most developed argument concerned the letters. They had been obtained through an illegal search of Chester's room without a warrant, he said, and without them the prosecution would have had no case at all. The evidence contained in the letters, he said, was hearsay and not admissible since it was not given under oath.

In rebuttal, Ward submitted a 111-page brief justifying all the points to which Mills objected. Ward, of course, was no longer the Herkimer County District Attorney. Since January of 1907 he had been a Herkimer County Court judge, but the Herkimer County officials agreed that it was Ward's case and no one could handle it as well as he could, so he was sent to Albany to make the arguments.

Ward told the judges that despite the minor objections raised by Mills, there was no other conclusion that the jury could have reached given all the other evidence. The suicide story, Ward said, was fabricated by Chester and his attorneys after they decided that the original story about an accident would never stand up. The trial was fair and impartial, he said, and circumstantial evidence was sufficient for conviction as long as the jury was convinced beyond a reasonable doubt of the defendant's guilt.

The letters, Ward said, while admitted by him, were also used by the defense in making its case. The fetus, he said, was enclosed in heavy wrapping paper and was not shown to the court or the jury, just to the doctor on the stand.

Many of Mills' points were minor, Ward said, and were the result of the extreme strain on both the prosecution and the defense during the three-week trial.

After two days of listening to the arguments, the Court of Appeals returned to its chambers and adjourned on January 31 without making a decision. The judges took the papers home with them during the recess and considered them in private. The court had a tradition of not making a quick decision in cases where a prisoner's life hung in the balance.

On February 18, the day after returning from its recess, the court issued its unanimous decision. The conviction was upheld.

The decision, written by Chief Judge Frank A. Hiscock of Syracuse, took the form of a point-by-point, dismissal of Mills' objections.

"No controversy throws the shadow of doubt or speculation over the primary fact that about 6 o'clock in the afternoon of July 11, 1906, while she was with the defendant, Grace Brown met an unnatural death and her body sank to the bottom of Big Moose Lake," said Hiscock in his opinion.

Among the most damning pieces of evidence, Hiscock said, was the fact that Chester had taken all of his luggage on the boat, while she left some of her things behind.

"We do not think the evidence fairly establishes any legitimate explanation for this latter conduct, and we are forced to the conclusion urged by the people that the defendant was then planning such a termination of the ride that he would not desire to return to the hotel and therefore was taking with him all of his possessions.

The court also defended the autopsy, which Mills had questioned. "The witnesses (the doctors) either saw what they described," Hiscock wrote, "or else with wholesale and wicked perjury they are attempting to sacrifice a human life by pretending to describe that which they did not see." The wounds on the body, he wrote, led the court to the opinion that Chester was responsible. "No reasonable theory sustains the possibility of their infliction after death and no reasonable theory accounts for their infliction before death save by the hand of the defendant."

Although there were no witnesses to the actual death and no way to tell what happened in any detail, Hiscock wrote, "it becomes a matter of small consequence whether he thus wounded her to insensibility, or worse, whether he flung her, partially conscious, into the water, there for a brief period to maintain a feeble struggle for life and thus produce those signs of drowning which presence is so earnestly asserted by counsel."

But Hiscock gave some hints that he was not entirely satisfied with Ward's version of what happened on July 11 either. ". . .

Limited as we are to a choice between two theories of the defendant's death," he wrote, "the one advanced by the people is strengthened, in our minds, if that were necessary, by the improbability and apparent untruthfulness of the one offered by the defendant."

Chester's version of what happened, Hiscock said, was one of "impressive unnaturalness" and did not explain very many of the facts. Although Ward's case was made up of circumstantial evidence, Hiscock said, the pieces, put together, "make such convincing proof of guilt that we are not able to escape from its force by any justifiable process of reasoning and we are compelled to say that not only is the verdict not opposed to the weight of the evidence and to the proper inferences drawn from it, but that it is abundantly justified thereby."

The fetus was rightfully brought into the courtroom, he said, because it was an important part of the people's case to show that Grace Brown was pregnant.

The only question on which the court had any serious doubts, Hiscock said, was on the matter of the letters. By reading them to the jury, he said, more importance may have been attached to them than was deserved. They contained many items that were not pertinent to the trial, he said, but most of the information in them was an important part of the case. Instead of objecting to the introduction of the letters as a whole, Hiscock said, Mills should have selected particular passages that he thought were objectionable.

Both the defense and the prosecution bent the rules to some extent during the trial, Hiscock said, but that was not unusual given the pressure on them. "We realize that human nature has limitations and that it is difficult for counsel, who for weeks have been engaged in such a struggle as was this case, tending to arouse the uttermost degree their zeal and anxiety, at all times to avoid transgression. Neither side was entirely free from it here."

"In conclusion," Hiscock wrote, "we think that no error was committed which substantially impaired the defendant's rights. We believe that the adverse verdict was not the result of any of these occurrences which were criticized by his counsel and which we could possibly say might better be modified or omitted in another trial."

In fact, he said, "no other result reasonably could have been expected in this case."

The court set the execution date for the week of March 30, just six weeks away.

The court's decision was the end of the line for Chester's case as far as the courts were concerned. The only possible further appeal would have been to the U.S. Supreme Court, but that could only happen if there was a question which involved interpretation of the Constitution. The only realistic chance to save Chester's life was an appeal to the governor, a routine procedure in all capital punishment cases and one that was often successful.

The governor of New York had tremendous power in capital punishment cases. With a single stroke of his pen he could commute the sentence to life imprisonment or he could sign a pardon and let the prisoner go free. The only real check on his power was public opinion.

The current governor, Charles Evans Hughes, had a very strict sense of justice, formed during his days as a lawyer and a law school professor at Cornell. While the previous governor had commuted the sentences of several murderers, Hughes had let it be known after his election in 1906, that he would not let mercy stand in the way of justice in such cases, and would not interfere, unless some new evidence or a last minute change in old evidence was produced. The prisoners on Murderers Row in Auburn, and their lawyers, made it their goal to postpone their execution dates until a new and possibly more merciful governor would take over.

Louisa read the decision in the Denver newspapers and immediately sent a telegram to Chester, saying, in part, "the end is not yet. Have faith in God." The telegram was received in Auburn the morning of February 19, the day after the appeal decision was made public, and it created a problem for Warden Benham. Officially, he had not yet received any word from Albany and it was his practice to wait for the official paper before telling a prisoner about the results of an appeal. He bent the rules enough to give Chester the news that morning. Chester, he said, took the news calmly and asked only that he be allowed to see his lawyers soon.

Henry MacIlravy was in New York City when he heard the news, but left immediately for Auburn to be with his most famous convert. Forced into a corner by reporters and asked to make a statement, MacIlravy said:

> This is the first and last statement I shall make. I do not consider Chester Gillette a hero by any means, nor do I look upon him as so vile a creature that the grace of God cannot save him . . . I have my personal opinion as to his guilt or innocence, just the same as everyone else has, but that in no way prompts me to withhold whatever spiritual comfort I can give him.
>     . . . I have seen Chester change from a careless, indifferent fellow into a serious-minded Christian. I have been very frank and told him exactly what I thought of him.

His sister, Lucille, also visited Chester just after the decision was announced. For months she had been visiting him each Wednesday, bringing him flowers, books and candy and singing songs for him in his cell. The other prisoners said they saw her as a "visiting angel" and that her songs were "the only ray of sunshine they ever saw."

Often, she would tell reporters what her brother had said to her. She said that Chester was always happy and never depressed. He often talked about going away and living quietly once he was set free. After the decision on the appeal was announced, she said Chester told her he thought it would be useless to appeal to Hughes for a pardon. According to Lucille, Chester said, "people may expect that I will set down and cry after hearing that the Court of Appeals would not grant me a trial, but I am not inclined to do any such thing. I am just as confident as ever that I can prove my innocence if given another chance and I am going to keep up hope to the very last minute. I am not going to die until I have to."

Chester compared his case to that of Harry Thaw, the other famous murderer of the time, whose appeal was held up for years thanks to the devious tricks of his lawyers. Thaw's case, in fact, was eventually dismissed. This is what Chester had to say about their cases, as quoted by Lucille:

> I don't believe that I am one hundredth as bad as Harry Thaw, but there is nothing before me but the

electric chair, and look at him, with freedom just ahead
of him. It isn't because he is crazier than I am, either,
but I am unfortunate enough to be born penniless. Hundreds saw him fire the bullet that killed White and they
want to electrocute me on circumstantial evidence.

When Chester found out that Lucille was repeating his
statements for the press, he demanded that she stop the practice.
Several reporters from New York City papers then attempted to
get clearance to visit Chester in his cell, some going to the extreme of seeking a court order, but these attempts were denied.

On February 26, just five weeks before the execution date,
Louisa, Frank and Paul Gillette boarded a train in Denver for
the 2,000-mile trip to Auburn and a last attempt to save the life
of their son and brother. Their goal was to seek an interview with
Hughes and ask that Chester's life be spared. They arrived in
Auburn on February 29 and went immediately to the prison with
Lucille, who had met them at the station. For Paul and Frank, it
was the first time they had seen Chester since 1905. The family
reunion lasted from 3 p.m to 5 p.m.

On the way out, Louisa told reporters, "Chester bears up with
wonderful spirit. Only once did he show any signs of breaking
down but he recovered and showed the same courage and bright
spirit he has shown all along. I can attribute this only to one
thing: his trust in God."

The Gillettes' plan was to circulate a petition seeking names of
well-placed people to present to Hughes. Louisa said they had
given up the idea that Chester could ever be pardoned and were
only seeking a commutation of the death sentence.

Louisa wrote letters to the governors of Colorado and Washington asking for their support. One of the tactics she used was to
tell everyone about Chester's conversion to Christianity. Since he
was born again, she said, he was a different person and should
not be condemned for what another Chester Gillette had done. It
seemed dreadfully ironic to her that she had tried all her life to
turn him into a Christian, and now that it had happened he was
to be killed for his past sins.

"The change has been very great in his letters home this year,"
she said, "so we have felt God was working a transformation in a
life. From a careless, thoughtless boy, he is now one who thinks

on serious things and weighs motives and influences as he never did before. His trouble has been brought on by his careless, easygoing nature and he realizes it. If people could only know him as he is, they would never think he is guilty. He cannot be a Christian and be guilty."

After meeting with Chester, the family split up to get as many names as quickly as possible. Frank went to Cortland, his boyhood home, while Louisa returned to Herkimer, where she met many of the people who knew her from her previous visit.

Since the petition has not survived, it is impossible to tell exactly who signed it or how many names were on it, but from newspaper accounts it appears that Frank had considerable success in Cortland, probably among Chester's friends and factory workers. But in Herkimer, most people refused to sign, even though they said they were sympathetic.

Louisa focused particular attention on the 12 jurors. Getting one of them to sign, she reasoned, would help influence the governor by indicating there was some doubt about the verdict. Louisa was very effective in her presentation, those who saw her said. She dropped to her knees and prayed that the juror would save the life of her son. But the closest she came to getting one to sign was Barrigan of Salisbury, who said he would sign if another of the jurors would also sign. The rest flatly refused to have anything to do with the petition. After nearly a week, the petition in Herkimer contained the names of a manufacturer, a dentist, two attorneys, a banker and a mail clerk.

On March 11, the family returned to Auburn, tired and somewhat depressed by their lack of success with the petition drive. Their last hope, Louisa said, rested with the governor.

"He has the reputation of being a very just man and so I expect to go with confidence in his sense of justice, to plead for the life of my boy, who has been condemned to death on probabilities and not knowledge."

The meeting with Hughes was set for Tuesday, March 17, St. Patrick's Day, and just 13 days before the scheduled execution. There were already rumors that Hughes had told his aides that he would not interfere under any circumstances, but that he would meet with Louisa and listen to her story. He had read the Court of Appeals papers and had said he was convinced Chester was guilty.

On the way to Albany for the meeting, Louisa said, "We have worked long and hard in this fight for (Chester's) life and I expect that the petition will be granted. I have secured a long list of names and believe that this ought to have some weight when carried to the eyes of the governor."

Louisa, dressed in black, walked from the train station to the governor's office, a few blocks away. She waited only a minute in the outer room before being ushered into the paneled office. She seemed to totter a bit as she crossed the large, carpeted and upholstered room and sank into the chair beside the governor's desk. Hughes gave her a courteous reception and asked her to tell her story.

Since the meeting was held behind closed doors, there is no description of exactly what happened. Louisa gave Hughes the petition and a letter from Governor Buchtel of Colorado. The letter made no mention of Chester, but described Louisa as a good and Christian woman who should be given every consideration. Buchtel was a Methodist clergyman who seems to have been particularly impressed by Louisa's crusade.

Commenting on the meeting much later, Hughes said that he was impressed with Louisa's lawyerly presentation of the facts and her appeal to reason rather than sentiment.

"I feel very much encouraged," she said when she emerged two hours later. "He gave the most earnest consideration and attention. I feel that his heart was in sympathy with me and my son and that if he were convinced that there was a doubt of Chester's guilt he would grant him commutation of his death sentence."

While Louisa returned to her family in Auburn, Hughes promised to re-read the information submitted to the Court of Appeals. Besides the facts in the case, Hughes had his own future to consider. He was being mentioned as a possible presidential candidate and a commutation of Chester's death sentence would have been an extremely unpopular action, one sure to cost him votes. There is nothing to indicate, however, that Hughes let anything other than the facts influence his decision.

Louisa, meanwhile, was waiting patiently, visiting Chester nearly every day, with special permission from the warden, and checking for news from Albany. On March 23, an unidentified

*Pass to Chester's execution.*

**WILLIAM O. DAPPING** - *Witness to the execution, Auburn newspaper reporter who knew Mrs. Gillette.*

THE WESTERN UNION TELEGRAPH COMPANY.
INCORPORATED
24,000 OFFICES IN AMERICA.    CABLE SERVICE TO ALL THE WORLD.
ROBERT C. CLOWRY, President and General Manager.

| Receiver's No. | Time Filed | Check |
|---|---|---|
| | | |

SEND the following message subject to the terms
on back hereof, which are hereby agreed to.                    190

To Gov Hughes

          Albany

Can you say before your god that you
have no doubt of Chester's guilt.
Please wire. If you cannot his blood
will be upon your head

          His mother

39 Seminary St

☞ READ THE NOTICE AND AGREEMENT ON BACK. ☜

*Telegram from Louisa to the governor that Dapping said was never sent.*

CHARLES EVANS HUGHES - *Governor
of New York in 1908.*

*Chester being led to his execution.*

*Chester in the electric chair.*

*Chester's grave.*

*Site of Chester's unmarked grave, according to Dapping.*

friend in Albany telephoned to say there was a rumor that the governor had decided in Chester's favor. "I pray God that the rumor may be true," she said.

Two days later, eight days after her meeting with Hughes and just five days before the scheduled execution, Louisa received a telegram from Robert H. Fuller, Hughes' secretary. It read, "Governor Hughes does not think himself justified in interfering with the decision of the Court of Appeals."

Louisa was shocked. "Can it be true?" she asked. "I do not see how he could have decided in this way with the evidence he had before him." She telegraphed a message to Hughes asking for more information. In reply, Fuller telegraphed, "He would not add to your sorrow, but in view of your explicit request, he directs me to say that he has not the slightest doubt of Chester Gillette's guilt or his duty not to interfere with the legal punishment of his crime."

The next day, the news was broken to Chester by MacIlravy, who showed him the two telegrams from the governor. Chester, as always, took the latest setback calmly.

Meanwhile, preparations for the execution were proceeding on schedule. Invitations were sent out to those selected to be witnesses and Edwin F. Davis, the state executioner, had been told when to appear.

During the week before the execution there were two distinct groups operating to save Chester's life. In Auburn, the Gillettes, now joined by Chester's Aunt Carrie from Spokane, and Bernice Ferrin, an acquaintance from Oberlin, were depending on the appeal to Hughes.

But when that effort appeared to be a failure, another group went into action. Fred Gillette, Albert Gross, Ella Hoag and possibly other friends of Chester had been quietly working behind the scenes while Louisa and Frank's efforts were attracting all the attention. They had been quietly collecting evidence that they hoped would help find Chester innocent at a new trial. When it became clear that there would be no other trial, they hired John H. Dugan, an Albany lawyer, who called on Hughes to tell him that new evidence was found that showed Chester was innocent of the crime. Since this was Hughes' only basis for interfering in such a case, he agreed to hear the new evidence.

Apparently, Louisa knew nothing of the other group's efforts up to this time. She was informed the Thursday before the scheduled execution, the day after she had been informed of Hughes' opinion. Louisa immediately took the train back to Albany, this time accompanied by Frank and Carrie Gillette.

They met briefly with Hughes Thursday night and he agreed to set up a full-fledged hearing on Saturday after he returned from a trip to Niagara Falls. Dugan said he was not requesting a commutation of the death sentence, but only a delay until the new evidence could be presented to a judge who would decide if there was enough to warrant a new trial. Louisa, commenting for reporters on the new developments, said:

> My boy Chester is innocent and now he will be saved.
> We are very hopeful, but, oh, we have been hopeful
> before. But we have now new witnesses and new evidence
> to show that he did not murder Grace Brown. Our
> evidence will have to do with the actual events of the
> death of Grace Brown. We have the witnesses and they
> will be here. I am sure if this evidence had been
> presented at the trial the verdict would have been
> different.

At 10 a.m. on Saturday, just 44 hours before the switch was to be pulled in Auburn, the Gillettes, the friends from Cortland and their witnesses gathered in Hughes' chambers once again. There was a crowd of press people eager to report the dramatic last-minute effort and there were even some curious observers, anxious to see what the new development was about.

The first witnesses called were Neva Wilcox, Ella Hoag, and Albert Gross, who presented a statement signed by other factory workers who had observed "spasms" when Grace was working there, evidence, they said, that she was an epileptic.

The next witness, Etoile Gillette, one of Chester's cousins, said that on an outing in September 1905, she had asked Chester if she could have the lining from his straw hat and he tore it out and gave it to her. This was the hat that had been found floating in the lake and evidence, Ward had said, that the lining was torn out so the hat couldn't be traced to Cortland.

Also presented was an affidavit from Albert H. Hamilton, an

Auburn pharmacist, who had acted as an expert witness at several murder trials. Reviewing all the evidence presented by the doctors in the case he said:

> In my opinion, all these things would be perfectly con-
> sistent with, first, an epileptic attack and a fall followed
> by death from complete and violent drowning. And I also
> say that if Grace Brown did have an epileptic seizure in
> the boat just before she entered the water, that she would
> be very likely to make a sharp, shrill cry and fall into the
> water and become at once submerged and would very
> likely in so falling strike her head against the boat,
> causing external injury to the side of the head . . ."

But the most unusual witness was a pale-faced, slovenly-looking boy of 20 named Douw Sanders of Scotia, New York, who spoke to Hughes behind closed doors.

Sanders told Hughes the remarkable story that he and another man had on several occasions "had relations" with Grace Brown and they had given her $75 to tell others that Chester Gillette and not they were responsible for her pregnancy. He produced diaries, letters and receipts with her name on them. The diaries showed the hotels that they had stayed in and some poems she had written to him.

Hughes, doubting Sanders from the first, assigned a detective to check on Sanders' background during a supper break in the testimony. Ward, who had been one of Hughes' law students at Cornell, was summoned to Albany to bring some of Grace's letters to compare the handwriting.

The detective, J. P. O'Connor, had no difficulty finding information on Sanders. He found a clerk who had watched Sanders make the entries in the diaries only a few days before. A few days previously, Sanders had been wearing a badge and telling people he was a postal inspector.

It's impossible to tell how Sanders became involved in the case. It's unlikely that anyone connected with the case put him up to it, and he was probably just a publicity seeker. Once he discovered there was a warrant out for his arrest, he ran away, to Canada according to one report.

The result of the Sanders episode was to throw doubt on

everything that had been presented at the hearing. The Saturday afternoon newspapers were full of large headlines like "Sensation in the Gillette Case," and "Last Minute Effort to Save Gillette," but Hughes seems to have taken the other evidence seriously.

The Gillettes left Albany Sunday morning before Hughes had made his final decision. They had to leave then in order to see Chester for one last time before his execution, now just 24 hours away. During the last few days, Chester had been busy writing in his cell. The rumors leaked out that he was writing a confession. Even Louisa said he was writing his own version of what happened at Big Moose. But what he was really writing were his last letters to the members of his family and a statement to be given out to the press after his execution. He had been moved from cell number two to cell number one, the one reserved for prisoners about to be executed. It was right next to the large metal door that led to the execution chamber. Through the door he may have heard some noises connected with the setting up of the chair and the controls in a small room behind it.

State electrocutioner Davis had arrived on Friday. With 110 executions in three states behind him, he was the most experienced executioner in the country, but no one knew where he lived or what he looked like. He carefully protected his identity so the families and friends of his victims could not seek him out. According to Department of Corrections documents, he seems to have been the only person in the state who knew how to operate the electric chair.

The chair was set up in a large room partly paneled and partly plastered. The chair itself was made of oak and had three legs. It was in the middle of the room, facing several rows of chairs or benches on which the witnesses sat. Behind the chair was a partition that hid the controls that connected the chair to the power house, where the electricity was generated via a dynamo powered by the water rushing through the Owasco Outlet.

A bell signal was used to communicate between the control room and the power room where the electricity was generated. Five rings meant ready. One meant turn on the current. Two meant more current. Three meant less current. One meant shut off the current and six was the signal that the execution was over.

Tests were run on the equipment all day Saturday and Sunday.

These involved placing a wooden board filled with electric light bulbs across the arms of the chair, connected to the electrodes. When the bulbs glowed, it meant everything was ready. When the current was turned on it made a loud hum that the prisoners in the next room could probably hear. There was a legend among the prisoners that the electric lights also dimmed when the power to the chair was turned on, but that was not likely since the chair had its own electrical system.

On Sunday afternoon, the Gillettes visited Chester for the last time, still without hearing from Albany. Louisa carried a white rose and his Aunt Carrie carried a red flower, but the guards would not permit Chester to accept them as they talked to him through a protective screen. Instead, they were placed in the corridor, where he could see them from his cell.

In describing the conversation later, Louisa said, "It was the hardest of all my duties to perform. It was so hard I almost excused myself by saying, 'they will take his life anyway.' "

"Chester," she told him, "if there is anything you have not confessed, you must confess it before you go."

"I have confessed everything to God and to Rev. MacIlravy," he said, "isn't that enough?"

"No," Louisa said, "you have told the world you are innocent and if you are not you must say so."

"If my conscience tells me I am right, is that not enough?" he asked.

"Not if God's word says differently," she said.

But Chester admitted nothing more, despite Louisa's urging. She said later that this conversation marked the first time she had ever doubted that her son was innocent of killing Grace Brown.

After his parents left, Chester summoned MacIlravy and gave him letters and presents that were to be given to each member of the family after his execution. To Paul, he gave MacIlravy's book, *A Young Man's Questions* and a very long letter, full of brotherly advice from a disgraced older brother to a younger:

> We have the best mother in the world and should be
> very proud of her and should do all we can to help her
> and make her happy. I didn't, but I am now in a position

where I can see things much clearer than I did when I was careless and thoughtless. Make things as easy for her as you can and then, if I am released, we can be such comfort to her.

I don't want to lecture, but there are some things I hope you may avoid. Girls will always be your failing as they were mine. They will make too much of you and so you will be led to do things you would not otherwise do. Be very careful in this respect. In this matter, as in all others, never be satisfied with any but the best . . .

I know what it means to get into debt and so warn you from that as I would from drink and gambling. Keep clean morally. Don't allow impurity to get into your life. This is a very hard matter, but one you should watch because it will be your failing as it was mine if you are not careful. This is the cause of my whole trouble. Never act toward any girl or woman other than you would have some other man act toward your sister . . .

I have not been a saint by a good ways and so perhaps I shouldn't lecture . . . please forgive me and redeem the Gillette name . . .

Whenever you are tempted to do wrong, look at it (the picture of Grace Brown that he enclosed with the letter) and remember your sisters.

He closed with a Bible quotation, "For God so loved the world that he gave his only begotten Son that whosoever believeth in Him should not perish, but have everlasting life."

In his letter to his mother, Chester wrote a poem and a message, "I want you to feel, mother, that I am fully prepared to die and that we may meet again some day. Don't worry about me, as there will be no need for it."

With the note was this poem:

### GOOD BYE, GOD BLESS YOU

I love the words, perhaps because,
    When I was leaving mother,
Standing at last in solemn pause,
    We looked at one another;
And I - I saw in mother's eyes,
    The love she cannot tell me;

A love eternal to the skies,
    Whatever fate befell me.

She put her arms around my neck,
    And soothed the pain of leaving;
And though her heart was like to break
    She spoke no word of grieving.
She let no tear bedim her eye,
    For fear she might distress me;
But kissing me, she said goodbye,
    And asked our God to bless me.

Say not 'good night', but in some happier clime,
Bid me 'Good Morning'.
God be with you till we meet again.

To his father he wrote:

> . . . Go ahead as you have heretofore, silently but bravely
> and courageously. You can know my peace is made with
> God and so we shall meet again some day. This is for the
> best and is only for a short time at most. We will all be
> together some day. I have done all I could to make my
> peace with God. So will wait for you on the other side.

Hughes, meanwhile, had spent the whole day thinking about
the case, "soul-searching," was how his secretary put it. At
dinner time, after the Gillettes had left Chester for the last time,
he walked to his office and issued a formal statement:

> I reached the conclusion that there was no ground
> upon which I would be justified in interfering with the
> execution of the judgment of the court . . . Whatever his
> power, the governor has no right to grant reprieves unless
> he can assign good cause and if the administration of the
> law is to be respected, petitions made at the 11th hour
> must show merit. I find none in the present case.

The statement that Grace Brown had been an epileptic had
already been denied publicly by Dr. Crumb, her family doctor,
and Hughes must have known about that. The epilepsy version of
what happened, he said, was "wholly untenable" and it would
have been impossible for Chester not to have known about it, yet
he did not mention it in his testimony.

> If reason is to be our guide and the established facts
> are taken into consideration, there is no escape from the
> conclusion that a brutal murder was committed and that
> the conviction was just. After examining the evidence now
> presented, I find nothing in it which in any way can
> affect the conclusion, or which furnishes any justification
> for executive action.

When she received this news from Hazel back in the Salvation Army barracks where they were staying in Auburn, Louisa fainted and a doctor had to be called to revive her. For a time, the other members of the family thought her heart had failed.

When she recovered, she composed a telegram to Hughes. "Can you say before your God that you have no doubt of Chester's guilt? Please wire. If you cannot, then his blood will be upon your head." The telegram was given to Paul to take to the telegraph office, but it was never received in Albany. The reason was revealed years later by William O. Dapping, a young reporter for the *Auburn Citizen*, who had become friendly with the Gillette family since their return to Auburn. He intercepted the telegram and later convinced Louisa that it would have hurt Chester's case.

The news was brought to Chester by MacIlravy a few minutes later. Chester, in a last opportunity for nobility, denied Sanders' charges and defended Grace's good name. MacIlravy and prison chaplain Cordello Herrick stayed with Chester and, according to their later statements, he made some admission of guilt to them. It's not known exactly what he said, since both ministers refused to repeat it, but most likely it was a simple statement that he was guilty of causing Grace's death, rather than a full account of what happened that day at Big Moose.

At 10 p.m. Warden Benham and Hughes had a telephone conversation about Chester. The sources differ as to who initiated the call. According to Hughes' version, "the night before Gillette's execution, I called up the warden of Auburn prison where the condemned man was confined. I will never forget the sensation as long as I live. The warden told me Gillette had made a confession that afternoon. That night I went to bed and slept soundly. It was my first refreshing sleep for a long time."

According to newspaper reports, however, it was Benham who

made the call to set the governor's mind at rest. If Hughes did call the prison, it is interesting to speculate why. Did he intend to postpone the execution after all? Had he had a last minute change of heart? Hughes never explained what his intentions were.

Chester slept from 11:30 p.m. to 4 a.m., when he was awakened by the guards and given a new uniform to wear, made of gray material and with slits in the legs where the electrodes would be attached. When MacIlravy and Herrick returned, Chester asked for a piece of cake and it was quickly brought for him. The three said prayers until just before 6 a.m., when the guards returned to tell them that it was time.

Casting a farewell glance around his cell, he stepped out into the corridor. The three other prisoners that were then in the cells had had the fronts covered with white cloth so they could not see what was going on, but they were all awake and knew. Brasch, his only friend among them, called out "good luck" from behind his curtain. Herrick recited the 23rd Psalm as they walked the 30 feet to the large metal door at the end of the corridor. On the way, Chester handed MacIlravy a copy of his last statement, addressed to the men of the country, and his diary, in which he had made the last inscription only a few minutes before.

Outside the prison, dozens of people were waiting just outside the gates and many had waited there all night. The official witnesses had begun to arrive at 5:45 and were escorted to the warden's office. It was a cold, gray morning and few people were stirring in the town other than the people at the gates. Benham read the order for execution and the witnesses followed him out the back door, down the back steps and out into the courtyard leading to the execution chamber. They had sat down on the benches for only a few minutes when they heard the steps and the murmur of the Psalm being read from the other side of the metal door.

When the door was slid open they saw him come in with the two ministers and the two guards. The witnesses who had seen Chester before, like Klock and Dr. Crumb, thought he looked no different than he had in Herkimer, except that he was thinner and paler. He wore a black bow tie and black oxford shoes. He didn't falter in his steps. There was no hint of a frown and some thought there was a faint smile on his lips.

Even though he knew some of the witnesses, he didn't look at them at all, but kept his eyes glued to the floor. He looked briefly at the chair, but his expression did not change. He walked straight to the chair and, without any assistance, seated himself as easily as if he were sitting in an easy chair. Without being told, he placed his arms on the wooden arms of the chair.

The guards rolled up his left trouser cuff, to the end of the slit, and strapped the electrode to his calf. On the other side, a connection was made at his thigh through another slit. The straps were connected, and the head strap, which also acted as a blindfold, with its metal cap, was placed over his head. The witnesses could now see only his mouth and chin.

There was a painful silence after the electrodes had been connected. Everyone was watching Benham and the prisoner in the chair. It was 6:13 and Chester had been in the chamber only a little more than a minute. One of the guards was watching Chester's breathing, waiting for him to exhale. If he were caught with his lungs full, an executed man sometimes made a noise that the witnesses found unpleasant. When Chester exhaled, the guard nodded, Benham nodded and behind the partition, Davis sent a single bell note to the power room.

A large knife switch in the power room was closed at exactly 6:14:03 by the prison clock and 1,800 volts at 7½ amperes travelled through the wires to the chair.

The witnesses saw Chester's body lunge against the straps on his arms, legs and chest. The current was gradually reduced to 200 volts and then shut off at 6:15:06. The body fell back into the chair and the doctors put their stethoscopes to his chest. At 6:18, the doctor went over to say something to Benham, who announced "the man is dead." The witnesses filed out of the chamber and back to the office to fill out some forms.

"Thank God Chester is out of his misery," Klock said on his way out.

Dr. Crumb, who was scheduled to help with the autopsy a few minutes later, said, "I caught a glimpse of his eyes and there was a queer, strained look in them that I'd rather not see again. But the fellow had all his nerve with him. I never saw anything so easy as his death."

Outside the prison, the guards gave out the word to the crowd, which slowly began to disperse. Herrick and MacIlravy were mobbed by the press when they came out, but all they did was hand out copies of two pieces of paper.

The first was very short. All it said was, "Because our relationship with Chester Gillette was privileged we do not deem it wise to make a detailed statement and simply wish to say that no legal mistake was made in his electrocution."

Pressed about the rumors of a confession, MacIlravy would only say, "No written confession was made. The only written statements Gillette made were the inscriptions in the books, the last letters and his final statement."

This statement, given out at the same time, said:

> In the shadow of the valley of death it is my desire to do everything that would remove any doubt as to my having found Jesus Christ, the personal saviour and unfailing friend. My one regret at this time is that I have not given Him the pre-eminence in my life while I had the opportunity to work for Him. If I could only say some one thing that would draw young men to Him I would deem it the greatest privilege ever granted to me. But all I can say now is, 'I know in whom I have believed and am persuaded that He is able to keep that which I have committed unto him against that day.'
>
> If the young men of this country could only know the joy and pleasure of a Christian life, I know they would do all in their power to become earnest, active Christians and would strive to live as Christ would have them live.
>
> There is not one thing I have left undone which will bar me from facing my God, knowing that my sins are forgiven, for I have been free and frank in my talks with my spiritual adviser, and God knows where I stand.
>
> My task is done, the victory won,
> Chester E. Gillette

This statement, which is not at all like Chester's other writing, may have been written by MacIlravy and only signed by Chester. The original copy at Auburn prison shows that it was typed out and only the signature added. The most interesting fact is that although Chester is said to have confessed, the last statement makes no mention of a confession. The only hint is that he said nothing was "left undone."

The Gillette family was gathered in the upstairs room at the Salvation Army headquarters. They had stayed awake all night, praying together that some miracle would yet save Chester's life. Louisa held clasped to her heart the Bible that had been Chester's last gift to her. Frank sat with one arm around his wife and the other around his three remaining children, who knelt at his feet, their faces hidden. Each of the children held the books that Chester had given them.

Just before 6:30, Captain Robertson, the head of the local Salvation Army, entered the room and spoke only two words: "It's over." Louisa gave a sharp cry and fell forward in her husband's lap. No one else moved. There was no other sound and no motion for several minutes.

Later that morning the family went to Tallman's Funeral Home where the body had been taken. At first, the family did not want to view the body. During the autopsy, Chester's brain had been removed and sealed in a jar, which was given to Dr. E. Anthony Spitzka of Jefferson Medical College in Philadelphia, a specialist in dissecting the brains of criminals. Louisa, finally, agreed to examine the body, but warned the others to stay away. "It doesn't look like Chester at all," she said. "He doesn't have his old smile."

At 10:30, Louisa held a press conference, but, fearing she could not deal with the New York City press corps, called only two Auburn reporters who had helped her during her stay there: William O. Dapping of the *Auburn Citizen* and Victor T. Holland of the *Auburn Advertiser*. They met in the upstairs room of Robertson's house.

Dapping, who was to spend the rest of his life in Auburn and won a Pulitzer Prize in 1929, said this meeting with Louisa was one of the most emotional moments of his life. Louisa ordered the two reporters to kneel beside the bed while she knelt on the other side. Dapping listened while she prayed that Dapping would never be involved in a similar tragedy. Then, she told them that she was convinced that her son was guilty of the murder of Grace Brown:

Though it is very hard for me to feel Chester was
responsible for Grace Brown's death, yet it was the wish
expressed to him continually by me that if he was guilty I
wanted him to say so before the world and in that triumphant death I feel that God has answered my dearest
wish and prayer.

And I am also so thankful to know that he did not
strike Grace Brown, as described by the prosecution. A
full account will never be given out, but he did not strike
Grace Brown.

His spiritual advisers will give out no more than they
have already done, but I will say one thing: Chester did
not strike that poor girl. This is true. I know it is true
and I am thankful to God for it - whatever else can be
laid to his charge, he struck her no blow.

Louisa never explained, however, how she knew that Chester
had not struck Grace. Perhaps MacIlravy told her more than he
told anyone else, or perhaps it was only wishful thinking on her
part. No further details of the confession were ever given out, as
Louisa had said they would not be.

Within two years after the execution, both MacIlravy and Herrick had moved out of New York and, as far as is known, never
spoke about the case again.

Just before 2 p.m. the next day, March 31, a horse-drawn
hearse left the Tallman mortuary in Auburn and a few minutes
later a streetcar bearing a family dressed in black followed it two
miles outside the city to Soule Cemetery, on a tree-covered
hillside.

The burial had been kept secret to avoid sightseers. Besides
the members of the family, only MacIlravy and his assistant, Mr.
Hartman, were present. MacIlravy brought a large flowering
azalea that he placed on the grave.

Since the grave was never marked, it is impossible to tell exactly where the burial took place. The burial card at the cemetery
says only "unmarked grave" and gives no location. According to
Louisa's description, it was on an eastern-facing slope, which
would place it near the back of the cemetery, over the crest of a
hill. A local Auburn legend says he was buried under what is now
the paved road at the top of the hill.

The hymns sung at the burial had been selected by Chester before his death. They included "Abide With Me," "Joy Cometh in the Morning" and "Until He Comes." At the end they sang a secular song that had been a favorite of Louisa's, "A Little Boy Called Taps."

During the Bible readings, which had also been selected by Chester, Louisa dropped to her knees and even the grave diggers had to wipe their eyes as they listened to her prayers while the dirt was thrown in to cover the inexpensive oak coffin.

In the trolley on the way back to Auburn, Louisa said, "Chester was taken away from the world most unjustly when he might have been some use to the world. If this is right, I fail to understand it. I do not believe that there is one person out of a hundred who believes in his heart in such a process of the law."

As she was about to leave New York forever, two days later, Louisa told the ever-present reporters, "Now that the last blow has been struck, I am only too glad to retire from the public eye and try to find peace and solace in the society of my husband and my three living children and in safe and sure reliance upon the God who has helped us bear up under the affliction that has come to us."

Frank Gillette, usually content to let Louisa speak for him, added in his whisper of a voice, "Now that it is all over I suppose there will be something else to interest the public and hope we will not be harassed further regarding our troubles of the past two years."

Within a year the Gillettes had moved to Houston, Texas, where no one knew about their connection to the famous murder case and they were able to live in peace.

Many in Central New York recalled the last time they saw one of the Gillettes, on April Fool's Day, the day after Chester was buried. Frank Gillette, the bearded, sickly man who had travelled 2,000 miles and worked feverishly to save his son, took the train from Auburn to Little Falls to call at District Attorney Rush Lewis's office for Chester's belongings.

They had been held in the district attorney's office in case they were needed as evidence in a new trial. Now, they had served their purpose and were no longer of any use to the people of Herkimer County. They were packed into the suitcase and handed to the father.

On his way back to the Little Falls train station, a crowd gathered to take one last look at the father of the person whose name had become so familiar to all of them. The last sight they had of him was a man in a black suit, walking slowly with a slight limp and carrying the suitcase with the tell-tale initials: C.E.G.

# PART TWO

## *The Legends*

CHAPTER TEN

# Purple Prose
# and
# Yellow Journalism

The 75 years of confusion about what really happened to Grace Brown and Chester Gillette began at nearly the same time their names were brought to the public's attention in the first newspaper articles of July, 1906. Part of the misconceptions and wrong information was the result of the normal way the facts came out in a criminal case, a little at a time with some of it in error.

But besides these routine mistakes of fact, there was a deliberate attempt by some of the jounalists covering the arrest and especially the trial to play the case for all it was worth. Some of the local journalists complained that the out-of-town reporters didn't even go to the trial at all but wrote their articles from the bar of the Palmer House.

Moreover, many of the facts about Chester's life were never included in any of the millions of words written about the case from 1906 to 1908. Little was known about his life before he came to Cortland and newspaper reporters seem to have made no effort, as they would do today, to ferret out every last detail of his life to show what circumstances led up to the crime he either did or did not commit. Interviews with his former friends, teachers and employers, for example, were nearly nonexistent.

Even simple errors of fact, like the statement that he had attended Oberlin College and not Oberlin Academy, were never corrected during his lifetime. None of his former friends ever seems to have stepped forward to tell what Chester was like during his formative years.

As a result, public opinion was formed based on a very few facts of his recent history: that he had come from a poor, but fundamentally religious family and had been abandoned at an early age, that he had been given a job in his rich uncle's factory and that he had seduced a fellow worker and taken her to the Adirondacks to do away with her.

Instead of digging out the facts, the national press was more interested in weaving fictional tales of passionate love triangles, suicide attempts, escape attempts, assassination plots, lynch mobs and plots to conceal evidence. Unfortunately for those interested in the case later, including its most famous chronicler, Theodore Dreiser, the fictions were accepted as fact.

The first newspaper report of the case was printed in the *Utica Daily Press* on Friday morning, July 13, the day after the body was found. Under the headline, "Body of Woman Recovered," it described the little that was known and said the death was probably the result of an accident. The search was continuing for "Carl Grahm," but there were "rumors of violence," helped by the fact that no Carl Grahm could be found in Albany.

But it was that evening's papers that first captured the public's attention with the first hint that an unusual crime had been committed. The headline over C. Floyd Hopkins' story in the *Utica Observer* was "The Big Moose Tragedy." From this point onward, the word "tragedy" was forever linked with the case. The next day's *Daily Press* used almost the same headline, "Big Moose Tragedy," to describe the latest developments. The reporter, William E. Wolcott, said there were still some doubts, not shared by Hopkins, that a crime had been committed. "Few give credence to the foul play theory," he wrote. "Most people believe the body of the man (now known to be Gillette) will be found."

After Chester's arrest, however, most newspapers abandoned

any thought that he might be innocent. Ward's statements after the arrest that Chester was "a degenerate" who deliberately knocked Grace unconscious and threw her overboard were given wide publicity. By this time, the national wire services and big city newspapers were reporting the case and it made the front page of more sensational newspapers. But at this point, the national press took little real interest in the case.

By Wednesday, July 18, a week after the murder, enough information was known for the local reporters to begin to piece together what had happened. Wolcott of the *Press* called it, "one of the most carefully planned and cunningly carried out schemes in the recent annals of crime." The only mistake Chester made, he said, was not jumping into the lake when he tipped the boat over so that his clothes would have been wet. If Chester had gone for help, he said, no one would have suspected a crime and he would have gotten away free.

"There has been during this spring and summer an exceptionally large number of stories in the papers of accidental drownings in northern lakes," Hopkins wrote, "all of which have blown over with little comment and the authorities are justified in believing that Gillette got the idea from these that it would be an easy and safe way to dispose of the intended victim."

The scene of the crime seemed to have been carefully chosen, he said, as was the decision to use Grace's real name but a false one for Chester at the Glenmore.

"If it had not been for the bruised condition of the girl's face," he wrote, "even then but little might have been thought of the matter. Right up to the time of his capture, Gillette moved shrewdly in all he did," but when he was arrested he fell apart and could not come up with a credible story.

The day before, Hopkins had written a similar piece, concluding that, "Those who will attempt any explanation say that he had tired of the girl and felt that if he married her he would lose the place which he had made in society in this city (Cortland). Vain from the attentions which he had received from others with good prospects before him in business life, and fearing exposure when Miss Brown should return, he decided to take her on a trip to the Adirondacks and make away with her."

But six days later, a *Utica Herald Dispatch* reporter, probably either George H. Waldron or George J. Winslow, wrote an article based on a different premise: that Chester Gillette may not have been guilty of murder at all.

The article, under the headline, "Did Brown Girl Jump in the Lake? Ended Life Rather Than Face Shame," contains all the main points used later in Chester's defense. Mills, in fact, may have been the source of some of the information, since he is mentioned prominently in the article. He had visited Chester the morning before the article was published:

> Despite the almost impregnable chain of evidence that District Attorney Ward and members of the Sheriff's office have forged about Gillette, it is today established by this paper that a widely divergent opinion of the tragedy is held by the natives in the northern wilderness and a largely proportionate majority hold to the accidental drowning theory.

The most interesting part of the story concerns an unidentified contractor from Lake Placid, who was never found and never testified, who overheard Chester tell Grace that he planned to leave her and Grace implored him not to leave until he had taken her for a ride on the lake. All of Grace's actions, the article said, are evidence of a girl desperately in love with a man who did not return her affections:

> It is believed that while in the boat, she pleaded to his manhood, but being unmovable, she jumped to her watery grave, and Gillette, thinking his story of the accident would never be believed by the authorities, rowed to shore and after taking out his effects, which he had taken with him, after determining to leave her, he overturned the boat and sent it adrift. They have no trouble accounting for the bruise on the side of her head, claiming that to have been inflicted by the grappling hooks, which were used to bring the body to the surface of the water . . .

The article concluded by saying that there was nothing in Chester's background that gave any indication that he was capable of cold-blooded murder.

Depending on which newspaper one read, therefore, readers were faced with conflicting accounts of what happened at Big Moose and even different analyses of what the "Adirondack woodsmen" thought had happened.

The Sunday after the *Herald Dispatch* article, another article, the first which resulted from any extensive investigation, was published in the *Syracuse Herald* by Edith Cornwall.

Cornwall, whose real name was Mary L. Parsons, was a member of the "sob sisters" school of journalism. At a time when women journalists were a novelty, the sob sisters made a specialty out of tear-jerking accounts that were grouped together under the heading of "purple prose." Her stories were widely read for their emotional impact, but she was known to often play fast and loose with the facts. A Vassar graduate, she often wore outrageous hats and was often sloppy about her personal appearance.

She was, however, the only reporter known to have actually visited Cortland and South Otselic and talked to the factory workers and friends who knew Grace and Chester. She talked with the Brown family in their home and later went to DeRuyter. Since South Otselic was not on a rail line, it was not an easy place for a reporter to visit.

Because of her reputation for inaccuracy, it is difficult to tell how much of her article is factual and how much of it was either made up or elaborated to the point of inaccuracy. While the description of Grace and Chester's relationship in Cortland meshes perfectly with the information that came out later in the letters (which had not yet been made public), she made the fairly basic error of getting all but two of Grace's sisters' names wrong.

It is from Cornwall's article that some of the earliest legends of the case have their origin. She is the first to have reported the opal ring story of how Chester and Grace met and the legend that Grace told one of her sisters that she thought it would be romantic to commit suicide.

"In all the annals of crime and misfortune," she wrote, "it is hard to believe that there has ever been recorded a more tragic or more cruel fate than that which befell Grace Brown . . ." Although the story had much in common with other stories, she said, there were elements "that lift it above the category of the commonplace and place it in the ranks of psychological phenomenon."

Cornwall painted a picture of Grace as an innocent country girl who moved to the city and met the ambitious young Chester. According to her version, Grace made little secret of the fact that she planned to marry Chester. Cornwall said Grace told both her mother and Maude Crumb that she was going away to get married. Neither of them ever said anything to anyone else that would confirm that. In fact, Ward never produced any witness at the trial who said Grace planned to marry Chester.

But Cornwall also uncovered facts that would have helped the defense. Grace, while she was home, had told her family and friends that she had "presentiments" that she would die soon, a statement found more clearly in the letters that Cornwall had not seen at this point.

In Cortland, she said, everyone she talked to, except Chester's close friends, were convinced he was a murderer.

Cornwall's article and others like it presented a problem for the Cortland newspapers. With the local story of the century breaking all around them, they found that so many socially prominent people were involved in the case that there was a lot of pressure not to write about it. The *Cortland Standard* took a compromise course. It used the wire service reports of the case as they appeared, but declined to put any of its own reporters on the story. There were no interviews with the factory workers or with Gillette's relatives and therefore an important source of information was lost.

For the next three months the newspapers reported the day-to-day events of the case from Herkimer. There were detailed reports of how Chester slept, what he ate and the efforts to obtain lawyers to defend him. Gradually, news about him began to appear less frequently until the start of the trial.

In 1906, murder trials, especially those involving a relationship between a man and a woman, were a major source of sensational copy for the metropolitan newspapers that specialized in "yellow journalism." In the frantic circulation wars that characterized the period, a sensational headline, some drawings or photographs, could make the difference between success and failure for newspapers whose sales depended on someone buying them from a boy on the street or from a newsstand. Newspapers filled much of the need that is today filled by television. Entertainment came first and accurate information took a back seat.

The Gillette case was just the kind of story these newspapers were looking for and during the second week of November, at least two dozen reporters, their copy runners, telegraph operators, photographers and artists descended on Herkimer. None of the Herkimer officials seemed to have been in any way prepared to deal with the onslaught. They certainly had no experience with this kind of thing, as officials in large cities had. Suddenly the sheriff, the district attorney, the jailors and the court officials became national celebrities. Their names, pictures and their every word soon appeared in the New York City papers, which were widely read in the Utica-Herkimer area.

The local officials were used to dealing with members of the local press. If a mistake was made in reporting, they could call the editor and complain. In effect, they had a certain control over what was written so that nothing got too out of line. But with the New York City reporters and the wire service writers, they had no way of checking what was written. When mistakes were made and deliberate misrepresentations were printed, they got angry but didn't know what to do.

For the New York City press corps, being sent to Herkimer was similar to being sent to Siberia. It offered little in the way of entertainment during the evenings. Most of the out-of-town journalists lived in the Palmer House and spent much of their time in the Palmer House bar. According to one account given later by one of them, one of the reporters took over for the bartender each night and dispensed drinks for his friends.

They were, however, under constant pressure from their editors to produce the kind of sensational copy each day that would justify the expense of sending and keeping them there. On some days this was no problem, since the reading of the love letters and Chester's testimony on the stand made terrific copy just as it came from the courtroom. But on other days there was only the routine testimony that would not make their editors happy.

So the reporters made up stories.

This was an accepted practice in 1906 in the yellow journals and was encouraged by the editors, who were under pressure from publishers to produce paper-selling sensations. Few of these stories seem to have been made up out of whole cloth. Usually they were based on some small details that changed the entire episode and made it much more sensational than it was. Many of these stories seem to have been made up in the bar room and not in the courtroom at all.

One article described a secret lover who wrote passionate letters to Chester each day and always ended by telling him how much she loved him. When a local reporter checked out this story, he found that the letters were from Lucille, Chester's sister.

The out-of-town reporters insisted on reporting that there were mobs outside the courtroom seeking to lynch Chester. While it was true that there were crowds trying to get in, there was never any attempt made at lynching. These reports seem to have had their origin in some crank letters Chester received saying that a group of people wanted to lynch him.

On one slow evening, several reporters borrowed some local clothing and went up to the jail, where they banged on the door and shouted, "We want to lynch Gillette." When they were satisfied that they had been heard, they changed back to their regular clothing, went back to the jail and inquired if it was true that a group of people had been there that evening talking about lynching. The next day, the poor jailor found himself quoted as confirming that a lynch mob had surrounded the jail and tried to get in.

The photographers were also under pressure to come up with photos of the principal characters. They succeeded to a great extent in capturing the witnesses as they went into the courtroom. At first, they purchased a photo of Chester and later caught him when he didn't have a newspaper or his hand in front of his face.

Getting a photo of Grace Brown posed a more difficult problem. There were several existing photos and drawings of her, but these had all been taken and used by the local newspapers and by Ward for use in the trial. A wire service photographer, under pressure to come up with a photo of Grace when none was available, talked a Herkimer drug store clerk into going outside with him where he snapped her picture. Thousands of people around the country thought that she was Grace Brown and even years later, the photo, which looks nothing like Grace, shows up in articles about the case and has led to years of confusion.

The reporters also encouraged local people to tell fantastic stories in order to get their names in the papers. A Hannah Monahan of Utica, for example, who had been employed at the Glenmore, described taking a boat carpet out of the boat that Grace and Chester had used. When she tried to wash it, she said, blood ran out of it. The Glenmore people denied it the next day, but the newspaper report was never corrected.

While many of these stories seemed harmless because the jury was prevented from reading them, they seriously poisoned public opinion against Chester, and seriously damaged the reputations of innocent people. Harriet Benedict seems never to have fully recovered from the mass of stories written about her alleged relationship with Chester.

Many of the most outrageous stories were printed on Mondays, and it is easy to see why. The reporters followed the practice of writing stories for the day they were published and then followed them up with additional details from later in the day for the next day's morning editions. But the late news from the Saturday sessions was printed in the Sunday paper. That left nothing to write for the Monday morning paper and the reporters were under pressure to come up with something new.

Some of these Monday stories backed the reporters into a corner. For example, when one paper reported that on the next day Chester and the entire court were to adjourn to the Mohawk River where Chester would get into the boat and re-enact the crime for the jury, the story was so good that the editor demanded the full story the next day. The river demonstration never took place, of course, so the reporter had to make it all up.

All of this hoopla was putting tremendous pressure on the reporters from the local newspapers who were attempting to write an accurate account of the trial. Their editors, who read the New York City newspapers every day, were furious when their reporters seemed to be missing the sensational developments they had seen in the *New York Journal* and the *New York World*. When the local reporters insisted that the events never occurred, they were forced to go to the Herkimer officials and get formal denials. Years later, these denials are invaluable in determining what did and what did not happen.

Quite a bit of resentment seems to have developed between the local and out-of-town reporters because of the process of getting the denials. It took quite a bit of time the local reporters could have been using to uncover their own stories. The readers in New York City and other cities, of course, never read the denials, and so got a very different impression of what was going on in Herkimer than did readers in Herkimer, Utica and Syracuse.

Here are some examples of the denials:

*Utica Herald Dispatch*, November 21:

Sheriff J.M. Richard this morning denied strenuously that there was cause for the slightest apprehension in his department or that any existed in the matter of pro-secuting Gillette. He was annoyed at a report he had read in a morning paper in this connection. Sheriff Richard laughed at the idea that any trouble was anticipated from the crowd that watched Gillette or from any feeling against the prisoner. The report to which the sheriff referred was to the effect that thirty or forty woodsmen and railroad men laid plans for action in case of a disagreement of the jury and that some of the hot heads were in favor of "rushing" the prisoner on his way to the courthouse today. That the officials had been notified and that the militia would be called out if the action grows worse was too silly, he said, to refute.

*Utica Herald Dispatch*, December 5:

The number of stories floating around Herkimer today were not less numerous than the "dope tales" which the representatives of the metropolitan journals in attendance at the trial have delighted in sending out during the past several weeks on the slightest provocation. For instance, this forenoon a tale recounting an alleged suicide attempt by Gillette a couple of evenings ago was doled out to those in a receptive mood. It appears that in Gillette's cell in the county jail there is a gas attachment, but the cock which regulates the flow of gas is outside the cell and beyond the prisoner's reach. The suicide story recounted how Gillette, by careful manipulation, had partially turned on the gas cock as he passed through the corridor to his cell the other night and that later in the

evening, when the deputy sheriff visited the prisoner, he
found the atmosphere in the latter's cell heavy with gas
. . . The jail authorities laugh at it and it is here repeated
only as an illustration of the methods employed by the
New York newspaper representatives to make sensational
yarns out of absolute falsehoods.

Nearly every day throughout the trial, the local newspapers
had to run such items, but eventually a story appeared that the
reporters could find no one to deny, the story that Chester had
confessed.

This story first appeared in the *New York World* and the *New
York Journal* on December 6, two days after Chester was convicted. Although the stories varied on details, they said that a few
days earlier, Chester, in speaking with Mills, had told an entirely
new story about what happened on the lake that day. For the first
time, according to the story, he admitted that he struck Grace
Brown. The conversation, the story said, had been overheard by
the jailors and reported to the sheriff.

The *Journal* went so far as to report what it said were Chester's
own words: "She stood up and came from her end of the boat
toward me and was crying and she said she was discouraged and
wanted to end it all. I took my tennis racket out of the straps of
my suitcase and struck her twice. She fell full length backward,
her head striking the seat. Then I dumped her overboard." Then
Mills is reported to have said, "You wretch, why didn't you tell
me this before?"

But according to the *World* version, Chester struck her once in
the boat and once again when she was in the water and came to
the surface. Both these articles appeared under the largest possible headlines, the *Journal's* under, "I Did Kill Grace Brown
- Gillette's Confession."

At first, all of this was treated as just another fiction, but it
became something else when Ward refused to deny it. All he
would say was, "You had better ask Sheriff Richard." But
Richard was out of town, as were Mills and Thomas, so there was
no one to immediately deny the story. The local papers decided
that they had to use the story, but included it under the careful
headline, "District Attorney Ward does not deny Gillette's
Confession."

According to the reports from the big city papers, Ward had attempted to get the two guards who heard the confession to testify at the trial, but Devendorf had told him that the evidence was inadmissible. A few days later, Mills denied that Chester had ever said anything of the kind. Richard, when he returned, declined to speak about the matter.

The best evidence that Ward believed that the incident took place, and the possible inspiration of the newspaper stories, was a single question during his cross-examination of Chester:

"Didn't you say to them (Mills and Thomas) the other night in the jail that you pushed the boat in shore, she came back by you and then you struck her?" Ward asked.

"No, sir," Chester said.

"Did you tell them that you struck her?"

"No sir."

"Night before last?"

"No sir, I never told them that."

Ward never mentioned the confession again after that, but it was, of course, a part of the public discussion of the trial and the matter was never cleared up. It could have been that Ward's question stirred the imaginations of the reporters and that they made up the rest at the Palmer House bar. Ward, since he had not heard the report himself, saw no reason to deny the report, just in case it proved true.

Granville S. Ingraham, the only member of the sheriff's department to write down his memoirs of the case, had no doubts that the confession story was true. He wrote, "After the verdict was rendered the public learned for the first time of the confession Gillette had made in his cell, that he had hit the girl in the head with a tennis racket as she came up beside the boat . . . Gillette had told his counsel only of suicide before that, now he told of blows struck. And Senator Mills' heart was not in his work."

But if there was a real confession, the people who actually heard it never told the full story, despite what must have been tremendous pressure from both the prosecution and the press. Most likely, the guards heard only part of what was said and made up the rest to make an interesting story and the reporters took it from there. It remains another of the unsolved mysteries.

*Sensational headlines during the trial from the* New York Journal.

Syracuse Post Standard *front page the day of the verdict.*

*Illustration from the* Utica Saturday Globe *showing how outside journalists portrayed Herkimer.*

*The reporters covering the trial filing their stories.*

After Chester's execution, the *Journal* printed an entirely different version of the old confession story, this one supposedly heard second-hand from Klock, who immediately denied that he had ever heard Chester make a confession. This version also quotes Chester directly as having said he hit Grace with his fist, then grabbed her legs and threw her overboard. When she came to the surface he hit her with the tennis racket.

The close of the trial brought an opportunity for the New York writers to unleash their flowing pens in a final summation of the case. For many of the reporters it was a time to write about their own feelings during the two weeks that they had watched the story unfold. These articles are important because they were certainly read by Theodore Dreiser and others who were interested in the case and helped to put the whole incident into perspective.

Charles Sommerville of the *Journal*, for example, wrote his summation published December 7 under the headline, "Rural Tragedy Made Famous By Love Letters," and it is a good example of the kind of writing that was used:

> Though the trial is done and there remains only the last incident when furtive-eyed Chester Gillette will go shambling with a corpse-white face to his shameful death in the Auburn electric chair, yet the tragedy of Grace Brown cannot die out of public interest for a long, long time.
>
> It has been altogether too wonderful - this tragedy of the Adirondacks - the story of a factory girl, an untaught, blue-eyed, child-woman of the hills who wrote as pure an epic of love and grief as ever was penned; who with all her sweet wisdom, yet laid her goodness, her whole tender, poetic, fine little self, body and soul, at the feet of a creature foul, brutal, monstrously cruel.
>
> Her god was in truth a devil but this wonderful little woman only found this out in the last few terrified minutes of her life. Trustingly she went with him out on Big Moose Lake. The boat purled gently through the waters, her great blue eyes smiled on him in love and confidence. She had suffered weeks of torture; weeks filled with frightened doubt that he would not come for her; weeks filled with an aching fear that in the end she would have to bury her face on her mother's bosom while

her lips staunched a secret of stinging shame: a shame
that all - her mother, her father, her sister, her brother
- would have to share with her . . .

The red summer sun fell back of the pines . . . And
she said nothing. She was contented. The love and trust
were shining full in her blue eyes.

Love and trust flew out of them. Wild fear flared in
them. Her dear dream was broken by the sudden sight of
a creature crawling toward her which she had never seen
before: a fiend with livid face and blue-thick lips with
little savagely glaring eyes.

She stammered out a few quick, frightened inquiries.
And then:

Chester! Chester!

He killed her. He struck her soft, gentle lips, her blue
eyes; he pounded the tennis racket that he used as a
weapon upon the thick hair that waved above a girlish
cheek.

Her head fell forward on the center seat of the boat,
thumping as it struck. She was still. As one might
dispose of a cat for whom one had no home, he dumped
her body into the lake . . .

And for a time the tragedy of Grace Brown and all that
has gone to make it so astounding remained hidden, save
as the men in the mountains talked of it, and a big,
youthful, tireless, rural district attorney placed himself
in the possession of as amazingly complete a case of
circumstantial evidence as has ever been uncovered; and,
what is more, found himself in the possession of a packet
of letters, stained by a wonderful girl's tears, soiled and
crumpled by the careless handling of a witless brute who
received them, a packet of letters whose contents have
now reached human eyes in half the world at least, and
have made those eyes shine with tears.

Way up where the Mohawk trails down to meet the
Hudson in the city of Herkimer, N.Y., Grace Brown's
love letters to Chester Gillette were read in open court
by the broad-shouldered, young district attorney, who
frankly wept as he read them.

Nobody for an instant suspected him of theatricalism.
And for a very good reason. The lips of every other man
and woman in the courtroom were quivering too, and the

lights in the courtroom danced in a haze in their sight.

Reporters, whose business it is to see first and feel afterward when they write, suddenly grinned in sickly fashion at one another, in acknowledgement of their unprofessional tears and the still more unprofessional conduct which consisted in having forgotten to make notes, because they had been utterly lost in the spell of the sweet simplicity, the straight, quaint grace of the written language of Grace Brown; the lovable touches of humor; the clean, high nature of her misplaced love; her gentle sorrow; her brave little plans for the future; her poignant grief at going away from her mother, her father, her sisters, the old home; her exquisite sentiment of regret at being called upon to desert the precious nooks and corners of the farm and all its childhood memories - all these things were in that packet of the letters of a factory girl.

Everywhere the wires carried the contents of that packet of letters. Editors threw out columns of other news in order that those letters should be fully read and known. Foreign correspondents, regardless of cable bills, wired the factory girl's letters to journals over the capitals of Europe.

The poor little tragedy of the foothills of the Adirondacks was suddenly heightened to a tragedy of world-wide fame because of the beauty, dignity and sweetness of the love letters of a poor farmer's child.

I have a correction to make. There was one person in the courtroom at Herkimer into whose eyes no tears came. It was Chester Gillette. He had read all those letters before. They had not affected him to one tender thought, to one moment of remorse, to one moment of honorable resolution. They had not stirred in his heart one pulse of pity.

They had whipped him into black anger against the girl. They moved him only to shut her tender mouth forever, they moved him to lure her out upon a lonely lake and batter murderously at the pretty head in which were formed such inately noble thoughts and sentiments.

From the first day he came into court with a half smirk and a glint in his evil little eyes toward girls in the courtroom whom he recognized as choices for his animal

fancy - a fancy that had, however, been kept in bounds
because these girls were of influential families, from
whom there would fall on him swift revenge for any
wrong he might commit against these daughters . . .

Gillette never loved anybody except Gillette. The
primitive motive of self is all that he ever understood. In
his cell after the day that he heard Grace Brown's letters
read, after days when he had been held up to contumely
in court, and jeered and cursed at in rage by the
populace as he made his way back from the courthouse to
the jail - he showed no sign that he cared at all. The only
time that a tear ever flushed his eye was when his counsel
described the horrors of the death chair, in pleading with
the jury not to send him there . . .

He always slept serenely. No hour is ever marred with
any lively vision of a summer evening in a lonely nook on
Moose Lake - of a girl's blood-stained face, of blue eyes
blinded by blows into a state of fright and agony. No
moan of remorse has ever come from his cot in the hours
of the night.

It is out of such prose that legends are made. Right and wrong
became much easier to distinguish than they had been in real
life. Grace Brown was all good and Chester was a monster.

But other reporters who covered the trial later said they were
not so sure that justice had been done in the Herkimer Courthouse during those weeks. Marlen Pew, a wire service reporter
who covered the trial and went on to a distinguished career in
journalism that included time as a Pulitzer Prize judge had this
to say about the trial in an article he wrote in 1931:

. . . The mystery in the death of Billy Brown was not
cleared by the conviction of young Gillette, nor his death
in the electric chair . . . I talked with the boy, fairly
candidly, and with the prosecutor and defense counsel,
scores of neighbors, many of the witnesses, and could
never decide in my own mind whether Gillette killed Billy
by striking her a blow on the head or face . . . or whether
he deliberately upset the boat and swam to shore while
she, unable to swim, sank beneath the surface, or
whether the wretched girl, in a frenzy because Gillette did
not yield to her pleading to make her his lawful wife and

cover her shame, had despairingly thrown herself overboard, as he claimed in his defense.

. . . Many persons who followed the case were left in
doubt by the admitted fact that Billy Brown also had a
suicide motive, and had actually discussed self-
destruction.

The end of the trial also enabled local reporters to unleash
their animosity towards the New York press. This took the form
of several editorials in which the many fictions were recalled and
chastised.

The most stinging of these was published in the *Utica Saturday
Globe* in an article headlined, "The Modern Munchausens," a
reference to a legendary German baron, Hieronymous Karl
Friedrich von Munchhausen, who spun fantastic and exaggerated stories about his experiences as a cavalry officer:

The Gillette trial furnished a splendid illustration of
the contrast that exists between legitimate journalism and
the faking sensationalism which brings disrepute to
printer's ink. The highest examples of newspaper decency
and accuracy were the reports of the Utica papers; the
worst exhibitions of indelicacy and mendacity were the
columns which the New York newspaper market was
flooded . . .

There was absolutely no excuse for the invented
sensationalism of this trial. The legitimate features
furnished enough dramatic and spectacle to satisfy a
normal editor . . .

The pity is the fruit of this investment was not all
sound. The rottenness and unreliability of metropolitan
journalism was thoroughly exposed at this trial. Some of
the reporters, male and female, who came from New
York taxed their ingenuity severely to produce 'stuff'
which would make 'special editions' sell . . . We were
asked to believe that the space between the Palmer House
and Court House was nightly patrolled by an armed band
of flannel-shirted woodsmen from the Adirondacks whose
ardor was so hot that they needed no overcoats to keep
from suffering, and who were waiting for the first
favorable opportunity to put a bullet into Gillette. Yet

four times a day Gillette walked back and forth between
Court House and jail and if anyone wished to do him
injury there was plenty of chance for it.

The article, which was accompanied by a cartoon showing a
whimsical group of backwoods hayseeds carrying guns and pitch-
forks out to lynch Gillette, then went on to expose some of the
specific articles that had been written.

The person who was most injured by all the stories of anarchy
in Herkimer County was Judge Devendorf. Because he was in the
middle of an important trial, he felt he could make no public
statements about the newspaper stories, despite the fact that he
was receiving letters from throughout the country criticizing him
for letting his courtroom be turned into a circus. A Buffalo paper
even went so far as to call for him to be removed from the bench.
After the trial was over, however, Devendorf felt free to express
his feelings.

On December 11, he told a reporter for the *Utica Daily Press*:

This was my first experience with such things. The
stories sent out of Herkimer during the Gillette trial were
outrages to public decency. I could relate a half dozen or
perhaps a dozen stories that had no truth to them whatsoever.

For instance, the publication of a picture of an armed
guard holding the crowd back, representing that the
militia had been called out, and that the fire department
had been called upon to help, and that Gillette tried to
escape and a number of other stories.

If the people who read newspapers demand such
stories, why don't they write them without any pretense to
their being true? Why don't they have the president
assassinated every day? And the governor assassinated?

Later that same day, Devendorf, reading yet another article
from New York complaining of the hoardes of people who had
stood in the way of justice in Herkimer, decided he would do
something about it. He called Ward to his office and showed him
the article. Before the day was out, subpoenas had been issued
for the publisher and editor of the paper and the famous author
of the article.

The paper was the *New York Sunday Telegraph*, a paper aimed at the upper class which dealt mainly with sports. The publisher was H. N. Cary and the editor was William E. Lewis. But it was the author of the article who attracted all the attention. His name was William Barclay Masterson, better known as "Bat" Masterson.

Masterson had become a living legend following the stories of his adventures as an Indian hunter, army scout and deputy marshal of Dodge City, Kansas. In 1902, however, he had moved to New York, following a love of boxing, to become a sports writer. In 1905, President Theodore Roosevelt had named him a federal deputy marshal. So it was not just another reporter who Devendorf was going after.

Masterson's article, spread out over two columns on the front page, was really a kind of editorial comment on the trial under the headline "New Style of Lynch Law in Northern New York, Mob Compels Jury to its Work in Gillette Case, Conviction Forced by Savage Threats of Herkimer County Bushmen." It was largely a rehash of things that had been written in other papers. Since it is very unlikely that Masterson attended the trial itself, his writing must have been based on information from other papers, including the Hearst papers.

The indictment of the three newspapermen included 17 specific charges, most of them dealing with errors of fact in the article and charging them with criminal contempt of court. Masterson had called the trial "a flagrant travesty of justice" and an "inexcusable insult to the intelligence and civilization of the state of New York" with "the entire proceedings subversive of law and order and a disgraceful mockery of justice."

Deputy Granville S. Ingraham, who had helped arrest Chester the summer before, took the train to New York to serve the papers. All three of the defendants were taken to the Court of General Sessions and had to find a bail bondsman to keep from spending a night in the Tombs prison. While waiting for the bondsman, Masterson, sitting in a roped off area of the courtroom, was interviewed by a reporter for the *New York Sun*.

"I've been through a great deal out in the West," he said. "Lived in Dodge City when it was the toughest town on the cattle trail, ran a vaudeville house, enlisted as a scout under General

Miles against the Comanches. And here in my sober 52nd year I get into trouble - for writing something in a newspaper. If that isn't a funny trick of fate, I don't want to know of one."

A bail bondsman secured Masterson's $500 bail and he was released. Lewis, however, failed to see the humor in it. Since the article was printed after the trial was over, he said there were no grounds for contempt.

"If it is contempt of court to print such an article after a trial is ended, when it can have no influence on the verdict of the jury, I want to know it," he said. "The *Morning Telegraph* did not use its columns in an endeavor to convict Gillette, as some newspapers did . . . We propose making a test case of this and settling the matter once and for all."

Lewis hired Clarence J. Shearn, a New York lawyer and advisor to Hearst, and made preparations for a First Amendment fight. Shearn came to Herkimer the next day and talked with Mills, apparently about seeking help with the defense. But Mills, who disliked newspapermen, declined to help.

The case opened on Monday, December 17. Masterson, Cary and Shearn were in the same courtroom where Chester had been tried, but Lewis was ill and remained in New York. If he had been there, the case might have been fought out to the bitter end. At 3 p.m. Devendorf opened the trial and granted Shearn more time to prepare his case.

The next afternoon, at 1:30, Devendorf sentenced the two journalists and Lewis in absentia to pay a $50 fine each in exchange for their pleas of guilty to the contempt charges. A plea bargaining had been arranged. Shearn admitted outside the courtroom that there had been inaccuracies in the *Telegraph* article, but said they were published without any attempt to commit contempt of court. Devendorf said the fines were levied as a notice to journalists that they should not repeat the same mistakes. Shearns, Masterson and Cary returned to New York on the 2:11 train and as far as is known never set foot in Herkimer again.

Soon afterward, Devendorf got his wish. With Chester in jail in Auburn there was little left for the big city papers to report. They all but ignored Louisa's lectures on behalf of her son, leaving the coverage to local papers. Chester's sisters were frequently chased in Auburn when they went to visit him, but for most people, Gillette was forgotten until March 1908, when the last-minute appeal brought the case back into the front page headlines once again. After his execution, the coverage stopped abruptly. In the following years, only the local newspapers revived the story. Letters written to friends by Louisa were published in the newspapers and whenever a juror or witness in the case died, his connection with the case was listed prominently in his obituary, often in the headline.

But if the newspapers had given up on the story, the legend weavers of the Adirondacks were just getting started. The case seemed to have struck a nerve in the public consciousness that was too strong to leave alone.

Among the earliest versions of the legend was a folk song, the author of which is unknown. But from internal evidence it appears to have been written after Chester's arrival at Auburn, but before his execution, since he is alive in the song. There are many different versions of the song. The one here was collected by Hugh Norton in the late 1930s from Frank Van Vranken of Benson, New York:

## "THE BALLAD OF GRACE BROWN AND CHESTER GILLETTE"

> The dreams of the happy is finished;
> The scores are brought in at last;
> A jury has brought in its verdict;
> The sentence on Gillette is passed.
>
> Two mothers are weeping and praying;
> One praying that justice be done.
> The other one asking for mercy,
> Asking God to save her dear son.
>
> All eyes are turned on the drama,
> A watching the press night and day,
> A reading those sweet, pleading letters,
> Wondering what Gillette would say.
>
> He is now in state's Auburn dark prison,
> Where he soon will give up his young life;
> Which might have been filled with sweet sunshine,
> Had he taken Grace Brown for his wife.

But Cupid was too strong for Gillette,
It was playing too strong with his heart,
For the one that had loved him so dearly,
Yet from her he wanted to part.

T'was on a hot sultry day in the summer,
When the flowers were all aglow,
They started out on their vacation;
For the lakes and the mountains to roam.

Did she think when she gathered those flowers,
That grew on the shores of the lake,
That the hand that plucked those sweet lilies,
Her own sweet life they would take?

They were seen on the clear crystal waters,
Of the beautiful Big Moose Lake,
And nobody thought he'd be guilty,
Of the life of that poor girl to take.

It happened along in the evening,
Just at the close of the day,
With the one that had loved him so dearly,
They drifted along on South Bay.

They were out of the view of the people,
Where no one could hear her last call.
And nobody knows how it happened,
But God and Gillette know it all.

It's unusually accurate for a folk song, even after being handed down for over 25 years, and perhaps most accurate of all was the line, "and nobody knows how it happened."

Written at approximately the same time was another song, "Entreating," by Maud E. Gould of Ilion. It was copyrighted in 1907 and published with a photo of Grace Brown and a scene of the rustic bridge from Big Moose Lake. On the cover was the caption, "dedicated to the memory of Miss Grace Brown of South Otselic, N.Y."

The song uses the words from Grace Brown's letters set to a haunting melody in a minor key. The lyrics are:

I'm lonely tonight, and I think of you, dear.
I'm lonely tonight, how I wish you were here.
This life's naught but sadness, the whole world seems dead.
The future's so dark and my heart's sore afraid.
There's nothing but trouble for me that I see.
Come take me away dear and don't let me be.

Dreaming, dreaming, dreaming of days that will be,
Longing, longing, longing for one dear face to see,
Oh, come and take me away, dear.
I cannot linger here.
My heart is breaking, for you I'm forsaking,
All I love most dear.

I'm bidding farewell to the nooks and the trees,
I'm bidding farewell to the flowers and the bees.
The orchard, the playhouse, that stood there within,
The little beehive and the moss-covered spring.
And there's mother, too oft I've wept on her breast,
To me she's but kindness, I love her the best.

Crying, crying, crying all the live-long day.
Sighing, sighing, sighing for one that's far away,
Oh, come and take me away, dear.
I cannot linger here.
My heart is breaking, for you I'm forsaking,
All I love most dear.

The folksong was sung around campfires in the Adirondacks, especially around lakes and many young women later recalled its association with campfire ghost stories. Strangely, however, there were never any reports of ghosts at Big Moose, the scene of the tragedy. Instead, they were reported to be seen at the Gillette Skirt Factory in Cortland, which was closed up in the World War I era, and around the courthouse in Herkimer. In Cortland, people reported seeing a man with a tennis racket near the factory. In Herkimer, a man and woman were reported to be seen in a rowboat.

As early as July 1909, these ghost stories were finding their way into the newspapers, when it was reported that the rowboat, which had been kept in the courthouse as a trial exhibit, had mysteriously disappeared.

The *Herkimer Telegram*, reporting on the missing boat, said:

> The stories have it that the grim tragedy is frequently
> re-enacted in the vicinity of the courthouse, that a boat
> with ghostly figures of a man and woman are seen as
> though rowing on water, the features of the man being
> those of Gillette, that at times a struggle ensues between
> man and woman, when following a piercing unearthly
> scream the latter is hurled from the boat and disappears.
> Those braver hearted, it is said, have rushed upon the
> spectral figures in an effort to solve the mystery, only as
> they reached the figures to have the scene vanish, they
> grasping but thin air.

Just three years after the trial, the case had become a
"mystery" and a ghost story, told around camp fires on moonless
nights. It was a story too good to be left untold, so it was told over
and over, and was waiting for some author to come and take it all
down.

# CHAPTER ELEVEN

# *Theodore Dreiser's 'An American Tragedy'*

A mong the millions of eager New York City newspaper readers who sought out the sensational daily articles on the Gillette trial in the early winter of 1906 was a 35-year-old magazine editor and sometime novelist named Theodore Dreiser. Each evening as he took the streetcar from his $40-per-week job at the *Broadway Magazine* at 7 W. 22 Street to his apartment at 439 W. 123 Street, he would have found it difficult to avoid all the newspaper boys screaming out the headlines recorded in six-inch type in the front pages: "Keep Gillette From Suicide" and "Gillette Doomed." He may, in fact, have clipped and saved these articles, as he saved so many other things, because of their value as a slice of American life that could be used in his writing.

To his friend, Richard Duffy, Dreiser suggested that the Gillette case would make a fine novel, but Duffy probably didn't consider this much more than a wild dream, considering Dreiser's current literary and economic status. His first novel, *Sister Carrie*, had been hailed as a literary masterpiece by Frank Norris, one of the founders and early advocates of the school of "naturalism" in American fiction. It was the story of the rise of a small-town girl in Chicago and New York who is jilted by lovers and finally achieves success in the theater.

What Norris found in the book was an accurate portrayal of a modern woman - the choices she was forced to make, the basic immorality of the characters she meets and society's failure to help her into a more proper course. But what the public saw in the book was a violation of all the taboos of literature. Carrie had sexual intercourse, she didn't act like a lady and, worst of all, she was not punished at the end of the novel for her life of sin. Although there was no questionable language and the sex was not described, the book had been virtually suppressed by Frank Doubleday, when he and his wife returned from Europe and found out what Norris had chosen for publication.

Dreiser insisted that the terms of his contract be fulfilled and that the book be published, but Doubleday cancelled all the advertising and promotions. Norris managed to get a few copies out to reviewers and some were released to bookstores, but the total sale was 456 copies. Dreiser's royalties came to a grand total of $68.40.

Six years later, he told his assistant at *Broadway Magazine*, Ethel Kelley, that he was embittered, discouraged and finished as a writer. Nevertheless, at the same time he could talk to others about a novel when he talked about the Gillette case, but it would take 20 years before it would be the basis of his most famous novel and his financial and critical success.

Dreiser was born August 27, 1871, in Terre Haute, Indiana, the son of a poor German Catholic immigrant who was often out of work. The family moved frequently as Dreiser's father looked for work and the family was split up several times, with Dreiser sent to live with relatives. One of his sisters eloped with a Chicago bartender who ran off with the receipts, and one of his brothers was in jail briefly for stealing. Another sister became pregnant and left the baby with his grandmother.

At 16, he left his family and moved to Chicago, where he worked in a hardware warehouse. An older woman paid for his tuition to Indiana University for a year, but he returned to Chicago and took jobs as a real estate clerk and a collections agent. At the age of 20, he became a newspaper reporter for the *Chicago Globe* and worked at several newspapers before moving to New York. Although he was never very good at straight reporting, his interpretive pieces, especially on class differences and the problems of the poor, were highly regarded by editors. But when he moved to New York in 1899, he found that his writing talents were not appreciated in the high-speed competition of New York journalism and he got only minor assignments and minor pay.

*Theodore Dreiser*

He got his start as a magazine editor through the efforts of his brother, Paul, who had changed his last name to Dresher and became a famous songwriter. Among his compositions were "My Gal Sal" and "On the Banks of the Wabash." They started *Ev'ry Month*, a magazine devoted to songs, stories and articles with mass appeal. He had some success as a freelance writer, specializing in interviews with tycoons and profiles of the urban poor.

Following the financial disaster of his first novel, however, he sank into a depression that included at least two suicide attempts. His brother placed him in a sanitarium and after his release he began a slow climb back up, beginning as a railroad yard worker.

The year of the Gillette trial also marked for Dreiser some new efforts at getting his novel republished. In 1907, the year Gillette spent in Auburn prison, he became secretary and editor of B. W. Dodge & Co. which republished *Sister Carrie* on May 18. The same year he also moved to a $5,000-per-year job as editor of Butterick Publishing Co., one of the nation's largest publishers of dress patterns and prim and proper women's magazines.

But the dedicated realist and author of the highly controversial *Carrie* could not act the part of a conservative editor for long and following a series of sexual incidents, and his pursuit of the 17-year-old daughter of a member of the Butterick staff, he was dismissed.

Jobless and estranged from his wife, Dreiser turned to fiction, writing *Jennie Gerhardt* in 1911, *The Financier* in 1912, *The Titan* in 1914 and *The Genius* in 1915. The latter was withdrawn from publication after John S. Sumner of the New York Society for the Suppression of Vice vowed to take the publishers to court. Dreiser didn't write another novel for 10 years. Instead, he wrote plays, poems, travel books, philosophical essays and became a crusader against Sumner's suppression and in favor of "breaking the bonds of Puritanism." By 1920, he was ready to write the novel for which he had been collecting information for most of his life.

In a series of articles written in 1935, Dreiser explained in his own words his fascination with a certain kind of murder case:

> It was in 1892, at which time I began as a newspaperman, that I began to observe a certain type of crime in the United States. It seemed to spring from the fact that almost every young person was possessed of an ingrowing ambition to be somebody financially and socially. In short, the general mood of America was directed toward escape from any form of poverty . . . Indeed, throughout this period, as I found, it was a rare American heart that was set, for instance, on being a great scientist, discoverer, religionist, philosopher or benefactor to mankind in any form . . . but his private obsession . . . was that the quick and sure way to do this was to get money . . . In short, we bred a fortune hunter deluxe. Fortune-hunting became a disease . . .
> In the main, as I can show by my records, it was the murder of a young lady by an ambitious young man.

Dreiser said he had found several variations on this type of crime, which he said was a peculiarly American one. The most common variation was the closest to the Gillette case:

> The third variation was that of the young ambitious lover of some poorer girl, who in the earlier state of affairs had been attractive enough to satisfy him, both in the manner of love and her social station. But nearly always with the passing of time and the growth of experience on the part of the youth, a more attractive girl with money or position appeared and he quickly discovered that he could no longer care for his first love. What produced this particular type of crime about which I am talking was the fact that it was not always possible to drop the first girl. What usually stood in the way was pregnancy, plus the genuine affection of the girl herself for her lover, plus also her determination to hold him . . . Nevertheless, these murders, based upon these facts and conditions, proved very common in my lifetime and my personal experience as a journalist.

The murderer found that he had to get rid of the lower-class girl in order to be free to win the rich girl. It was a sacrificing of love for ambition, he said. Dreiser said he soon found evidence that it was society, not the murderer, who had made the murder necessary.

By 1920, Dreiser had collected a half dozen cases which fit his archetypal theme and the problem was to either choose one to fictionalize or somehow merge them all into a single story. Among the cases he considered were those of Carlyle Harris, Clarence Richsen and Roland Molineux.

Harris was a young medical student in 1894, when Dreiser first arrived in New York. While an intern in a New York hospital he secretly married a young girl from a poor family. When he later fell in love with an attractive young society woman, he gave his wife some poisoned powders which caused her death. Harris was tried and executed.

Dreiser was attracted to this story, especially because he had met Harris' mother and she had told him that the pressure to "get up in the world, be famous, marry money" was the reason for her son's crime.

Richsen was a young Baptist minister in Hyannis, Massachusetts, who seduced a female parishoner named Avil Linnel. When he was offered a transfer to Cambridge and the possibility of marriage to a wealthy woman, he poisoned his pregnant paramour. Dreiser wrote six chapters of a novel based on this case before giving up, apparently because a minister was not working out as the main character and because Dreiser, who did not care for organized religion, was having trouble identifying with his protagonist.

Roland Molineux was a yachtsman, connoisseur and amateur chemist who found himself in competition with another man for the hand of Blanche Chesebrough, a wealthy young socialite. He was accused of sending a poisoned box of candy to a suitor through a friend who, like Molineux, was a member of the Knickerbocker Athletic Club. Mrs. Kate Adams accepted the candy by mistake and died of poisoning. Like the Gillette case, the trial became a newspaper sensation and Dreiser had no trouble finding newspaper clippings of the case.

In 1914, he obtained permission through a lawyer friend to examine the Molineux case court records and began to write a novel called *The Rake*. He copied out much of the court testimony of the case and many minute details. Again, this experience was put to good use when he finally began work on the novel that was to become *An American Tragedy*.

He abandoned *The Rake* after only a few chapters, probably because it deviated somewhat from his archetypical pattern: it had two men and a woman instead of the more typical two women and a man. For a time, he studied another murder, that of William Orpet, a Midwesterner who jilted one girl for another and was indicted for murder by poisoning. But Orpet was acquitted and therefore did not fit into Dreiser's plan.

It wasn't until 1919 or early 1920 that Dreiser finally decided on the Chester Gillette - Grace Brown case as the best possible example of an "American" tragedy. The first real evidence that Dreiser was studying the case is a letter dated August 13, 1920, to the county clerk in Herkimer requesting a copy of the trial transcript.

Dreiser gave several versions of why he finally decided on the Gillette case. In a letter to a Mr. Beyer dated December 16, 1926, he wrote, "I had thought and brooded on the Chester Gillette murder case for many years before I ever set pen to paper, because the ramifications of that particular case seemed to reach out into all of the life of America and as a result, An American Tragedy."

But in a series of pieces he published in *Mystery Magazine* nearly a decade later, Dreiser wrote, "The Gillette case had come to my attention eighteen years after the tragedy and two years before I completed the book."

Although it's impossible to tell exactly when Dreiser decided on the Gillette case, it's not difficult to see why he found it to be the most appealing of those in his collection. In the *Mystery Magazine* article he wrote:

> Furthermore, in my examination of such data as I could find in 1924 relating to the Chester Gillette-Billy Brown case, I had become convinced that there was an entire misunderstanding, or perhaps I had better say non-apprehension of the conditions surrounding the victims of that murder before the murder was committed. From these circumstances, which I drew not only from the testimony introduced at the trial but from newspaper investigations and information which preceded and accompanied the trial, I concluded that the murder was not one which could either wisely or justly be presented to an ordinary conventional, partly religious, and morally controlled American jury and be intelligently passed upon.

In other words, Dreiser thought the lawyers, the judge, the jury and the journalists at the trial had failed to see that it was more than just a factory worker on trial, it was the American dream.

The dramatic aspects of the case, many of which were manufactured by the newspaper reporters in 1906, afforded more opportunities to transform the story into a novel with universal implications. The factory, for example, was an easy symbol of America, where raw materials were converted into goods by workers, but where the riches went to the factory owners.

Secondly, there were the letters. The concept of the dead girl, reaching out from the grave to convict her own murderer in her own words was a highly dramatic touch and especially appealed to Dreiser, who planned to rewrite the letters to make them fit his pattern.

Thirdly, a factory worker like Chester would make a much better symbol of the common man than a clergyman or a medical student. These professionals had their own myths and symbols that tended to get in the way in Dreiser's early attempts.

Fourthly, Dreiser saw that the class difference between the two women was much clearer between Grace Brown and Harriet Benedict than in the other cases. This was partly due to the newspaper exaggeration, of course, but it was certainly true that Grace Brown was many steps below a lawyer's daughter like Harriet. Ward's courtroom addresses, that Dreiser read in the transcript and in the newspaper articles, brought out the very idea that had attracted Dreiser to the theme: the abandonment of "Miss Poor for Miss Rich."

But most important of all for Dreiser, the more he learned about Chester Gillette, the more he came to realize how similar their backgrounds were and the more he came to sympathize and identify with the plight of the murderer.

Dreiser and Gillette shared an early life of strict religious observance accompanied by poverty. They both had had to face the problems of moving to new homes with their families every few months or so: the lack of close friends, the breaking off of relationships, the feelings of disorientation. They both had rebelled from an early religious life to develop an unusual fondness for women. They both had spent a brief time at college before deciding to leave and both had lived in Chicago and worked at menial jobs in unattractive places like railroad yards.

Once Dreiser decided on the Gillette case, he researched it mainly through the New York City newspapers that had made so many errors in reporting the trial. Several Dreiser scholars have done lengthy studies comparing the novel to the trial transcript and newspapers and have arrived at the general conclusion that the *New York World* was Dreiser's primary source.

The *World*, like many of the more sensational papers of 1906, had exaggerated Gillette's relationship with Harriet Benedict to stress the love triangle aspect. Dreiser either did not know of the exaggeration or chose to ignore it. In fact, in many ways, he exaggerated even more than the newspapers because it was important to fit his archetype.

But the newspapers contained very little information on Chester's early life. They reported that his family had been Salvation Army workers, that they had been Dowieites and that they were too poor to attend the trial.

With these few details as a basis, Dreiser invented an entirely fictitious early life for his Gillette character, Clyde Griffiths (the name chosen to keep the C. G. initials that Chester had used in his aliases). While Dreiser's portraits of Mr. and Mrs. Griffiths are very close to Mr. and Mrs. Gillette, as is his portrayal of the lives of Salvation Army workers, nearly all of the first part of his book is purely imaginary as far as the Gillette case is concerned. In fact, as Dreiser scholars have pointed out, the early life of Clyde Griffiths is much closer to that of Theodore Dreiser.

For example, in the novel, one of Clyde's earliest family problems is the pregnancy of his elder sister. Chester, of course, had no elder sister and there was nothing similar in his background. It was Dreiser who had the pregnant sister whose baby was raised by his grandmother. Clyde leaves his family in Kansas City to work as a bellhop after being involved in an auto accident. Like Gillette and Dreiser, he ends up in Chicago working at a menial job.

Much of this early part of the novel was written in Los Angeles, where Dreiser probably had no access to newspaper files on the Gillette case. He had written 20 chapters when he moved back to New York in October, 1922. Here there were plenty of Gillette newspaper files available, but Dreiser stopped work on it for a time, even though he had already promised his publishers, Boni and Liveright, a "big new novel."

It wasn't until the summer of 1923 that he took up the writing and research again and decided to make a trip to Upstate New York for a first-hand look at the scenes of the action. With him on the excursion was Helen Richardson, his literary assistant and mistress, who many years later was to become the second Mrs. Dreiser. In her autobiography, she recounted the trip in some detail. They took the Maxwell car they had purchased in Los Angeles and followed the dirt roads through the Delaware River

Valley northward from New Jersey to Monticello and finally to Cortland.

"Upon our arrival," she wrote, "we drove around to different sections to get a general impression of the city as a whole - the best residential section, the factory section and the poor streets of the town."

In his diary for that day Dreiser wrote, . . . "Beautiful scenery. Bright, cool day. No car trouble. At Cortland, 7 p.m. Stop at the Cortland House. The fine house. A good room but we resent being compelled to stay in town. The beautiful Glen just south of Cortland. Greeks running restaurants everywhere."

Dreiser spent that night and part of the next day in Cortland, but it's unknown whom he spoke with. It's very likely that he did talk to someone involved in the case, or perhaps picked up some details from someone he met on the street. Among the people who still lived in Cortland who could have answered any of his questions were Chester's friends, Albert Gross and Fred Tyler, both of whom were now successful businessmen; Rowland L. Davis, the lawyer who visited him in Herkimer and was now a Supreme Court Justice; Myron P. Crain, Chester's old landlord, Mrs. Florence Gillette, N.H.'s second wife, or even Harriet Benedict, who was now Mrs. Levi Chase.

Although neither of them wrote about it, they certainly went to see the factory, which by now had been converted into a shirt factory, the Newton Shirt Co., but still had the cornerstone identifying the building as the Gillette Skirt Co. From Cortland, Dreiser and Helen drove to South Otselic and asked for directions to the old farmhouse where Grace Brown had lived. Helen described it in her memoirs:

> The narrow country road leading to her home was
> about as Dreiser described it in the book. I wondered as
> we rode along how a young girl could have lived so far
> away from everything in so bleak a spot at a time when
> automobiles were scarce and one had to travel three miles
> behind a horse to the general store. The lone house up on
> the hill under great trees had all of the lorn feeling that
> he later put into its description. It might seem charming
> to one who had always lived in cities, but for a girl who
> had never seen anything it must have been a rather drab

existence to return to after knowing Cortland and the
little gaiety she encountered there. A haunting note
prevailed in this atmosphere that Teddie caught and
played on with variations throughout the book.

Again, it's impossible to know who Dreiser spoke to in South
Otselic. He must have asked someone how to find the farm and
almost anyone would have known where "the Brown farm" was,
even though the Browns had moved out of it in 1906. Dreiser may
not have realized that the farm had been abandoned for years
and that may have led him to describe it as much more run down
than it had been at the time the Browns lived there.

In his diary he wrote . . . "We motor from here (Cortland) to
South Otselic (McGraw, Solon, East Freetown, Cincinnatus,
Pitcher, North Pitcher). The farmer who knew Frank Brown.
The old house. The four trees. Armenian farmers. We talk about
it. Back to DeRuyter. . . . The Tobes house, DeRuyter. We
motor on toward Cazenovia where we stop . . ."

From South Otselic they followed the route of Grace's last
journey from DeRuyter to Utica and to Old Forge, where they
had their car serviced in preparation for the trip over the nearly
impassable roads to Big Moose. They checked into the Glenmore
Hotel on July 3, just as Chester and Grace had done on July 11,
1906, and the next day they took a rowboat out onto the lake.
Helen described what happened then:

> As we were getting the boat, Teddie asked the boatman
> if he had ever heard of the Gillette case. The attendant
> said yes, he knew all about it; he had been working there
> in the same capacity at the time. Describing the boy as
> dark and swarthy, young and good-looking, he even
> pointed out the actual spot where the murder had taken
> place, a bend in the lake completely hidden from
> everything excepting the shore line of trees all around.

The boatman they talked to was certainly not Robert Morrison, who had rented the boat to Chester, but may have been
another boatman, who may also have been there in 1906. Dreiser
rowed to the spot indicated as the site of the murder and Helen
wrote that they "found ourselves drifting into a quiet, deathlike

stillness," and "the mood of the most dramatic note of the *Tragedy* seized us both. Here it was that girl had met her death, and her unheeded cries had rung all over the waters that closed about her."

The "hypnotic spell" of the place frightened Helen and she said she was afraid Dreiser might get the idea that he would like to murder her so that he could write about it later.

"Maybe Teddie will become completely hypnotized by this idea and even repeat it, here and now," she wrote.

Helen said she felt like someone looking over the top of a tall building, deciding whether to jump. The spell was broken by the call of a bird that Dreiser later used in the death scene of his novel.

"Kit Kit, Kit Ca-a-ah," was how Helen described it. "Was it the departed soul of Grace Brown hovering near the scene of her untimely death? I thought it might be. The sensation and mood of this moment never left me and never will. A death moment . . . or as near as one could come perhaps."

Dreiser described the scene much less vividly in his diary. He wrote, "Put up at the Glenmore on the lake. $10.00 for room, dinner and breakfast. No bath. We row on the lake and listen to the music & watch the dancers. It rains from 3 A.M. till dawn." The next day, the Fourth of July, he wrote, "Bright, cool day. Talk to the guide who found Grace Brown's body. His recollections of Gillette and her. We motor back to Eagle Bay."

Later on the Fourth of July, Helen and Dreiser went to Herkimer, where they visited the courthouse and the jail across the street. But because it was a holiday, they may not have been able to go inside. In Herkimer, there were many people he could have spoken to who knew much about the case. Charles Thomas, one of Chester's lawyers, Irving Devendorf, the judge or Austin B. Klock, the lawman who knew Chester best and who arrested him and attended the execution. Again, it is not known whom he spoke with.

Although it is not included in either Helen's story of the trip or in Dreiser's diary, it is known that he went alone to Dolgeville to visit Mrs. George Ward, widow of the district attorney who prosecuted Chester. She showed him a scrapbook that Ward's secretary had kept and the original copies of Grace and Chester's letters.

Soon after this trip, he and Helen returned to New York. The best guess is that Dreiser actually talked to very few of the people connected with the case, since so much of the novel seems to be based on the newspaper accounts. In fact, he seems to have ignored many of the facts that would have been obvious from his trip. Many of the characters and scenes were significantly altered, often for dramatic effect and to better fit in with his theme.

His Lycurgus, for example, resembled Cortland only superficially. He locates it halfway between Utica and Albany, about 150 miles from its real location and describes it as cut in half by a river with factories and poor people's homes on one side and rich homes on the other side. Whatever city that describes, it is not Cortland. His Lycurgus is also much bigger than Cortland was in 1906. He describes Lycurgus as having 25,000 people, while Cortland had only 10,000. He made Samuel Griffiths, much more wealthy and prominent than N.H. Gillette had been in Cortland. By increasing the size of the city, he heightened the difference between rich and poor that did indeed exist in Cortland in 1906.

Since Dreiser visited Central New York in 1923 and not 1906, he moved the date of the events forward to the present, when automobiles were more common and styles were different. By doing this, however, he reduced to a great extent Grace Brown's dilemma, since by 1923 an unmarried mother was not as great a social disgrace as she would have been in 1906.

Dreiser worked on his novel in a rented cabin in the Catskills near Monticello after he returned from his journey and was involved in his own love triangle. Helen Richardson was constantly asking him about his plans to divorce his wife and marry her. She read to him from *Wuthering Heights* and typed his work after he had handwritten it, but he refused to discuss marriage with her. In the meantime, she found a letter, one of many written to him by women admirers, and left him for a time.

In a December 1923 interview with the *New York Times*, Dreiser described the philosophy of his new novel:

> Realism is not literature, it is life. That is where most
> of our present-day writers are making their big mistake.
> They set out to write a novel of realism and then proceed
> to ignore life entirely. They choose one dark, dank, ugly
> corner of life and spend themselves lavishly upon it,
> forgetting that life consists of many corners and many
> open spaces.

Meanwhile, his publishers were impatient for the novel. He promised it would be ready by the fall of 1924, but could not meet that deadline. "For some reason," he wrote them, "this book is harder than any I ever wrote. I might as well be chipping it out of solid rock." The publishers did not like Dreiser's title, *An American Tragedy*, and suggested changing it to *Clyde Griffiths*, the name of the Chester Gillette character.

While writing two or three chapters a week in 1924, Dreiser also found time for further research. He went to the Cluett and Peabody collar factory in Troy, New York, to study the making of shirt collars, which he had decided to use instead of a skirt factory. He also visited Dr. Abraham Arden Brill, an Austrian-born psychiatrist who had studied under Jung, to discuss the psychology of a murderer like Gillette. He consulted attorney Arthur Carter Hume, who had an office in the same building on Union Square. Much of the legal advice on the arrest and trial probably came from Hume.

Since much of the trial is taken virtually unchanged from the *New York World*, Dreiser had to have had either a scrapbook or the newspaper files from the New York Public Library to use as a guide.

The manuscript had grown to a monstrous size. W. A. Swanberg, Dreiser's biographer, estimates that it must have been at least a million words long before it was edited down by his two assistants. By the time his editors were through with it, it had been cut to 385,000 words, still too long for a single book, so it had to be published in two volumes. When the proofs arrived in August 1925, Dreiser was still not satisfied with the execution scene and told his publishers, who were trying to meet an October publication date, that he wanted to do further research and make additional changes.

Although he had already visited Sing Sing prison to research the final scenes, he had not been to Death Row because regulations prohibited it. Now he pulled some strings with important acquaintances such as James M. Cain, editor of the *World*, and his friend H. H. Mencken and a special court order was issued for him to visit Death Row and talk to a condemned prisoner, Anthony Pantano.

The book was finally published on December 12 at what then seemed like an outrageous price, $5 for both volumes. A special limited and signed edition was sold for $12.50.

But the book that insiders had already known was based on the Gillette case, over a generation before, was not really about the Gillette case at all. Dreiser had made so many changes in the characters and the plot that it had become a completely different story. Some of the changes, such as changing the names and playing fast and loose with New York State geography, may have been an attempt to prevent libel suits, but most of the changes seem to have been made to force the story into the framework that he had set up years earlier.

But the most important change Dreiser made was in the character of his protagonist. Although he comes from the same background and is put into the same kind of situation, Clyde Griffiths has little else in common with his model, Chester Gillette. In transforming a careless and thoughtless pleasure seeker like Chester into a victim of society and his own dreams and ambitions, Dreiser used more imagination than history and had to leave out key facts.

Clyde, unlike Chester, never went to anything like Oberlin Academy and while the hero of the novel is a somewhat shy and withdrawn youth with an overriding ambition to fulfill his dreams of wealth, status and luxury, there is no evidence that Chester had any of those qualities. Chester showed little in the way of ambition. He drifted through his short life living from day to day, drifting from one place and one job to another in a careless existence from which any extensive planning or goals seem to have been absent. He was a popular ladies' man who made friends easily and loved to tell stories about his adventures in the West.

In the novel, Clyde confines his attentions to just two women - Roberta Alden (Grace Brown) and Sondra Finchley (Harriet

Benedict). He spends most of his life working out in detail ways of escaping into a life of luxury. He thinks out every step in detail before making a decision and he weighs all the alternatives. He is much more naive and much less cool and sophisticated than Chester really was.

While the basic outline of the story is so identical that pieces of the testimony are interchangeable between the real case and the novel, by skillfully adding and changing details, Dreiser was able to change the net impact of the case so that Clyde, not Roberta, becomes the victim.

Clyde, like Chester, is working in Chicago when his rich uncle from New York suddenly appears and invites him to come work in his factory. There, like Chester, he meets a young farmer's daughter, whom he secretly dates. Like Grace, Roberta gets pregnant and both had to find a solution to the pregnancy without marriage.

But there are just as many dissimilarities. There is no evidence that Chester was left on his own by his uncle as much as Clyde was. All the evidence shows that while Chester lived with his uncle for only a short time they remained on good terms and he visited them often.

But in the novel, Clyde goes through a period when he is all but forgotten by his uncle and has to make his own way. Later his uncle suddenly remembers him and invites him to parties at his house.

Chester's relationship with Grace Brown was no secret at the factory the way Clyde's was with Roberta. In the novel, Clyde hides his relationship with Roberta even from his closest friends because there was a rule against factory managers dating their employees. At the Gillette factory there seems to have been no such specific rule, but many of the managers warned Chester it was not a good idea, and he merely told them that it was none of their business. In the novel, Clyde is Roberta's direct supervisor while Chester worked in a different department than Grace, although they met often.

Dreiser's theme made it necessary for him to significantly change the role of his Harriet Benedict character, Sondra Finchley. His description of her appearance and her character is so much closer to reality than what was given in the newspaper accounts that he almost certainly had been given more information about her in Cortland. Dreiser took this information and added it to the newspaper fictions about a secret romance and a possible engagement and turned it into a full-blown relationship. While it is certainly possible that there was more to Chester and Harriet's relationship than was made public and that some of it was covered up, it seems very unlikely that anything like what Dreiser described could have existed. Harriet seems to have been more embarrassed about being dragged into the case than concerned about Chester. And, of course, Chester went out with many other women during his last year in Cortland. The reason Harriet was singled out later was because it was her misfortune to have her photograph on the film that was found in Chester's camera when he was arrested. Ward used the other woman idea in his presentation at the trial.

In the novel, Sondra is with Clyde when he is arrested and comes to visit him when he is in prison, something that is very unlikely to have happened in real life. While Harriet Benedict was given some preferential treatment at the trial, in that she was allowed to use the back door to avoid the press and certainly wasn't pushed very hard by Ward when she testified, Dreiser took the preferential treatment a step further. In the novel, Sondra not only avoids testifying, but her name isn't even used. By an agreement between the lawyers she is referred to only as "Miss X."

Large portions of the novel's trial testimony, the letters and the opening and closing statements are so similar to the trial transcript that they were barely rewritten. Clyde's final statement, given out after his execution, is virtually identical to Chester's.

The timing of the events was also significantly altered by Dreiser when he moved all of the events, beginning with Roberta's pregnancy, ahead by a month. This seems to have been done so that the trial could be held in October instead of November, which enabled Dreiser to make more of the political differences between the defense lawyers and the district attorney because his trial started before, instead of after, the election.

The scene of the tragedy, "Big Bittern Lake," is much the same as Big Moose Lake, but Dreiser made Clyde much more familiar with the area than Chester had been. In the novel, Clyde visited the area and planned the murder before he took Roberta to the lake. There is no evidence at all that Chester had ever been to Big Moose before July 11, 1906. Dreiser also places Sondra Finchley in the Adirondacks so that Clyde can visit her after the murder. While Chester did meet some Cortland women in the Adirondacks after the murder, Harriet Benedict was in Cortland throughout this time and never went to the Adirondacks at all that summer.

One of the most important changes Dreiser made was in the "murder" itself. Clyde, as Chester may have done, planned the murder out in detail before he left Cortland, planning his route, how the murder would be done, how he would cover up the crime and how he would escape. But at the final moment, he finds he cannot go through with it. While he is in a trance, thinking about it, Roberta startles him and he accidentally hits her with his camera tripod, knocking her out of the boat. He deliberately makes the decision not to rescue her and leaves her to drown.

A tennis racket was probably too brutal a weapon for Dreiser to use to convince readers that Clyde was innocent, even though Dreiser mentions that Clyde had a tennis racket with him.

When the critics were presented with the novel, it was already well-known that the book was based on the Gillette case and charges of plagiarism surfaced almost immediately. But they seem to have been whispered in literary circles before they were made public. In 1928, Morris Ernst and William Seagle wrote about it in their study *Obscenity and the Censor*. Although the passage does not mention Dreiser by name, it is indexed under his name, indicating that his name was removed at the last minute. They said Dreiser copied the letters that had been made up by reporters.

In the authors' haste to condemn Dreiser they relied too heavily on the stories going around and did not do their homework. Dreiser did rewrite Grace and Chester's letters, even if he did retain some of the key phrases and their basic tone. Also, the letters are among the few things that the reporters at the trial did not have to make up.

Dreiser certainly had access to the real letters at Mrs. Ward's home in Dolgeville and probably was able to obtain one of the pamphlets that had been published during the trial for 15 cents. He did not have to depend on the newspaper versions of the letters.

Ernst and Seagle's comments, however, are evidence that the general public believed Dreiser had put together his novel with scissors and paste using the newspapers and the trial transcript.

Only a few of the original reviewers mentioned the Gillette case and none of them complained of plagiarism. Robert S. Gorman, writing in the February 1926 issue of "Book Review," for example, said:

> It will, of course, be inferred that *An American
> Tragedy* is based in part on an actual murder trial that
> was once a country-wide sensation and this is true. One
> has but to go to the yellowing files of old newspapers and
> read there of the Chester Gillette - Grace Brown tragedy
> at Big Moose in 1906 to discover where Dreiser found the
> inception of his book. But the author has taken this
> actual story and transforms it to a significant exposition
> of a phase of American life. He has lifted it to the heights
> of tragedy by building up the character, which is based
> on Chester Gillette, into the weak-willed vacillating
> person that is necessary to the theme.

The major criticisms of the work were that it was poorly written and overly long, frequent criticisms of Dreiser's other works. It was highly praised by the *New York Tribune* and *Saturday Review* and many more reviewers gave it mixed reviews.

The public, however, found something it liked about the novel. Some of it may have been from older readers who remembered the Gillette trial from 20 years before. But for most, its mixture of sex, murder and a criminal trial and execution may have been its attractions. In any case, it was Dreiser's first financial success, the source of his fame and fortune.

By the end of 1926, more than 50,000 copies had been sold and Dreiser's royalties totalled $47,647. He had sold the rights for a play based on the book and he became a sought-after celebrity, making the rounds on the book circuit. Sales of his other books picked up and he began receiving letters asking for his photograph and autograph.

His publishers, triumphant that their long cultivation of Dreiser had finally paid off, set up a nationwide contest with a $500 prize for the best answer to the question, "Was Clyde Griffiths guilty of murder in the first degree?"

Meanwhile, in Cortland, Big Moose and Herkimer, remaining principals of the Gillette case were slowly finding that they, too, were becoming sought after. For some, like the witnesses from Big Moose, it was a welcome tourist attraction. But to some people in Cortland, it was like the reopening of a partially healed wound. They began to wonder if they would ever be able to forget the case and live in peace.

# CHAPTER TWELVE

# *Films*
# *And*
# *Folklore*

The impact of *An American Tragedy* on the people who were familiar with the Gillette case was somewhat subdued, considering what happened in later years. No one seems to have made a big deal over the fact that the popular novel was based on something that had happened there 20 years ago, but it is obvious that the fact was well-known.

In an article in the *Syracuse Herald* on November 8, 1927, about a year after the novel was published, reporters J. Walter Franz and Frank Early found that the basis of the novel was known only too well in Cortland.

"It was the subject of serious concern in the Franklin Hatch Library administration whether *An American Tragedy* by Theodore Dreiser, founded unmistakably on the Gillette case, could be left on open shelves, and it was quietly withdrawn from circulation." They added that a New York columnist, who they did not identify, had reported that the book was not available in Cortland bookstores.

In Herkimer, however, those involved in the Gillette case seem to have welcomed the fact that interest in the case was reviving.

In February 1927, retired Judge Irving R. Devendorf was asked to speak at the Men's League of the Reformed Church in Herkimer, and he, in turn, asked them to choose a topic. Predictably, they chose the Chester Gillette case, one of Devendorf's first cases in his 21 years as a judge. He noted in passing that the case was the basis for Theodore Dreiser's popular novel, and then went on to speak for two hours about the trial.

When Charles D. Thomas died in 1930, his obituary contained a paragraph about his connection to the famous novel: "Among the famous cases with which he was connected was the murder trial of Chester Gillette, since immortalized by Theodore Dreiser in what has been termed by eminent critics one of the greatest of American novels, *An American Tragedy*.

"Immortalized" was probably not too strong a word as far as the witnesses and jurors were concerned. It is a mark of how important they considered their participation in the case, that included in their obituaries was a reference to the case.

When Dreiser was mentioned for a Nobel Prize in 1930 (losing to Sinclair Lewis), it was another excuse for the *Herkimer Telegram* to retell the whole Gillette story once again in its columns.

Would all of this interest in the Gillette case have existed if Dreiser had chosen another case as the basis for his novel? Probably not, but interest in the case seems to have been revived occasionally even before the novel was published. In 1921, for example, the *Syracuse Herald* ran a long Sunday illustrated article about the trial.

But the real revival of the case didn't come until 1931, when Dreiser's *Tragedy* became one of the first "talkies," a motion picture with sound that played in Herkimer, Old Forge, and Norwich, near South Otselic, but probably not in Cortland.

Dramatist Patrick Kearney had adapted the novel into a play as early as 1926 and the idea of filming it came at nearly the same time. Horace Liveright, Dreiser's publisher, produced the play and had asked for 50 percent of the motion picture rights, but observers doubted it would ever be filmed because of its sexual content.

Jesse Lasky and Walter Wanger of Famous Players rejected the script for a movie, but Quinn Martin of the *New York World* insisted the book would make "the greatest film yet produced" and Lansky was encouraged by this and other enthusiastic movie people.

Dreiser, Liveright, Lasky and Wanger met at the Ritz Carlton Hotel in mid-March 1926 to discuss the project, but the negotiations quickly led to a fist fight. The 200-pound Dreiser ordered the 130-pound Liveright to stand up and prepared to start a fight. Liveright refused to stand up so Dreiser threw a cup of coffee in his face and stormed away. A few days later, Dreiser sold the rights for $80,000 for himself and $10,000 for Liveright. But that was far from the end of the matter.

When Dreiser's friend Sergei Eisenstein visited Hollywood in 1930, Paramount (the successor of Famous Players), suggested that he and Ivor Montagu film the movie version of the novel and plans were made for a $1 million, 12-reel extravaganza. Eisenstein's script focused on the criticism of American society in the book and Dreiser, who read the finished script, praised it. Paramount, however, was not so happy and finally cancelled the project, saying it could not afford a $1 million movie.

Instead, an entirely new script was written by Samuel Hoffenstein which focused on the detective story and the courtroom aspect of the novel and left out the social criticism. This version was approved for production. Dreiser got an additional $55,000 for the sound rights and Josef von Sternberg was assigned to direct.

When Dreiser read the script, however, he called it "nothing less than an insult to the book - its scope, actions, emotions and psychology," and demanded that the script be abandoned. To his friends, he complained that Clyde had been transformed into a sex-starved, drug store cowboy and complained to Paramount that the script was "a cheap, tawdry tabloid confession story." In a newspaper interview he referred to Hollywood as "Hooeyland" and said his novel had been transformed into "a Mexican comedy."

On June 15, he invited a large group of literary figures to view the finished film with him in New York. The 840 pages of the novel had been reduced to 11 reels. Philips Holmes, Silvia Sidney and Frances Dee played the principal parts of Clyde, Roberta and Sondra. After the screening, the group generally agreed that the movie version was inferior to the novel, even though the director had included some of the additions Dreiser had suggested.

Dreiser got a court injunction against Paramount and the case was heard in White Plains on July 22. Paramount's attorneys argued that the book was "cold-blooded plagiarism" of the Gillette case. Dreiser had to be restrained to keep from interrupting the court procedings, but the judge sided with Paramount and the picture opened a few days later.

Reviewers called the picture "a triumph," with their only reservations being the parts that had been added at Dreiser's insistence. Mordaunt Hall, writing in the *New York Times*, called the trial scene "emphatically stirring, so much so that not a sound was heard from the perspiring throng," and made up for the "uninspired" sequences at the beginning and end of the film.

Two months later, the film played in Herkimer, where the owners of the Fox Liberty Theater were well aware of the local connections of the story. Local people who were involved in the Gillette case were contacted and by the time the film opened on September 22, the lobby was filled with scrapbooks, newspaper clippings and mementos.

Grace Brown's letters were on display, courtesy of W. Randall Whitman, who said he kept them in a safety deposit box at the Herkimer County Trust Company. He permitted them to be displayed only after the theater owner agreed to protect them in a glass case and assigned a policeman to guard them at all times. In just 25 years their value seems to have increased considerably.

But the highlight of the display was the murder weapon itself, the tennis racket, which was displayed courtesy of an "anonymous donor," who is known today to have acquired it from Ward's chauffeur. A.P. Zintsmaster contributed some of his original photographs.

Among those who went to see the movie during its four-day run in Herkimer were some of the main characters in the real case who had the unusual experience of seeing themselves portrayed in a film based on a novel based on themselves. Judge Devendorf went to see it on the second night and said he enjoyed every minute of it:

I thought the acting was very good, and that the film

pointed a moral lesson. Of course, it was impossible to
provide the background of evidence provided at the trial
by 103 witnesses. I thought the acting of the district
attorney in the film particularly realistic.

Of course, there were two instances in the movie
version which never happened, the clash between the
attorneys and the arrest of the man in court who shouted
out, "Why not kill him now?" I can understand why
these things were added to the movie version, being
needed to relieve the tension. I had determined not to see
the film and rejected offers to see it in New York and
other places but I changed my mind yesterday and I was
pleased with the production. There was little feeling
expressed in the courtroom here by the spectators against
Gillette and the trial was one of the most orderly in local
history.

The other principals of the trial, Ward, Mills and Thomas did
not live to see themselves portrayed on the screen.

A few weeks later, in early November 1931, the film reached
Norwich in Chenango County, New York, just a few miles from
South Otselic. The Fox Colonia Theater, seeking to promote the
movie the way Herkimer had successfully done, placed an advertisement in the Norwich Sun advertising the film as "a true story
that happened at our very doors." The theater lobby was used,
once again, to display a series of newspaper articles on the
Gillette case donated by James Rose, manager of the *Norwich
Sun*; a scrapbook donated by Mrs. Walter White and original
telegrams and letters. The first night, 2,106 people saw the
movie, a house record, and a total of 6,174 saw it by the end of its
three-day run.

While all of this was certainly interesting to the residents of
Chenango County, one person, at least, was not happy with the
developments at all. Minerva Brown, now a widow and living
with one of her daughters, was not one of the thousands who
went to see the movie, but most of her friends and neighbors did
and told her about it and how it portrayed the Browns as dirty,
poor and illiterate. That was, of course, an accurate transcription of the novel, but not of real life. Minerva, upset that her
sorrow of 25 years before should be reborn as a public slander

upon her family, decided to take Paramount to court.

The case was prepared by the firm of Searl & McElroy of Syracuse and filed September 24, 1932. It sought $150,000 in damages for the movie's libelous portrayal of Minerva, Frank and their daughter, Grace. Minerva complained that the movie contained "false, untrue, slanderous, libelous and defamatory matter," that portrayed the family as "illiterate, unkempt, slovenly, neglectful" persons who forced their daughter "through lack of care, to seek her own livelihood as a mere child" and that she had permitted her daughter to carry on "clandestine relations with Chester Gillette, or others." The result, she said, was that she had become "an object of contempt and ridicule among her friends, neighbors," and had been made to appear as "poor white trash and a disreputable, untidy product of the hills, without decent care for her daughter and as contributing to the condition in which her daughter found herself."

This was certainly a development that Dreiser and Paramount had not even considered in all their long planning for the filming of the novel. Paramount's lawyers asked that the case be dismissed because there was insufficient evidence, but their petition was denied. Undoubtedly, the Chenango County Judge, Riley H. Heath, thought Minerva was justified in taking the big-time corporation, with its millions of dollars, to court. Paramount, convinced that the libelous aspects of the film were being overstated, arranged for Heath to see the film at a special showing in Norwich in November. They didn't deny that the film was based on the Gillette case, but denied any libel in the film itself.

On December 6, Paramount, in an attempt to convince Minerva that the film was not as bad as she had been led to believe, scheduled a private screening for her in the Paramount Building in New York City. Minerva probably was somewhat surprised because much of Dreiser's description of the run-down Brown farm was not included in the film. Minerva, however, picked out a single piece of dialogue that backed up her complaint. In a scene between Clyde and Roberta, Roberta says, "Clyde, I am afraid you will want to marry instead a girl of education and wealth."

Paramount now found itself in a difficult situation. It had already gone to court against Dreiser, claiming that the author had plagiarized his novel from the Gillette case. Now, in order to win this case, it would have to prove that the film was not based on the Gillette case. The Paramount lawyers probably did not get much sleep.

The first action they took was to get the case transferred out of Chenango County. They argued successfully that it would be impossible to obtain a jury there that was not partial to Mrs. Brown. In July 1934, the case was transferred to Tompkins County Court in Ithaca.

A few months later, on November 13, 1934, the matter was settled out of court. Paramount was probably convinced that no jury would side with it against Mrs. Brown and so agreed to compensate her. It is unknown how much she received, since the settlement was not made public, but it was probably considerably less than the $150,000 she had asked for.

Minerva is probably the only person involved in the Gillette case who received any financial gain from the popularity of the novel and the film.

By this time, as her lawsuit shows, the lack of ready facts about the original case and the easy availability of the fictionalized version of the story were leading to considerable confusion about what did and what did not happen in 1906. Even many of the people involved in the original case seem to have forgotten essential facts or got them confused with the novel and the film.

Inez Wallace, a 10-year-old resident of Big Moose in 1906 and a newspaper writer in the 1930s, attempted to contrast the novel and film with the real story in an article published in several newspapers called "When An American Tragedy Really Happened - I Was There!" She saw Grace and Chester twice, once at the Glenmore and later in the rowboat and watched the men searching for the body.

Unfortunately for history, however, her memory failed her on some key points. She said Chester escaped from Big Moose to where "the wealthy girl with beauty and position awaited him," which was pure Dreiser. The tennis racket, she says, was found coated with blood. Even the date was mistakenly given as July 14 instead of July 11.

The result of her article and many more like it over the years was that the Gillette case and Dreiser's novel became confused to

*Publicity still from the movie* A Place in the Sun.

*The only historical marker about the Gillette case,
located in front of George Ward's home in Dolgeville.*

the point that no one was sure exactly what had happened. In the numerous retellings of the story, handed from person to person, it changed the way a folktale changes, a little at a time. People who had read the novel adopted Dreiser's version because the true story had yellowed and faded with the clippings and the scrapbooks.

Interest remained strong and on January 13, 1942, an anonymous letter to the editor in the *Syracuse Post Standard* requested that the matter be cleared up. "With what concern was Chester Gillette employed, silk mill or corset factory and where? This is long ago and I have heard different opinions."

Three days later, his question drew no fewer than seven responses, all from people who either remembered the case or who had been at the trial. Some quoted scrapbooks and others quoted more recent accounts of the case in *Intimate Detective Magazine*. But few backed up an interest in the case with basic historical research.

The exception was Eleanor Waterbury Franz, a historian from Dolgeville, Ward's home town, who dug out the old newspaper accounts and borrowed the original letters and files from George Ward's widow to write "The Tragedy of the North Woods" in the Summer, 1948 edition of *New York Folklore Quarterly*. This served to set the official record straight, but not for long.

George Stevens, director of such films as *Gunga Din*, *The More the Merrier*, and *Woman of the Year*, had been interested in *An American Tragedy* since at least 1947 and was convinced that it would make an excellent film based on, as Dreiser had intended, an indictment of America's false standards. He met with Dreiser and convinced him that a new movie would right the wrongs of the old one.

Ivan Moffat, his assistant, even researched the original Gillette case and wanted to use some of the facts that Dreiser had changed. But that film was never made for several reasons. First of all, Paramount wanted to stay as far away as possible from the original Gillette case to avoid the kind of lawsuit that Minerva Brown had filed. The late 1940s to early 1950s was the era of the blacklist and Paramount rejected Stevens' original script as too un-American.

The original screenplay was written by Harry Brown and

Michael Wilson. Anne Revere, who played the Louisa Gillette role in the movie, read that first script and called it "superb. They kept to the plot, which was based on an actual killing and subsequent trial in Upstate New York. But the characters in this version made perfect sense. They were almost archetypal. The murderer was more frankly ambitious - conniving." Most of her best scenes in this version, she said, were later cut out.

Paramount demanded a revision by the original authors and Moffat and the result was less social criticism, more love story. Even the title, "An American Tragedy" was too un-American sounding for 1949, even though it had been fine in 1931. For a time, the script was called "The Lovers," reflecting the new emphasis of the script and Paramounts' attempt to make the most out of the real life love story of its leading man and lady, Montgomery Clift and Elizabeth Taylor. Eventually, however, the name was changed to "A Place in the Sun."

Frustrated in his original idea by the political climate, Stevens chose to make the film stylistically innovative. The scenes were carefully planned to flow into one another and extreme closeups were used as special effects. Perhaps in an effort to avoid another lawsuit like Minerva Brown's, the names of all the places and people were changed yet again. Chester, was not Dreiser's Clyde Griffiths or even someone with C. G. initials. Instead, he became George Eastman. Harriet Benedict became Angela Vickers and Grace Brown, played by Shelley Winters, became Alice Tripp. George Ward was played by Raymond Burr, who was soon to become a famous television lawyer as Perry Mason.

Stevens, in describing his attraction to the story, said "the greatness of *An American Tragedy* lies in the fact that it is all things to all people . . . In the main this might have been the love story of any Johnny or Mary in America."

The filming began in October 1949 at Paramount Studios in Hollywood and right away Stevens and the other members of the crew knew that Clift had decided this was to be his Academy Award role. Stevens, if he had studied the original case, was probably aware of how much Clift looked like Chester Gillette and Clift put everything he could muster into his preparation for the role. He even spent a night on death row in San Quentin to get that part of the story right.

He seems to have had a feeling for the role of Chester Gillette as much as for the role of Clyde Griffiths when he said, describing his role, "He's the kind of guy who has some charm but basically he conceals and dissembles about everything. He's tacky and not that bright."

Among the innovations Stevens used was having his actors and actresses rehearse their parts without dialogue so their expressions would help add to the story. He used mood music during the filming and dubbed in the dialogue later. It is full of slow motion and close up effects and Dreiser's loon is heard throughout the soundtrack.

Four months and 400,000 feet of film later, the last scene in the prison was shot and the film was completed. The result probably would not have pleased Dreiser, who died before the film was completed, but it did manage to contain more social criticism than the original version.

In this version, the class difference between Grace and Harriet is even more pronounced. The factory is a bathing suit factory for which the Harriet character is a model. Perhaps most disturbing, however, is the 1950s setting. The poor pregnant factory girl is an even less sympathetic character in the 1950s than she was in 1926 and the story seems very different when the Chester character crosses the lake in a speed boat.

Stevens, his cinematographer, his writers, and his costume designer all won Academy Awards. Clift and Winters were nominated, but lost. Charles Chaplin called it "the best film ever to come out of Hollywood."

Soon after the film was released, an author named Charles Samuels, intrigued by the story, set about writing what was, at the time of its publication, the only non-fiction version of the story. *Death Was the Bridegroom*, however, was not all it could have been. It was part of a "famous murder trials" series of paperbacks published by Fawcett Publications in 1955 and could have been the factual account that was so much needed to set the record straight. But Samuels seems to have been in a hurry to produce the work and seems to have done little or no original research on the case.

Nearly all of the information in the book can be traced back to the original transcript of the trial and the *New York Sun* newspaper account. It deals almost exclusively with the trial and not with the events that came before or after. Louisa's appeals and lectures and Chester's execution are dealt with in the last four paragraphs.

But the book inspired at least one researcher to track down the original story and save as much of it as he could for posterity. In the summer of 1957, Sexton Beer, a carpet salesman from Latham, who read the book, set out on a tour of the places mentioned in the book and sought out the few remaining people who had first-hand knowledge of the events.

"We read the story and were overwhelmed with the depth of this thing," Beer said in an interview in 1959. "We fell in love with the story and we fell in love with the girl . . . For some reason we have become obsessed in the atmosphere of Grace Brown, 53 years later."

Beer and his wife visited Big Moose, Herkimer, South Otselic and Cortland, where they found that people were still not ready to accept their own past. The head of the Cortland Historical Society, Mrs. Clara Elder, agreed to help him in his research only after he promised not to let on what he was doing. When Beer photographed Chester's and Grace's former boarding houses, he placed his wife in the picture so no one would suspect he was really taking a photo of the house.

The next year, on the 50th anniversary of Chester's execution, William O. Dapping, the young reporter who had prayed with Louisa Gillette the night after her son's death was the subject of a nationally distributed Associated Press feature about the case. In it, Dapping revealed for the first time why the "blood upon your head" telegram had not been sent and included a picture of where Chester had been buried, long a mystery.

By this time, the last surviving participants in the trial seem to have had mixed feelings about the story. Some, like Dr. J. Mott Crumb, Grace's family doctor who attended the execution, was fed up. In an interview with the *Syracuse Herald American* in 1956, just months before he died, he said he had "told and retold the story so often that it had become a virtual nightmare."

But at Big Moose Lake, retelling the legend had become one of the essential features of a visit to the lake that people looked forward to each time they returned. After many of the principal characters passed away, the role of chief storyteller fell to Roy Higby, the 13-year-old boy who had been on the steamer when the body was found and claimed to be the one who first spotted it.

Higby, too, had told the story over and over throughout his life, but unlike Crumb, be seems never to have grown tired of the job. He even had his version of the story run off on a duplicating machine so he could give a copy to everyone who asked for it when they came to see him at the Higby Club on the shore of the lake.

While Higby's account of the Big Moose part of the story was accurate, his retelling of the other aspects of the case showed a heavy influence of reading Dreiser. He said the "other woman" was referred to at the trial as "Miss X," as it was in the novel but not in real life. Higby's most startling revelation however, was a statement he claimed Ward had made many years before. Higby said that after Chester's execution, at a meeting in Utica of Higby, his father and Ward, Ward told him that if young Roy had been called as a witness and had told about using the pike pole to probe for the body, the defense would have used it to explain the marks on Grace's body. If that had happened, Higby said Ward told him, Chester would have gone free.

Higby told the story years after the other witnesses who could have denied it had died. In 1966, however, an Associated Press reporter picked up a copy of the statement. The result was another nationwide sensation; sixty years later a witness who remained silent was finally telling the story that had not been told at the trial. The long-lost piece of evidence was finally restored.

It was, of course, a lot to say about the memory of a 13-year-old boy, especially when everyone who could deny the story was no longer alive to do so, but it was an occasion for yet another retelling of the story.

In the 1970s, however, a new generation of researchers began to sort through the accumulated legends for what truth remained to be found. Operating from the two major scenes of the story, Cortland and Herkimer, they helped to sort the facts from the fictions.

Henry D. Blumberg became interested in the case when he held the position once held by George Ward, district attorney of Herkimer County. After plodding through the transcript in the county clerk's office and studying the available resources in the Herkimer County Historical Society, he organized showings of the two films in the courthouse where the trial had taken place and then re-constructed the actual trial for a full-dress performance in 1977. The courtroom was packed every night, just as it had been in 1906. Blumberg himself played his famous predecessor.

Dr. Joseph Brownell, a geography professor at the State University of Cortland had the tougher, but at least as fruitful task of rediscovering the facts in Cortland. He visited the sites and researched the records there for years and will someday write his own account of his research.

Today, interest in the case is still so strong that the Herkimer County Historical Society has turned the old jail where Chester was once kept into a museum. Several people still call there each month and ask about the Gillette case.

Why is there so much interest in the case, 80 years later? Dreiser and the films, of course, inspire those who read and see them to find out the facts behind the fiction. But those who have spent years researching the facts feel that the story is one that has suffered for years from retellings. The real story, the one that the public has forgotten since 1906, is much better than the versions that exist in the current folklore.

As George Stevens said, "the greatness of *An American Tragedy* is that it is all things to all people . . ." Those familiar with the real case, however, know that the real story is much more interesting than the fiction, even though it is much more difficult to find.

# Notes

For those interested in more information about the Chester Gillette case, the best sources of information are the transcript of the trial and the newspapers in Central New York that covered the events without the sensationalism of the New York City papers and many of the wire service accounts.

There are two versions of the transcript. The original complete version is in the Herkimer County Clerk's office but is in very poor condition and access to it has been restricted. Fortunately, there is a condensed version that has been published and is available in many locations. This is the version that was sent to the New York Court of Appeals. Copies of it are available in many large law libraries in New York. Copies are also located in libraries in Utica, Cortland and Ilion and historical societies in Cortland and Herkimer. While the condensed version does not contain every word spoken at the trial, most of what was eliminated was the swearing in process and other legal matters. The testimony included is an accurate record of what witnesses, lawyers and the judge said.

While the transcript is the best record of what was said at the trial, it does not deal with what went on in the courtroom while it was being said, nor does it deal with events that took place after the trial. For these events, the best record is contained in the newspapers.

Generally, the best accounts are the ones closest to the events. The two Herkimer papers, *The Citizen* and *The Telegram*, had, by far, the most complete and detailed accounts. However, neither of these papers is on microfilm and access to the bound volumes has been restricted because of their age. The Herkimer County Historical Society has several files of clippings about the case from the Herkimer papers, but there are some gaps in the coverage.

The best complete newspaper accounts that are available on microfilm are the Utica newspapers: *The Daily Press*, *The Observer*, *The Daily* and *Sunday Tribune* and *The Saturday Globe*. *The Globe's* photographs and drawings are available nowhere else. For the period between the trial and the execution, the two Auburn papers, *The Citizen* and *The Journal*, have information that is not included in other accounts. The Albany and Cortland papers have little about the case that is not available elsewhere.

The main value of the New York City newspaper accounts is to show the extent of the sensational coverage of the trial and execution. The worst of these were *The American*, *The Journal* and *The World*, the latter of which Theodore Dreiser used as the basis of his book. Other New York papers, such as *The Tribune* and *The Sun*, were more accurate but there is little in them that is not available in the Central New York papers.

Other documents and collections of materials that relate to the case are stored in archives at the Herkimer County Historical Society, Syracuse University, Oberlin College, and the Cortland County Historical Society.

Following is a chapter by chapter description of sources used in the preparation of this book.

### KEY TO ABBREVIATIONS:

TT - Trial Transcript (Appeals Book Version)

UDP - *Utica Daily Press*

UO - *Utica Observer*

UHD - *Utica Herald Dispatch*

USO - *Utica Sunday Observer*

HT - *Herkimer Telegram*

CS - *Cortland Standard*

SH - *Syracuse Herald*

INTRODUCTION: The most complete account of the finding of the boat and Grace Brown's body at Big Moose Lake is the testimony of those who were there that day. See TT testimony on Robert Morrison, Florence Morrison, Grace Luce, Frank Crabb, and Charles Kirwin. Also useful is Roy Higby's account in *A Man From the Past* (Big Moose Press, 1974). Some of the details are provided in UDP and UHD July 12 to July 16, 1906.

CHAPTER ONE: Information on the early history of the Gillette family is included in records compiled by the Cortland County Historical Society, especially in files marked Gillette, Osborne, and East Scott. Also helpful are property and census records in the Cortland County clerk's office. Louisa Gillette's birth record is on file in the Massachusetts archives.

Information on the Gillette family in Cortland is in *Book of Biographies, Cortland County, New York*, no author, (Buffalo: Biographical Publishing Company, 1898) pp. 123-127. General information on early Cortland is contained in *The Geography and History of Cortland County* by Cornelia Baker Cornish, (Ann Arbor: Edwards Bros. Inc., 1935).

A brief biography of Frank Gillette's family and a photograph from 1900 is included in a *War Cry* article. The family is also listed in the 1870 and 1880 Montana census and the 1900 California census.

A description of Wickes, Montana at the time the Gillettes lived there is included in *Montana, High Wide and Handsome* by Joseph Kinsey Howard (New Haven: Yale University Press, 1943); and *Montana, A History of Two Centuries* by Michael P. Malone and Richard B. Roeder (Seattle: University of Washington Press, 1976). Additional information on Montana was provided from records compiled by the Montana Historical Society Library, Helena. Although a record of Chester's birth date has not been found, the date was given at the trial and on his death certificate.

Louisa's statements about Chester's early life are from newspaper interviews given in December 1906 and January 1907 and contained in UDP and UHD and many other newspapers.

Information on Spokane history is included in *A History of the State of Washington* by Lloyd Spencer and Lancaster Pollard (New York: American History Society, Inc., 1937) and *History of the City of Spokane and Spokane County, Washington* by N.W. Durham (Chicago: S.J. Clarke and Co., 1912). Other details of life in early Spokane were provided by Raymond J. Fisher of the Eastern Washington Genealogical Society.

The Gillettes are listed in the Spokane Falls and Spokane city directories beginning in 1887 and continuing through 1900, as is information of Gillette's Restaurant and the occupations of Chester's father and uncles. Articles about the family are in *The Spokane Chronicle*, March 18, 1896, March 21, 1896; March 23, 1896, January 29, 1893 and *Edwards History of Spokane County, Washington* (1905).

The information about Chester's school life in Spokane is in UDP December 8, 1906, and HT, same date.

Salvation Army history at the time the Gillettes were involved with it is included in *Marching to Glory, the History of the Salvation Army in the United States* by Edward H. McKinley (New York: Harper and Row, 1980) pages 36-47, 54-58. Louisa's descriptions of her life in the Army are in UHD, January 24, 1907. Details of the Gillettes' Army career up to 1900 are in the *War Cry*, January 20, 1900.

Louisa's *War Cry* articles are included in nearly every issue of the *War Cry* during 1900 and 1901, including details of the journey to Hawaii and events there. The *War Cry* is on file at the Salvation Army School for Officers Training, Rancho Palos Verde, California. Articles about them are included in the *Hilo Tribune*, October 6, 1900. The "Seventh Annual Report for the Salvation Army, Hawaiian Islands Division" is in the possession of the Hawaiian Historical Society, Honolulu.

Lucien Warner is listed in *Who Was Who* and *Cyclopedia of American Biography*. His autobiography is *Lucien C. Warner, The Story of My Life During Seventy Eventful Years 1841-1911*, privately printed. Copies are in the Cortland Historical Society and Columbia University Library.

Chester's Oberlin College records and a file of letters about him, including one from his mother are in the Oberlin College Archives. Recollections of former students about him are in the *Oberlin Tribune*, December 7, 1906. Information about subjects and classes is from the "Oberlin College Catalogue 1900 to 1902." Chester's Oberlin College notebook is in the *Dapping Papers* at the Syracuse University Archives. The history of the Gillette Skirt Factory is among papers at the Cortland Historical Society.

Information of John Alexander Dowie and Zion City is in *History of Lake Country* by John J. Halsey, undated; *The Chicago Chronicle*, March 15, 1907; *New York Times*, March 10, 1907. Information of the Gillettes in Zion is included in *Leaves of Healing*, October 18, 1902. Louisa's description of how the family came to Zion City is in *Leaves of Healing*, December 6, 1902. Copies are in the Zion Public Library.

The lives of railroad brakemen at the turn of the century are described in *Workin' on the Railroad*, Richard Reinhardt (Palo Alto: American West Publishing Co., 1970) pages 84-84, and *The American Railway*, Thomas Clarke (New York: Arno Press, 1976).

N. H. and Harold Gillette's journey to St. Louis and later Zion City is described in CS, November 12, 1904.

CHAPTER TWO:    The early history of the Brown, Browning and Babcock families can be followed through census and property records in the Chenango County Clerk's office. Also see the Henry Brown citation in *Biographical Sketches of Leading Citizens of Chenango County,* (Buffalo: Biographical Publishing Co., 1898) and *History of Chenango and Madison Counties* (D. Mason and Co., 1880). Essential to the story are family records maintained by Mrs. Clifton Bowers of South Otselic and scrapbooks of the *South Otselic Gazette* and *South Otselic Herald* known as the "Cox Scrapbooks." Also used were scrapbooks owned by Florence Andrews of South Otselic, "The Otselic Town Directory," and "Browning Genealogy" at the New York State Historical Society. Also see *History of Chenango County* by Carrie Frank Lynch, (1929).

The history of Frank Brown's farm, its mortgages and the legal procedures through which he lost it are in the Chenango County Supreme Court files at the courthouse.

The description of the Brown farmhouse is from personal examination of the existing building and interviews with neighbors about what it was like in the past. Many details of the day-to-day life of the Browns are included in the "Cox Scrapbooks" 'personal' columns. It lists all movements of the family as well as births, deaths and marriages. *The Cortland Democrat* also contains this kind of information in its South Otselic column. A detailed description of South Otselic in 1903 is included in the *South Otselic Gazette*, October 8, 1903.

Frank Brown's description of Grace is in UHD, November 23, 1906. History of the factory is from several sources, including the *Cortland County Chronicles*, Cortland Historical Society, *Cortland 1958*, pages 275-277; *Grip's Historical Souvenir of Cortland*, (Cortland: Standard Press, 1899) pages 57-58. A description of the fire is in CS, January 9, 1904.

Chester's arrival in Cortland is in CS, April 3, 1905. Harold Gillette speaks about Chester's character in UHD, July 25, 1906. Mrs. Clara Elder, who was later Cortland historian, lived on East Main Street when Chester lived there. Her memories are included in letters to Sexton Beer at Cortland County Historical Society.

Details of life in the factory are taken from the testimony of workers at the trial. A description of the death of Robert Hawley and the funeral are in the *South Otselic Gazette*, September 13 and September 19, 1906. Theresa Harnishfager talks about Grace's leaving in UHD, November 19, 1906.

CHAPTER THREE:   The Glen Haven excursion on Decoration Day is described by Georgia Hoag, TT, Vol I, page 522. Josephine Patrick testimony about her visit to the factory, TT, Vol. I, pages 628-633, Robert Wilcox testimony, TT, Vol, I, page 607. Albert Raymond's testimony about visit to Little York, TT, Vol. I, pages 528-539.

There are several versions of the letters available, all very similar. They are included in the trial transcript. There is a published booklet available at the Herkimer County Historical Society and the New York State Historical Society. The original letters are the property of Mrs. Vosburgh of Dolgeville. Copies of the originals are in the "George Ward Papers" in the Syracuse University archives.

Harriet Benedict testimony: TT, Vol. 1, page 604. Fourth of July at Little York is described in CS, July 5, 1906.

CHAPTER FOUR:   The journey is constructed from the trial testimony of the witnesses who saw Chester and Grace with some additional details added by newspaper reports. Among the important sections are testimony by Chester himself as well as Albert Gross, N. H. Gillette, Neva Wilcox, Harold Gillette, Ella Hoag, Myra Coy, Ralph Weaver, Fred Brown, Harold Williams, Morrell E. Tallett, Josephine Patrick, Charles H. Dube, Royal K. Fuller, Meyer Neuman, Clara Greenwood, Thomas E. DeDell, James A. McAllister, Andrew Morrison, Robert Morrison, Edward O. Stanley, Bernard Foster, Irving Crego, Harold Parker, James S. Hart, Albert J. Styles, George G. Boshart, Everett H. Johnson, George F. Delmarsh, Frank A. Williams, Minnie E. McDuffy, Gertrude M. Dean, Edward E. Whitford, Gladys Westcott and Rev. Cathbert Frost.

CHAPTER FIVE:   George Ward's biography is in *History of the Mohawk Valley Gateway to the West* (Chicago: Clarke and Co., 1925) pages 717-719. The story of the arrest and Ward's part in it is in UO and USO, July 15 and 16.

The report of the autopsy is in the "George Ward Papers" at Syracuse University. The Hotel Martin register incident is in UDP, July 18, 1906. For other details of Chester's imprisonment and search for evidence see the UHD and UDP, July to October, 1906.

The "Gillette Not Deserted" article in is CS, August 11, 1906. Theresa Harnishfager's visit and interview are in the *Norwich Sun*,

November 16, 1906. Chester's letter from his mother and Chester's reply are included in the "George Ward Papers." The Mills letter to Ward is included in the "George Ward Papers."

CHAPTERS SIX AND SEVEN: Day to day coverage of the trial, some of it running to several pages each day, was included in all of the Central New York newspapers and a lesser amount was carried in the New York City newspapers. The trial transcript is the best source for what was said in the courtroom, but the better newspaper accounts add to it by describing how it was said and what else was going on in the courtroom. The newspapers also describe what went on in the evenings after adjournment.

A biography of Charles D. Thomas is in the HT, December 26, 1930. A biography of Albert M. Mills is in the HT, September 17, 1919.

Thanksgiving descriptions of jury and Gillette and Hatch's letter to his family are in the Herkimer County Historical Society archives. Ward's annotated copy of the published letters is included in the "Ward Papers."

CHAPTER EIGHT: The Denver interview with the Gillettes is in HT, December 2, 1906 and UHD, December 6, 1906. Louisa's account of her journey to Herkimer is included in the December, 1906 *New York Journal* articles on file at the New York City Public Library.

Devendorf's recollections years later are in the Herkimer County Historical Society. There are several versions of the post-sentencing news conference with Gillette. Among them are CS, December 11, 1906.

Louisa's Utica lecture is described in UHD, January 21, 1907.

CHAPTER NINE: Chester's letter to his mother and her return letter are in the "George Ward Papers." Information about Henry MacIlravy is included in the UHD, January 20, 1908 and UDP, December 9, 1908, UHD, April 11, 1908.

Charles Evans Hughes' involvement in the case is included in his papers at the Library of Congress, Box 166 of "Beerits' Memorandum," pages 27-29. The second meeting with Hughes is described in the *Albany Times Union*, March 28, 1906, and March 30, 1906.

Descriptions of the electric chair and its operation are included in the *Auburn Citizen*, October 6, 1908. Descriptions of the execution and the last days of Chester's life are in the *New York Times*, March 31, 1908; *Auburn Semi-Weekly Journal*, March 31, 1908. Chester's last letters and his mother's impressions of them are quoted in *Auburn*

*Semi-Weekly Journal*, April 10, 1908. His last letter to his brother is printed in full in *Auburn Citizen*, September 14, 1908. William O. Dapping's retelling of the events in Auburn just before and after the execution were published in the *Syracuse Post Standard*, March 30, 1958. Gillette's last statement and MacIlravy and Herrick's statements are on file at Auburn prison. A list of witnesses to the execution and a pass to enter the prison that day are in the "Dapping Papers," Syracuse University Archives.

CHAPTER TEN:   First press accounts of the case were published in UDP, July 13, 1906 and July 14, 1906, and UO and UHD, July 14, 1906. Press reconstructions of the crime can be found in UDP, July 18, 1906 and UO, July 17, 1906. For some of the sensational stories about the case printed in New York City newspapers see the *New York Journal*, *New York American* and *New York World* from November 11 to December 13, 1906. For denials the New York stories, see UHD, November 21, 1906, UHD, December 5, 1906. The confession story can be found in the *New York Journal* and *New York World*, December 6, 1906.

   Marlen Pew's account of the trial is from *Editor and Publisher* in the 1930s. Folk songs about the case are in the collections of the New York Historical Society in Cooperstown. Copies of "Entreating" are in the Herkimer and Chenango County Historical Societies.

   Deputy Ingraham's account of the case was published in a booklet that is available at Hamilton College, the Herkimer Historical Society and the New York State Historical Society.

CHAPTER ELEVEN:  The best biography of Dreiser is W.A. Swanberg's *Dreiser* (Scribners, 1965). Other books useful in understanding the novel and its relation to the Gillette case are: Dorothy Dudley, *Dreiser and the Land of the Free* (New York: Beechhurst Press, 1946), pages 461-465; Helen Moers, *Two Dreisers* (Viking, 1969); Jack Salzman, *Theodore Dreiser The Critical Reception* (David Lewis, 1972); Morris L. Ernst and William Seagle, *To Be Free . . . A Study of Obscenity and the Censor (Viking, 1928); Helen Dreiser, My Life With Dreiser* (World, 1952) especially chapter eight; John F. Castle, *Making of An American Tragedy*, University Microfilms #5017, unpublished doctoral thesis comparing the novel to the Gillette case; Donald Pizer, *The Novels of Theodore Dreiser, A Critical Study* (Minneapolis: Minnesota Press, 1976) pages 203-289.

   Theodore Dreiser's diaries were published by the University of

Pennsylvania Press in 1982. His trip to Central New York is on pages 400-403. Dreiser's descriptions of his sources for writing the novel are in "Resources for American Literary Study," Volume II, Number 1, Spring, 1972.

The impact of the novel on Central New York can be found in the SH, November 8, 1927.

CHAPTER TWELVE:   The impact of the novel on Cortland is described in SH, November 8, 1927. Charles Thomas' obituary is in the HT and in the Herkimer Historical Society files. For a description of the fight over the movie script and rights, see Swanberg.

The legal papers on the Brown-Paramount lawsuit are in the Tompkins County Supreme Court offices, Ithaca, New York. The ghost stories are in the files of the Herkimer Historical Society. The Inez Wallace story is from the *Cleveland Plain Dealer* and is in the files of the Oberlin College Archives. The *Syracuse Post Standard's* letter on the case was published January 13, 1942 and the responses were published January 16, 1942.

Eleanor Waterbury Franz's story was published in the Summer, 1948 edition of *New York Folklore Quarterly*. "Sexton Beer's Papers" can be found in the Cortland Historical Society and the "William O. Dapping Papers." Henry Blumberg's re-enactment of the case is in his file at the *Utica Observer-Dispatch*. A transcription of a talk he gave on the case is at Cortland Free Library.

See also: Charles Samuels, *Death Was the Bridegroom* (Gold Medal Books, 1955).

# *Photo Credits*

Photographs from the *Utica Saturday Globe*, courtesy of the Oneida County Historical Society: frontispiece; page 5 bottom, 25 bottom, 48 top, 61 bottom, 89, 90, 128, 207, 208 bottom, 209, 210, 211 bottom, 212, 227, 228, 229, 230, 231, 251, 254 bottom, 282 bottom right, 283, 284 top, 317.

Oberlin College Archives: 26 top.

Collection of Mrs. Wilda Bowers of South Otselic, New York: 47, 48 bottom, 50 top.

George Arents Research Library: 157 top, 281, 282 top and bottom left, 284 bottom.

Grip's Historical Souvenir of Cortland: 62, 63.

Paramount Pictures: 357, 358.

Herkimer County Historical Society: photos of Irving Devendorf, Albert Mills and Charles Thomas.

Brian Boyle: 126 top

Wildwood Enterprises, Old Forge, N.Y.: 5 top

Collection of the author: pages 23, 24, 25 top, 26 bottom, 49, 50 bottom, 61 top, 62, 63, 64, 65, 125, 126 bottom, 127, 129, 157 bottom, 158, 185, 186, 187, 188, 208 top, 211 top, 252, 253, 254 top, 315, 316.

# *Index*